UNDERSTANDING DOGMAS AND DREAMS

CHATHAM HOUSE STUDIES IN POLITICAL THINKING

SERIES EDITOR: George J. Graham Jr.
Vanderbilt University

UNDERSTANDING
Dogmas and Dreams
A TEXT

Nancy S. Love
Pennsylvania State University

Chatham House Publishers, Inc.
Chatham, New Jersey

Understanding Dogmas and Dreams: A Text

Chatham House Publishers, Inc.
Post Office Box One
Chatham, New Jersey 07928

Publisher: Edward Artinian
Cover design: Lawrence Ratzkin
Production supervisor: Katharine Miller
Composition: Bang, Motley, Olufsen
Printing and binding: R.R. Donnelley and Sons Company

Library of Congress Cataloging-in-Publication Data

Love, Nancy Sue 1954–
    Understanding dogmas and dreams : a text / Nancy S. Love
        p.   cm. — (Chatham House studies in political thinking)
    Includes bibliographical references and index.
    ISBN 1-56643-044-5 (pbk.)
    1. Political science.   2. Right and left (Political science)
    3. Ideology.   I. Title.   II. Series.
    JA71.L68   1998
    320.5 — dc21   97-4916
                                                                              CIP

Printed in the United States of America
10   9   8   7   6   5   4   3   2   1

Contents

Preface

Political ideologies are the value-laden, conflict-ridden, philosophical substance of modern politics. They have been variously described as "decontested meanings," "social levers," "ethical impulses," "metaphysical illusions," "accepted values," and the "social imaginary." Behind these different definitions lies general agreement that ideologies perform an important political function: they bridge the gap between theory and practice. Their role as the "translators" of ideas into action is what prompts my continued interest in studying them.

In keeping with that interest, I have written this book not only for students of political theory but also for those who study American government and comparative politics. Wherever possible, I have illustrated the effects of theoretical ideas with examples from practical politics. These include discussions of Lani Guinier on proportional representation, Charles Murray on affirmative action, Vaclav Havel on posttotalitarian politics, Murray Bookchin on sustainable communities, Audre Lorde on multicultural feminism, and many more.

I have also written this text to complement the selections from primary sources published in *Dogmas and Dreams: A Reader*. To maintain continuity, some of the introductions to those readings reappear here. However, these analyses offer students a much broader and deeper understanding of their subject. This text provides a companion to the reader and a comprehensive study of political ideologies.

My interest in the complex connections between historical developments and normative theories began when I was a graduate student at

Cornell University. I want to thank Isaac Kramnick, in particular, for introducing me to the study of political ideologies. Benjamin Ginsberg, Peter Katzenstein, Theodore Lowi, and Sidney Tarrow may also see their influence here.

More recently, conversations with colleagues (too numerous to name) in philosophy, political science, and women's studies at Penn State have greatly increased my understanding of ideologies. So have my students by sharing their convictions and their questions during class discussions. The Department of Political Science also provided me with invaluable research assistants, Margaret Farrar and Jamie Warner. My thanks as well to Carmen Heider, Speech Communication, Krystopher DeVyver and Eric Georgette, Political Science, who proofread much of the text.

At Chatham House Publishers, Chris Kelaher assisted in the early stages of manuscript preparation, and Nancy Benson and Katharine Miller saw the project to its completion. My special thanks go to Edward Artinian, who conceived of the project and supported it throughout.

They helped make this a better book. Any errors that remain are my own.

The End of Ideology — Again?

*The charge of utopianism is sometimes best under-
stood more as a symptom of the condition of those
who level it than an indictment of the projects against
which it is directed.*

— Alasdair MacIntyre

In the 1960s Daniel Bell declared the "end of ideology" in the advanced industrial societies of the West. Ideology, as he defined it, was
"an all-inclusive system of comprehensive reality, . . . a set of beliefs, in-
fused with passion . . . [that] seeks to transform the whole of a way of
life."[1] Ideological politics was largely irrational, a politics of image,
myth, and symbol that aroused popular emotions in support of revolutionary causes. From this perspective, the end of ideology was a positive development. According to Bell, a more rational "politics of civility" had replaced the rhetoric of left and right with its roots in the
nineteenth century. A "rough consensus" on political issues now existed, the terms of which were "the acceptance of a welfare state; the
desirability of decentralized power; a system of mixed economy and of
political pluralism."[2] Social progress would continue, but it would now
be based on realistic assessments of empirical conditions.

Ironically, many scholars attacked Bell's end-of-ideology thesis by
arguing that it also was ideological. The ensuing debate is not important here, except as it sheds light on similar arguments emerging today.
Shortly before the demise of the former Soviet Union, Francis Fukuyama declared the "end of history" in terms reminiscent of Bell's position.[3] Many scholars interpreted the subsequent defeat of socialism as
the triumph of liberal capitalism. Like Bell's earlier claims, their arguments rest on several shared, and questionable, assumptions.

What are the assumptions behind these accounts of the end of ideology? First, the end-of-ideology thesis fails to recognize that the status quo (e.g., "the American Way of Life and anticommunism") is also an ideology.[4] As we see, it is a common feature of ideological politics to assume that "their" (the "enemy's") beliefs are "ideology." "Our" ideas are, in contrast, the absolute, complete, objective, rational "Truth." Such claims are obviously simplistic and self-serving. Yet they raise an important question: by what criteria can we assess the truth claims of various ideologies? To acknowledge that different values exist is not to suggest that all are equally fair, good, and just. This is a problem to which we return on multiple occasions.

A second, and related, assumption by those who proclaim the end of ideology is that widespread conformity indicates genuine agreement. Instead, consensus might reflect the power of ideology to suppress conflict and silence opposition. Vaclav Havel describes how Czech citizens "act[ed] as if" they agreed with the Soviet system in order to survive. They did not need to believe in it, only to accept it, to be willing to "live within a lie." According to Havel, "[ideology] offers human beings the illusion of an identity, of dignity, and of morality while making it easier for them to *part* with them."[5] Because it bridges the distance between self and society, ideology inevitably exists in some tension with personal experience. The relationship between abstract concepts and actual lives is another issue we explore further later.

Third, it is a mistake to assume that the demise of what Bell calls "easy 'left' formulae for social change" is the end of ideology per se.[6] As we later see, ideologies serve many social functions (e.g., communication, legitimation, and socialization), besides mobilizing the proletariat. It seems likely that ideologies continue to unify Western democracies, especially as the media increasingly influence politics. Further, as Bell recognizes, alongside the old ideologies of the West, new ideologies associated with national liberation and group identities have emerged among oppressed people. According to Bell, these ideologies are parochial and instrumental, whereas earlier ones were universal and humanistic. We may question this distinction, but it suggests the importance of considering how ideologies develop historically. Otherwise, we may confuse a change in ideology with the end of ideology.

Fourth, proponents of the end-of-ideology thesis often ignore their own role in creating and sustaining ideologies. They assume that their ideas are somehow above or outside the political fray, or both. Yet, as Theodore Lowi points out, political science is a discipline that serves the state it studies.[7] It is hardly surprising that free elections, a central feature of American democracy, are also a key component of standard definitions of democratic government. Who, we might ask, has the greatest interest in a "politics of civility"? Donald Hodges suggests that bureaucrats, intellectuals, technocrats, and "the disillusioned and exhausted ex-militants of the Left," are the most likely candidates.[8] Robert Haber draws the relevant conclusion: "the 'end of ideology' is a status quo ideological formulation designed to rationalize the incorporation of intellectuals into the American way of life."[9] We later see that political theorists who denigrate ideologies may espouse a similarly self-interested position.

Last, and most important, those who celebrate the end of ideology often adopt a definition of ideology that is itself anti-ideological. The terms of the debate are, quite literally, skewed from the start. Ideology connotes a politics of dangerous dreams, illusory ideals, and utopian schemes. But is this necessarily the case? Isn't hope for something better also a source of social progress? It is the loss of hope that concerns Alasdair MacIntyre in the epigraph to this chapter. He describes critics of utopianism as those who "not only inhabit contemporary social reality but insist upon seeing only what it allows them to see and upon learning only what it allows them to learn, [and] cannot even identify, let alone confront the problems which will be inscribed in their epitaphs."[10] His words are harsh. That is because the place of values in politics is at issue. Max Weber, in an effort to make politics "rational," first declared the separation of facts from values. According to Weber, "an empirical science cannot tell anyone what he *should* do—but rather what he *can* do—and under certain circumstances—what he wishes to do."[11] For Weber, empirical science yields "unconditionally valid" knowledge of social reality, whereas the validity of values is "a matter of faith." Many scholars have questioned the fact/value distinction, claiming that natural science may be value neutral but that politics, including political science, is always value laden. Scientific objectivity, they suggest, should not be confused with moral indifference. In Kurt Lewin's words: "science gives more freedom and power to both the doctor and the murderer, to democracy and Fascism. The social scientist should recognize his responsibility also in this respect."[12] MacIntyre's—and our—focus here is a slightly different but closely related question: might a politics without hope be as dangerous, if not more dangerous, than the utopian schemes that preceded it?

Friedrich Nietzsche claims it is "a general law: every living thing can become healthy, strong, and fruitful only within a horizon; if it is incapable of drawing a horizon around itself or, on the other hand, too selfish to restrict its version to the limits of a horizon drawn by another, it will wither away feebly or overhastily to its early demise."[13] If ideologies form horizons, then what might follow the end of ideology? According to Eric Hobsbawm, "worse visions and more dangerous dreams, such as religious fundamentalism, nationalist zealotry, or, more generally,...racially tinged xenophobia" may fill the ensuing moral vacuum.[14] This possibility, in some cases already a reality, suggests that we should reassess the merits of ideology. We might begin by reconsidering the meaning of the term. Has ideology always had pejorative connotations? If not, how did it acquire them? By exploring these questions, we can better understand the current controversy and the continued importance of ideology.

Defining Ideology: A Brief History

The *Oxford English Dictionary* provides two standard definitions of ideology.[15] The first is descriptive or neutral: ideology is the "science of ideas." This definition, indeed the word ideology, originated with Destutt de Tracy, a French Enlightenment philosopher. Contemporary social scientists who study ideologies as belief systems adopt this usage. A second definition is critical or deprecatory: ideology is "ideal or abstract speculation" and "unpractical or visionary theorizing." This understanding better fits popular usage, especially pejorative references to ideologues as dogmatists. Both definitions are common today, but there is some historical distance between them. As John Thompson points out, few today would proudly proclaim themselves ideologues.[16] Yet de Tracy and his followers once did just that. Why were they proud to be Ideologues? The answer to this question also begins to address another: why study ideologies?

The history of ideology begins with de Tracy's notion that ideas originate in sensory experience and that their origins can be studied scientifically. De Tracy contrasted ideology with metaphysics: "ideology, on the other hand, was very sensible since it supposes nothing doubtful or unknown; it does not call to mind any [supernatural] idea of cause.... Its meaning is very clear to everyone."[17] For de Tracy, the science of ideas had positive political connotations. Ideology constituted a challenge to existing authorities; philosophers and priests were superfluous if ideas were "very clear to everyone." Since everyone could understand ideas, everyone should discuss them and decide among them. De Tracy explicitly associated his sensationalist psychology with democratic politics. He was a French revolutionary, a defender of individual freedom and representative government. A friend attested to de Tracy's (and his compatriots') political aspirations: "*Ideology* they told me would change the face of the earth, and that is exactly why those who wish the world to always remain stupid (and with good cause) detest Ideology and the Ideologues."[18]

This historical background further complicates the definition of ideology by suggesting a third and largely forgotten meaning. According to de Tracy, ideology was a democratic philosophy, a defense of popular intelligence. The science of ideas, today a neutral definition, originally had positive connotations and only later developed negative ones. Napoleon, de Tracy's contemporary, first used ideology pejoratively. He referred to the Ideologues as a "metaphysical faction" and, less flatteringly, as "dangerous dreamers" and "windbags . . . who have always fought the existing authorities."[19] Here, too, the term had political connotations. In his famous denunciation of ideology, Napoleon says:

> We must lay the blame for the ills that our fair France has suffered on ideology, that shadowy metaphysics. . . . Indeed, who was it that proclaimed the principle of insurrection to be a duty? Who adulated the people and attributed to it a sovereignty which it was incapable of exercising? Who destroyed respect for and the sanctity of laws by describing them, not as sacred principles of justice, but only as the will of an assembly composed of men ignorant of civil, criminal, administrative, political, and military law?[20]

Like de Tracy, Napoleon links ideology and democracy, but his linkage is a negative one. With their democratic dreams, the Ideologues destroyed the illusions necessary for social order and human happiness.

The Ideologues' claim that democratic ideas, that ideology would "change the face of the earth," surely sounded utopian in eighteenth-century France. Genuine democracy remains a distant prospect more than two centuries later. Yet Western history reveals slow, steady progress toward democratic ideals. Why, then, have the negative connotations Napoleon associated with ideology persisted? Why is ideology so often dismissed as dogmatic, irrational, metaphysical, simplistic, or utopian thinking, or all these things? Most important, why does the intellectual history of ideology portray it as incompatible with democracy?

Karl Marx, a nineteenth-century German philosopher, took the next significant step in the history of ideology when he provided socioeconomic explanations for philosophical ideas. Marx knew de Tracy's work and probably adopted the term "ideology" from him. Like Napoleon, Marx criticized the Ideologues' idealism and associated ideologies with metaphysics. Unlike Napoleon, Marx traced the origins of ideology to the class conflicts that underlie even democratic politics. According to Marx, ideologies have three basic characteristics. They are social, functional, and illusory forms of consciousness. Marx argues that societies develop belief systems that fit their historical contexts. Class relations are the most important influences on forms of social consciousness. Marx says, "the ideas of the ruling class are in every epoch the ruling ideas, i.e., the class which is the ruling *material* force of society, is at the same time its ruling *intellectual* force."[21] Ideologies function for the ruling class as legitimating illusions. They make its rule seem natural and its interests seem universal when, in fact, history involves continual conflict between classes.

For Marx, ideology obstructs democracy by preventing subordinate classes from understanding the sources of their oppression. Marx fears that democracy, when narrowly construed as political emancipation, is itself an ideology. Political emancipation gives citizens rights but without eliminating the economic oppression that prevents them from exercising those rights equally and freely. For example, workers are not "free to choose" their employers or the conditions of their employment as long as they must work to stay alive and they live in a company town. Marx distinguishes political emancipation from human emancipation. The latter involves a genuine, that is, economic, social, *and* political democracy. Such a democracy provides people with the economic resources they need to develop their capacities and exercise their rights. Only after people see through the ideological illusion of "bourgeois democracy" does Marx think they will organize fully to emancipate themselves.

The question that arises here is: why would people believe ideological illusions? Sigmund Freud, the next major figure in many histories of ideology, offers an answer. Freud's focus is religion, not ideology, but he suggests that they have a common origin: "Having recognized religious doctrines to be illusions, we are at once confronted with the further question: may not all cultural possessions, which we esteem highly and by which we let our life be ruled, be of a similar nature? Should not the assumptions that regulate our political institutions likewise be called illusions?"[22] To understand the human need for illusions, it is necessary to look briefly at Freudian psychology. According to Freud, the psyche has three parts: id, ego, and superego. The id involves the basic instincts, eros (libido) and thanatos (aggression). The ego mediates between those instincts and reality, balancing internal desires with external demands. The superego is the conscience, the site of internalized social values, which helps the ego control the id. For Freud, social life requires individuals to repress or redirect their instincts, or both. Needless to say, this is a painful process. But, along with its prohibitions, society provides substitute gratifications. As the locus of social values, ideologies not only discipline individuals but also provide a largely unconscious sense of security. According to Freud, most people do not really want to be free; taking responsibility for themselves is too frightening for them.

The presence of an "unconscious ideology" may explain why social norms persist long after legal reforms. Bem and Bem offer such an explanation for the tenacity of sexism. An unconscious ideology reinforces traditional sex roles, virtually guaranteeing that most American women "choose" to bear children and accept primary responsibility for raising them. As they put it, "Discrimination frustrates choices already made. Something more pernicious perverts the motivation to choose."[23] Perceived threats to psychological security systems can also explain political violence. According to Erich Fromm, the appeal of fascism is its promise of an "escape from freedom" through obedience to the "Führer," a surrogate father.[24] In psychological terms, ideology is undemocratic because it encourages individuals unconsciously to accept the status quo instead of determining their own values.

Of the many other figures included in histories of ideology, I now discuss only one: Karl Mannheim.[25] His work is important because he states what Marx and Freud imply: ideology is often a conservative force in history. Mannheim distinguishes between ideology and utopia. An ideological perspective values the status quo and reinforces it by obscuring other alternatives. Ideology, in this sense, accompanies attempts by a ruling class to prevent its own demise. In contrast, a utopian perspective values what does not yet exist and promotes the changes necessary to create it. Utopias can also obscure, specifically, by neglecting ideological (and other) barriers to change. But whereas ideologies, especially those held unconsciously, restrict political activity, utopian ideas tend to encourage it. Again, democracy, which requires an active citizenry, is incompatible with ideology.

Popular intelligence to popular illusions: that summarizes the history of ideology. De Tracy's democratic philosophy is followed by Napoleon's shadowy metaphysics, Marx's false consciousness, Freud's wish fulfillment, and Mannheim's social conformity. In these (and many other) philosophies, Napoleon's pejorative usage persists, but it assumes a new meaning. The recurring theme is not the association of ideology with democracy but the tensions between them. No wonder those who treat ideology as a pejorative term conclude that democrats should not be ideologues and that the end of ideology is a progressive development. Yet this conclusion neglects the promise of ideology as de Tracy defines it—as the democratic science of ideas. Might we reclaim that promise today as an alternative to the end of ideology and an antidote to more dangerous dreams? If so, the study of ideology is extremely important.

Why to Study Ideology

The standard reason political scientists give for studying ideologies is their significance in modern politics. Ideologies perform several crucial functions. Most important, ideologies legitimate political systems by establishing the basic values to which they should adhere. Another function, socialization, is closely related. Ideologies help socialize individuals by giving them a shared identity, consisting of customs, language, roles, symbols, values, and so on. Through these shared meanings ideologies facilitate communication between different individuals. Ideologies also mobilize people, whether by class, group, nation, party, race, or sex. Contrary to Mannheim, political scientists use the term ideology to refer to sources of both stability and instability, concord and conflict, stasis and change, in politics. According to Roy Macridis, "the dynamics of politics . . . lie in the ideas people develop."[26] Leon Baradat concludes, "a clear understanding of current ideologies is essential to anyone who hopes to grasp the political realities of our time."[27]

Although ideologies still perform these political functions, I have suggested another, more important reason for studying ideologies: the need for values in politics, especially democratic politics. Political scientists' standard definitions ignore this dimension of ideology. Ideology is "a set of closely related beliefs, or ideas, or even attitudes, *characteristic of* a group or community" or "a value or belief system *accepted as* fact or truth by some group."[28] These definitions parallel the neutral—and neutralized—usage we saw from the *Oxford English Dictionary.* They suggest that everyone has an ideology. That you have an ideology. But what is it? The one "characteristic of [your] group or community"? And why do you have it? Because it is "accepted as fact or truth"? In a democracy, these answers are woefully inadequate. What such definitions ignore is the political problem, the problem of democracy that de Tracy raised. Ideologies not only perform the functions political scientists analyze. They also raise claims to moral truth that require justification. In a democracy, these claims should not be ascribed to citizens or imposed on them. They can be justified only through extensive discussion of competing ideas, followed by egalitarian decision-making processes. Studying ideologies, then, increases citizens' ability to assess competing truth claims and make informed choices among them.

Even democracy, to be true to itself, must be a topic of debate. It is not enough to *be* a democrat. Democracy, as John Stuart Mill tells us, cannot survive, let alone thrive, on dogma and sloth. Murray Edelman recently said that the American "'public' is mainly a black hole into which the political efforts of politicians, advocates of causes, the media, and the schools disappear with hardly a trace."[29] Apathy, indifference, quiescence, and resistance—these words describe the citizens of postideological politics. They suggest that modern citizens should (re)learn how to participate in democratic politics.

To resurrect ideology as de Tracy viewed it, as the democratic demonstration of ideas, is difficult today. Most of us no longer share de Tracy's confidence in sensory experience. The laws of nature—empirical, metaphysical, or both—are no longer so self-evident as they were when Jefferson wrote the Declaration of Independence. The source of moral standards today is, at best, citizens' considered, collective judgment. Since those standards should not be ascribed or imposed, the conditions under which citizens exercise judgment become crucial.

Jürgen Habermas has attempted to specify those conditions, to provide criteria by which democratic citizens can assess value claims. As part of his theory of democratic discourse, he describes an ideal speech situation characterized by three conditions. First, anyone should be able to raise any issue for discussion. Second, during discussions, everyone should speak sincerely and seek understanding. Third, any decisions reached should be applied equally to all. Habermas describes these conditions as "complete symmetry in the distribution of assertion and dispute, revelation and concealment, prescription and conformity, among the partners in communication."[30] They are, he argues, linguistic approximations of truth, freedom, and justice. Many obstacles prevent actual democracies from realizing these conditions. Without equal educational opportunities and some economic security, individuals lack the ability, energy, and resources to debate political issues. Habermas has been criticized as a utopian thinker. Still, the ideal speech situation can help guide efforts to recover a positive—and democratic—sense of ideology.

Political Ideology and Political Theory

Unfortunately, political theorists often distinguish between philosophy (or theory) and ideology in order to denigrate the latter. According to Roy Macridis, "what separates theory or philosophy from ideology is that while the first two involve contemplation, organization of ideas, and whenever possible, demonstration, ideology incites people into action."[31] He adds that because they are oriented toward collective action, "ideologies are inevitably highly simplified, and even distorted versions of the original [philosophical] doctrines."[32] David Ingersoll and Donald Matthews agree that ideology is easily distinguished from philosophy, but their argument has a less critical cast. They claim that "what is often called the Age of Ideology came about as a reaction to classical philosophic thought and its apparent lack of concern with processes by which change could be effected."[33] Unlike philosophy, ideology oversimplifies in order to motivate action.

What is at stake in these efforts to divide and rank systems of ideas? The ideology/philosophy distinction raises the issue of the relationship between theory and practice. In doing so, it reinvokes the end-of-ideology debate. Bell also argued that ideologies translated ideas into action: "ideology is the conversion of ideas into social levers."[34] From his status quo position, this conversion process carried pejorative connotations. Other scholars have taken a more positive approach. Roy Macridis argues that history involves a dialectic between philosophical ideas and social needs. An ideology emerges when they converge and, by mediating between theory and practice, plays a crucial role in political change. Without ideology, "heartfelt demands arising from the social body may fail for the lack of ideas; and ideas may go begging for a long time for the lack of relevance to social needs."[35] Macridis implies that the presence of ideology does not necessarily result in ideological politics. Robert Haber makes this crucial distinction explicit. He stresses that the translation of ideas into action varies with social movements and political contexts. Simplification may be necessary, but demagoguery, dogmatism, and dehumanization are not, as long as the translation process involves democratic institutions and procedures. To argue otherwise is to call not only for the end of ideology but for the end of politics altogether.[36]

Perhaps that is some political theorists' unconscious intention. According to Richard Ashcraft, the dominance of philosophical methods in political theory has led to the denigration of political ideologies. Ashcraft notes that these methods divorce theory from history and politics. Political theorists "link historically-rooted political theory with ideology, and great political theory with trans-historical philosophy."[37] This distinction is difficult to sustain; it is also self-serving. It allows political theorists to ignore how their ideas are shaped by their political context. Philosophical arguments, it implies, are above politics, outside history, or both. If so, political theorists are spared from analyzing their assumptions, including the distinction between great philosophical and minor ideological texts.

This suggests a final and a more scholarly reason for studying political ideologies. Approaching philosophy as ideology contributes to the creation of a more democratic political theory. Many political theorists are engaged in this effort. Benjamin Barber has called for a philosophy that "renders judgment in political terms rather than reducing politics to the terms of formal reason."[38] Terence Ball has undertaken conceptual histories to reinvigorate our sense of politics (and political science) as argument.[39] William Connolly long ago defined a "responsible ideology" as "one in which a serious and continuing effort is made to elucidate publicly all of the factors involved in its formulation and in which a similar effort is made to test the position at a strategic point by *all* available means."[40] John Thompson has developed a "potentially positive usage" of ideology as "the social imaginary."[41] Although Destutt de Tracy is seldom acknowledged, he is no longer alone in understanding political ideology as a democratic philosophy.

How to Study Ideology

I have suggested three reasons for studying political ideologies: to understand modern politics, to discuss and to choose among political values, and to democratize political theory. But how should ideologies be studied?

To be understood properly, ideologies should be situated in history. We already have seen one example of how important context can be. De Tracy, Napoleon, Marx, Freud, and Mannheim used the same word, "ideology," to convey very different meanings. In other cases, the same meaning may be communicated by different words. In the mid-nineteenth century, a liberal was someone who espoused a free market and limited government. Today, most Americans associate the label "liberal" with supporters of welfare programs and big government. In popular discourse, those once called "liberals" are now commonly referred to as "conservatives." Yet philosophers describe the range of positions from free market to welfare state with the same term, "liberalism." There are two important relationships to consider here, one between words and concepts, and another between philosophical and popular meanings.

In a recent article, Michael Freeden suggests how they converge. He argues that political concepts (e.g., liberty, equality, power, justice) are the "building blocks" of political theories. Ideologies impute meanings to concepts by placing them in a structured relationship with other concepts. For example, liberals and conservatives employ the concept and, in this case, also the word, "liberty," but their definitions of it vary based on its relation to equality. As Freeden puts it, ideologies "aim at cementing the word-concept relationship. By determining the meaning of a concept they can then attach a single meaning to a political term. Ultimately, ideologies are configurations of *decontested* meanings...."[42] Of course, the meanings of liberal and conservative also vary with the context. The increasing use of prefixes and, to a lesser extent, suffixes (e.g., neoconservative, postmodern, anarchafeminist) may indicate a period of ideological change. Perhaps a new terminology is needed to describe contemporary ideologies. But this need not suggest the end of ideology.

Understanding ideologies also requires a particular approach to learning: "connected knowing."[43] Most people are (or have learned to be) "separate knowers." Gaining knowledge means separating oneself—one's beliefs, concerns, ideas, and values—from the subject of study in order to master it. This epistemological stance involves analyzing, doubting, criticizing a position from above or outside. Of course, such an objective stance is difficult, if not impossible, to achieve. Instead of feigned objectivity, I suggest the more empathic and interactive relationship between student and subject called "connected knowing." A connected knower cares about how others understand themselves and tries to understand them in their own terms. Connected knowing also involves suspending the self, but for a very different purpose. Connected knowers are willing to enter into another worldview, to adopt another perspective, for the purpose of increased understanding. Does this mean that one should become a liberal, a conservative, even a fascist and a socialist? Yes, at least temporarily. "Separate knowing" is also an important skill; it enhances analytical and critical capacities. But separate knowing is an inappropriate way to begin studying an ideology. Only after one understands another viewpoint thoroughly can one criticize it effectively. Besides, consciously adopting another perspective can make us more aware of our own unconscious ideology. By exploring a variety of viewpoints, you may also find that other ideologies provide valuable insights.

Studying ideologies this way is risky business. It changes people, making them aware of their own assumptions and enabling them to assess them. But you should demand no less of yourself. Ignorance, especially when it reinforces our interests, can be bliss, but it is also true that an unexamined life is not worth living. Democracy does not thrive on dogma and sloth. A democracy asks its citizens to consider the relationship between ideas, language, and power—including their own.

Human beings have the unique capacity to reflect on and, as necessary, reassess their basic values. Only by exercising this capacity can citizens retain "the ethical impulse of utopian thinking" and reject the undemocratic tendencies that all too often accompany it.[44]

Notes

1. Daniel Bell, "The End of Ideology in the West," in *The End of Ideology Debate*, ed. Chaim J. Waxman (New York: Funk and Wagnalls, 1968), 96.

2. Ibid., 99.

3. Francis Fukuyama, *The End of History and the Last Man* (New York: Free Press, 1992).

4. Robert Haber, "The End of Ideology as Ideology," in Waxman, *End of Ideology Debate*, 184.

5. Vaclav Havel, *The Power of the Powerless: Citizens against the State in Central-Eastern Europe* (Armonk, N.Y.: M.E. Sharpe, 1985), 28.

6. Bell, "End of Ideology," 103.

7. Theodore Lowi, "The State of Political Science: How We Become What We Study," in *Discipline and History*, ed. James Farr and Raymond Seidelman (Ann Arbor: University of Michigan Press, 1993).

8. Donald Clark Hodges, "The End of 'The End of Ideology,'" in Waxman, *End of Ideology Debate*, 388.

9. Haber, "End of Ideology," 205.

10. Alasdair MacIntyre, *Three Rival Versions of Moral Enquiry: Encyclopaedia, Genealogy, and Tradition* (Notre Dame, Ind.: University of Notre Dame Press, 1990), 235.

11. Max Weber, "'Objectivity' in Social Science," in *The Methodology of the Social Sciences,* trans. and ed. Edward Shils and Henry Finch (New York: Free Press, 1949), 54.

12. Kurt Lewin, *Resolving Social Science* (New York: Harper & Row, 1948), 213, quoted in Waxman, *End of Ideology Debate*, 8.

13. Friedrich Nietzsche, *On the Advantage and Disadvantage of History for Life,* trans. Peter Preuss (Indianapolis: Hackett, 1980), 10.

14. Eric Hobsbawm, "Lost Horizons," *New Statesman & Society* 3 (14 September 1990): 17.

15. *Oxford English Dictionary,* 1933, s.v. "Ideology."

16. John Thompson, *Studies in the Theory of Ideology* (Berkeley: University of California Press, 1984), 1.

17. Antoine Destutt de Tracy, "Memoire sur la Faculté de Penser," MIN I 323, quoted by Emmet Kennedy in "'Ideology' from Destutt de Tracy to Marx," *Journal of the History of Ideas* 40, no. 3 (July–September 1979): 353–68, at 354–55. For a more extensive discussion of de Tracy, see Emmet Kennedy, *A Philosophe in the Age of Revolution: Destutt de Tracy and the Origins of Ideology* (Philadelphia: American Philosophical Society, 1978).

18. Biran to Abbé Feletz, 30 July 1802, *Œuvres de Maine de Biran*, 6:140, quoted by Kennedy in " 'Ideology,' " 357–58.

19. Napoleon, "Response à l'adresse du Conseil d'État," in *Moniteur*, 21 December 1812, quoted in ibid., 358–59.

20. Kennedy, " 'Ideology,' " 364.

21. Karl Marx and Friedrich Engels, *The German Ideology*, ed. C.J. Arthur (New York: International Publishers, 1977), 64.

22. Sigmund Freud, *The Future of an Illusion*, trans. W.D. Robson-Scott (New York: Liveright, 1955), 59. My remarks here parallel those of Mostafa Rejai, s.v. "Ideology," in the *Dictionary of the History of Ideas*, vol. 2, 1973.

23. Sandra L. Bem and Daryl J. Bem, "Homogenizing the American Woman: The Power of an Unconscious Ideology," in *Feminist Frameworks: Alternative Theoretical Accounts of the Relations between Women and Men*, 2d ed., ed. Alison M. Jaggar and Paula S. Rothenberg (New York: McGraw-Hill, 1984), 12.

24. Erich Fromm, *Escape from Freedom* (New York: Avon Books, 1965).

25. Karl Mannheim, *Ideology and Utopia*, trans. Louis Wirth and Edward Shils (London: Routledge and Kegan Paul, 1948).

26. Roy Macridis, *Contemporary Political Ideologies*, 4th ed. (Boston: Scott, Foresman/Little, Brown, 1989), 12.

27. Leon P. Baradat, *Political Ideologies: Their Origins and Impact*, 3d ed. (Englewood Cliffs, N.J.: Prentice Hall, 1988), xii.

28. John Plamenatz, *Ideology* (New York: Praeger, 1970), 15; and Lyman Tower Sargent, *Contemporary Political Ideologies: A Comparative Analysis*, 10th ed. (Belmont, Calif.: Wadsworth, 1996), 3. Italics mine.

29. Murray Edelman, *Constructing the Political Spectacle* (Chicago: University of Chicago Press, 1988), 7.

30. Jürgen Habermas, "Towards a Theory of Communicative Competence," *Inquiry* 13 (1970): 371.

31. Macridis, *Contemporary Political Ideologies*, 3.

32. Ibid.

33. David Ingersoll and Donald Matthews, *The Philosophic Roots of Modern Ideology: Liberalism, Communism, Fascism* (Englewood Cliffs, N.J.: Prentice Hall, 1986), 7.

34. Bell, "End of Ideology," 96.

35. Macridis, *Contemporary Political Ideologies*, 3.

36. Haber, "End of Ideology," 186.

37. Richard Ashcraft, "Political Theory and the Problem of Ideology," *Journal of Politics* 42 (August 1980): 687–705.

38. Benjamin Barber, *The Conquest of Politics: Liberal Philosophy in Democratic Times* (Princeton: Princeton University Press, 1988), 194.

39. Terence Ball, *Transforming Political Discourse: Political Theory and Critical Conceptual History* (Oxford: Basil Blackwell, 1988), 13.

40. William Connolly, *Political Science and Ideology* (New York: Atherton Press, 1967).

41. Thompson, *Studies in the Theory of Ideology*, 6.

42. Michael Freeden, "Political Concepts and Ideological Morphology,"

Journal of Political Philosophy 2, no. 1 (1994): 156.

43. For this distinction, see Mary Field Belenky et al., *Women's Ways of Knowing: The Development of Self, Love, and Mind* (New York: Basic Books, 1986), chap. 6. These authors find that "connected knowing" is more common among women than men.

44. Seyla Benhabib, "Feminism and Postmodernism," in *Feminist Contentions: A Philosophical Exchange,* ed. Linda Nicholson (New York: Routledge, 1995), 30.

2

Liberalism and Democracy

Democratic government is a purpose held in common, and if it can be understood as a field of temporary coalitions among people of different interests, skills, and generations, then everybody has need of everybody else. To the extent that democracy gives its citizens a chance to chase their own dreams, it gives itself the chance not only of discovering its multiple glories and triumphs but also of surviving its multiple follies and crimes.

— Lewis Lapham

Democracy, Liberalism, and Capitalism

From ancient Athens to nineteenth-century England, democracy, like ideology, had negative connotations. According to C.B. MacPherson, "everybody who was anybody knew that democracy ... would be a bad thing—fatal to individual freedom and to all the graces of civilized living."[1] Democratic Athens executed Socrates for his philosophical teachings. Led by Cromwell, the radical Protestants beheaded King Charles I of England. The French revolutionaries, who declared the Rights of Man, created the Committee of Public Safety, which orchestrated the Terror. Even the American Revolution had its democratic excesses. Shays's Rebellion was a catalyst for the constitutional convention. What was "wrong" with democracy? How did popular sovereignty threaten individual freedom and moral community? How have democrats tried to resolve these tensions? Why does democracy now have positive connotations?

A brief history of three related concepts—democracy, liberalism, and capitalism—begins to answer these questions. *Democracy* is derived from two Greek words: *demos* and *kratos*. *Demos* refers to the people, more precisely, the citizens of a polis, and *kratos* refers to their power or rule. *Demo-kratos* literally means rule by or power of the people as citizens.[2] But this says little about who the people are and how they are to rule. Ancient and modern democrats interpret rule of the people in very different ways.

In Athenian democracy, the *demos* was the largest class of citizens, those who claimed sovereignty by free birth. The poorer classes made up this numerical majority. Aristotle regards the poverty of the *demos* as the defining feature of democracy. Like later critics of democracy, he assumes that economic status shapes moral character, and that the many poor are likely to be "petty," "mean-spirited," and "envious." Conversely, he regards the rich as "useful," "worthy," "best," "well-born," and "notable."[3] Fearing that the poor may put their class interest above the common interest, Aristotle places democracy among the bad regimes.

Since the Athenian *demos* ruled directly, the many poor had considerable power. All citizens participated in the assembly, which met ten times a year and made major decisions (e.g., whether to wage war, how to levy taxes). Between assembly sessions, a Council of Five Hundred administered Athenian law. Council members were chosen by lot (or sortition), and the poor were eligible to serve. Citizens were equal before the law, and they shared duty on huge juries, like the one that convicted Socrates. According to Aristotle, participation improved the moral character of the *demos* and promoted collective wisdom. When Aristotle writes that "man is by nature an animal intended to live in a polis," he means that only in a political community do human beings realize their full potential. Politics develops citizens' ability to speak, to reason, and to judge wisely. In Athens, noncitizens were called *idiotes,* which literally means a private person, but also by implication a fool. Women, slaves, children, and resident aliens comprised this vast category of people. Citizens were a relatively small proportion of the Athenian population, roughly 10 percent. Only they were truly free, since only they could become fully human.

Because citizens had an active, broad, and direct role in politics, Athens is regarded as a participatory democracy. Scholars often use Athenian democracy, specifically the trial of Socrates, to illustrate how popular sovereignty threatens individual freedom. From an Athenian perspective, a different picture emerges. Socrates' execution may reflect a flaw in the Athenians' moral character, but it was not a violation of his rights. In democratic Athens, public and private were not separate spheres. The polis was a civic body—an organic whole—analogous to the human body; politics was a way of life, not a part of it. The Athenians who condemned Socrates revealed their lack of "liberality," an Aristotelian virtue. Aristotle portrays liberality as the mean between the excess of prodigality and the defect of meanness. Liberality suggests moral limits on citizens' property, since the polis cannot survive a large gap between rich and poor. More important here, liberality refers to the quality now called "civility." Prior to the seventeenth century, "the term 'liberal' still functioned chiefly as a derivative of liberality, the classical virtue of humanity, generosity, and the open mind."[4] A "liberal" person was courteous, moderate, prudent, and reasonable. By some accounts the Athenians were "illiberal" in condemning Socrates, but they did not violate his rights, except by modern standards.

In modern democracies, liberty no longer refers to a moral virtue developed through political activity but to freedom from restraint, especially from government control. Benjamin Constant, an eighteenth-century French philosopher, captures the difference: "whereas for modern men, liberty signifies a protected sphere of noninterference or independence under the rule of law, for the ancients it meant entitlement to a voice in collective decision-making."[5] The modern concept of liberty takes shape in the seventeenth-century writings of John Locke, the father of liberalism. Since the origins of liberalism and capitalism are closely connected, the two concepts are best understood together.

Capitalism refers to a free-market economy. Historically, capitalism supplanted feudalism throughout Europe from the seventeenth to the nineteenth centuries. C.B. MacPherson describes the changes that occurred: "instead of a society based on custom, on status, and on authoritarian allocation of work and rewards, you had a society based on individual mobility, on contract, and on impersonal market allocation of work and rewards in response to individual choices."[6] His final phrase, "in response to individual choices," captures the connection between capitalist and liberal philosophy: they are the economics and politics of "free choice."

According to Isaac Kramnick, liberal ideology developed "to persuade men [sic] that it was both possible and right for them to further the progress of the Industrial Revolution by launching a revolutionary attack against the established political order."[7] Against that order, liberals declared individual rights to life, liberty, and, above all, property, and they created a limited government to protect newly freed markets. Kramnick argues that more than coincidence explains the simultaneous publication in 1776 of Thomas Jefferson's Declaration of Independence and Adam Smith's *Wealth of Nations*. As Milton Friedman later points out, liberal democracies continue without exception to have capitalist economies (though the obverse is not true).

The relationship of liberalism to democracy is more tenuous. Despite their rhetoric of rights, early liberals were far from democratic. John Locke's *Treatise of Civil Government,* discussed in the next section, provides a justification for Britain's Glorious Revolution of 1688. After the revolution, Parliament further restricted the suffrage, extended terms of office, and conducted numerous uncontested elections. In America, most states legally limited suffrage with property, race, and/or sex qualifications until 1920. In the 1780s, only 10–15 percent of the population had the right to vote in Massachusetts. In Virginia, the percentage was even smaller.[8] Early liberals' views of the *demos* paralleled those of the ancient democrats (whom they often read). The propertied classes would be least likely to abuse political power, especially since the state protected their property.

Liberalism became democratic only when the people demanded it. In the process, democracy, like liberty, was redefined. With liberalism, politics became an activity far removed from people's daily lives, a perception that persists today. For example, a consumer health advocate defines "being political" as "being interested in the government, national issues, political parties, legislation—things that are far away." She does not understand herself as "politically involved": "I'm completely non-political. The only time I am political is when I vote, and I don't always do that." Yet she is "interested in taking action on things that immediately affect me like my health, my neighborhood, day care for my children, and things like that."[9] A liberal democracy requires only an occasional vote—for a candidate, not a policy—from its citizens. Joseph Schumpeter provided the standard (re)definition of democracy in modern, liberal terms: "[it is] that institutional arrangement for arriving at political decisions in which individuals acquire the power to decide by means of a competitive struggle for the people's vote."[10] Liberalism replaces participatory democracy with a more or less representative government.

The rest of this chapter examines how liberalism gradually became democratic and how democracy was simultaneously "liberalized." In a famous passage, C.B. MacPherson describes the process: "By admitting the mass of the people ... the liberal state did not abandon its fundamental nature; it simply opened the competitive political system to all the individuals who had been created by the competitive market society. ... In so doing, it neither destroyed nor weakened itself; it strengthened both itself and the market society."[11] Whether it also strengthened democracy remains an open question.

In a liberal democracy, liberalism is the dominant partner. For modern liberals, participatory democracy still has negative connotations. Only the right to liberty, as freedom from restraint, makes democracy tolerable. As we explore liberalism's victory, we cannot neglect the costs for democracy. What remains of moral community in modern democracies? According to Robert Bellah, many people "only rarely and with difficulty understand" themselves "as interrelated in morally meaningful ways with . . . other, different Americans."[12] In his interviews, Bellah searches for a common language, a shared morality, a way citizens could speak of something beyond their interests. Is popular sovereignty the primary threat to modern democracy? Or does liberal individualism also pose major problems?

Liberal Individualism and Natural Rights

With his *Treatise of Civil Government,* a defense of the Glorious Revolution of 1688, John Locke became the founding father of liberal ideology.[13] The state of nature, natural rights, the social contract, limited government, and legitimate revolution—these Lockean concepts continue to define rights-based liberalism. Liberals' commitment to individual freedom informs all these concepts.

Locke argues that freedom and equality are the natural condition of humanity. In the state of nature, individuals can act as they choose, since no one has the power to rule over anyone else. The only restraint on natural men is the law of nature, which tells them not to harm themselves or one another. Locke initially says that the law of nature is "plain to a rational creature," but he also claims that people must "consult" and "study" it.[14] When violations of it occur, everyone is authorized to judge and to punish the offender. Locke admits that conflicts frequently occur in the state of nature and that they often lead to a state of war because "there is no [higher] Authority to decide between the Contenders."[15]

According to Locke, the major source of conflict in the state of nature is inequality of property. Individuals have a natural right to life, liberty, and property. The right to property arises from the right to, or a property in, our person. For Locke, "property" refers not only to the objects people consume and possess but also to their capacities, most important, their capacity to labor. Since people own their labor, they become owners of the objects on which they labor. Locke spells out this logic in the following passage:

> Though the Earth, and all inferior Creatures be common to all Men, yet every Man has a *Property* in his own *Person*. This no Body has any Right to but himself. The *Labour* of his Body and the *Work* of his Hands, we may say, are properly his. Whatsoever then he removes out of the State that Nature hath provided, and left it in, he hath mixed his *Labour* with, and joyned to it something that is his own, and thereby makes it his *Property*.[16]

The law of nature places moral limits on the right to property, at least at first. People cannot take more than they can use, and they must leave enough for others to survive. Since surplus goods would quickly spoil and enough exists to provide for all, these moral limitations coincide with people's natural inclinations. According to Locke, the law of nature is quite effective until people introduce money to the state of nature. Money circumvents the natural morality that limited property acquisition. Since money does not spoil, property is no longer restricted to immediate use. More important, the prospect of greater wealth encourages the development of industry. Originally, conditions in the state of nature were merely adequate, not luxurious or penurious. With economic development, scarcity becomes a problem.

Locke recognized that land, the dominant form of property in seventeenth-century England, was a limited resource. He thought a money economy would replace landownership with employment opportunities. In a crucial passage, Locke assumes that workers sell their labor—the "property" of their person—for a wage and that the products they produce then rightly become the property of their employers:

> Thus the Grass my Horse has bit; the Turfs my Servant has cut; and the Ore I have digg'd in any place where I have a right to them in common with others become my *Property*, without the assignation or consent of any body. The *Labour* that was mine, removing them out of that common state they were in, hath *fixed* my *Property* in them.[17]

Wage labor makes the separation of owners and workers, and owning and working, possible. "I" now own what "I" dig, what "my" horse bites, and what "my" servant cuts. As we discuss later, the labor theory of value with which Marx analyzes and criticizes capitalism already exists in Lockean liberalism.

So do the conflicts between classes that prompt people to adopt a social contract. In the state of nature, conflict arises when someone "meddle[s] with what was already improved by another's labour." In Locke's words, the "quarrelsome" and "contentious" violate the property rights of the "industrious" and "rational." It is the "corruption, and vitiousness of degenerate Men" that make government necessary.[18] With these adjectives, Locke suggests that property owners are not only more industrious and rational but also more ethical. It is "Other" people—servants, women, idiots, and children—who neither know nor follow the law of nature. Idiots and children may be less rational, though they are not necessarily less moral. But are women and servants (or, more generally, wage laborers)? According to Locke, members of these groups depend on someone else (e.g., a husband and/or an employer) to survive, and their dependence prevents them from developing their rational capacities. In *The Reasonableness of Christianity*, Locke makes their limitations painfully clear:

> you may as soon hope to have all the day-labourers and tradesmen, the spinsters and dairy-maids, perfect mathematicians, as to have them perfect in ethics this way: hearing plain commands, is the sure and only course to bring them to obedience and practice. The greatest part cannot know, and therefore they must believe.[19]

Lockean liberalism is not democratic even in the modern sense of representative government. Less rational individuals bring fewer rights, including less property, into political society. Locke distinguishes two forms of consent—"express" and "tacit"—in the formation of the social contract.[20] The "industrious" and "rational" explicitly agree to unite in society and to form a government. The rest of the people —"the greatest part"—tacitly consent simply by remaining within its jurisdiction. Not surprisingly, property owners create a government that remedies the "inconveniences" of the state of nature. It is a government of laws whose purpose is limited to protecting individual rights, especially to property.

According to Locke, if government abuses its powers, then sovereignty reverts to the people. Jefferson follows Locke's logic in the Declaration of Independence. He establishes the rights of man, reviews a "long train of abuses," mostly against property, and concludes that revolution against England is justified. Locke did not worry about whether a right to revolution potentially threatened the social order. (Jefferson was less sanguine and more radical.) Locke assumed that property owners would revolt only with just cause and that they would soon reestablish a legitimate government. A century elapsed before popular majorities pursued revolution beyond the objectives of "respectable classes" in America and France.[21]

So far, I have presented Locke's theory quite literally, as if the state of nature really exists or existed. Locke occasionally suggests as much. He says that "all *Princes* and Rulers of *Independent* Governments all through the World, are in a State of Nature." He uses the "*Indian,* in the woods of America" as a example of "Men in that State."[22] But to leave the matter here is to miss Locke's brilliance. By deriving the social contract from a state of nature, Locke sets aside or abstracts from the actual conditions of human society. This theoretical move has three important effects.

First, since individuals are born free and equal, they are solely responsible for their fate, including their economic welfare. For Locke, freedom consists of "being left alone," more precisely, in "being alone."[23] Locke knows that few, if any, people live beyond the bonds of society. A shared culture, history, language, morality, and so forth shapes most people's lives. When Locke takes people out of this social context, he leaves only their property as a measure of worth, a source of identity, and a sign of freedom. The result is a "thin self" whom C.B. MacPherson calls the "possessive individual."[24]

Second, since "once upon a time" everyone had an equal opportunity to acquire property, existing economic inequalities are morally legitimate. They merely reflect differences in ability, effort, luck, talent, or all of these. As an abstraction from society, the state of nature serves a dual purpose for Locke. It allows him to attack a feudal hierarchy that determined social status by noble or ignoble birth and to defend a new—liberal capitalist—hierarchy that ostensibly bases class standing on merit alone.

Third, since the social contract has a prepolitical origin, politics remains a minor part of most people's lives. According to Robert Dahl, the liberal individual is "homo economicus," not "homo politicus." "He" cares about "primary activities involving food, sex, love, family, work"; politics "lies for most people at the outer periphery of attention, interest, concern, and activity."[25] The state of nature sets up liberals' distinction between private and public, individual and citizen. In both cases, the latter is derived from the former, and subordinated to it.

What happens when the "quarrelsome" and "contentious" demand full rights and potentially threaten private property? Locke's writings anticipate tensions between liberalism and democracy, and suggest how liberals might resolve them. In a "liberalized" democracy freedom is being alone, inequalities are morally legitimate, and politics is peripheral. Once democracy no longer requires active citizens, liberals can safely admit the masses to the(ir) political system.

An Economic Interlude: The Invisible Hand

Although his liberalism fits a capitalist ethos, Locke wrote in a mercantilist era when European governments actively regulated industry and trade. A century later, Adam Smith supplied the next major component of liberal ideology: the idea of a naturally harmonious and prosperous economy, or the free market.

Smith assumes that no one is self-sufficient. Since people depend on others to meet their needs, they have a natural "propensity to truck, barter, and exchange one thing for another."[26] That propensity promotes a division of labor that fosters "the great multiplication of the productions of all the different arts." Smith illustrates the advantages of a division of labor with his famous story about making straight pins: "one man draws out the wire, another straights it, a third cuts it, a fourth points it, a fifth grinds it at the top for receiving the head...." A lone worker can produce one pin a day, but ten people performing different tasks can make 48,000 in the same time period.[27]

According to Smith, people are motivated to cooperate by self-interest, not benevolence:

> It is not from the benevolence of the butcher, the brewer, or the baker that we expect our dinner, but from their regard for their own interest. We address ourselves, not to their humanity but to their self-love, and never talk to them of our own necessities but of their own advantages.[28]

The division of labor is closely tied to market forces because people will produce only what they can exchange. Smith claims that current prices provide the information necessary to balance supply and demand. No one controls the market, nor should they. Free competition ensures that economic exchanges are mutually beneficial; otherwise, people would not participate. In adjusting economic activities to market forces, the individual is "led by an invisible hand to promote an end which was no part of his intention.... By pursuing his own interest he frequently promotes that of the society more effectually than when he really intends to promote it."[29] Smith concludes that free markets encourage "a general plenty [that] diffuses itself through all the different ranks of the society."[30]

Smith regards political efforts to improve market processes as presumptuous follies.[31] Only three duties of the sovereign are consistent with his "system of natural liberty." They are:

> first, the duty of protecting the society from the violence and invasion of other independent societies; secondly, the duty of protecting, as far as

possible, every member of the society from the injustice or oppression of every other member of it, or the duty of establishing an exact administration of justice; and, thirdly, the duty of erecting and maintaining certain public works and certain public institutions, which it can never be for the interest of any individual . . . to erect and maintain.[32]

Although Smith prefers laissez-faire economics, his three duties open the door for departures from it. According to Vernon Van Dyke, they are "potentially extensive," especially the third one. Interpretations of it could range from merely providing an economic infrastructure to widely promoting the general welfare. Adam Meyerson concludes, somewhat paradoxically, that "Smith offers an intellectual framework for a generous and compassionate government consistent with a competitive market economy."[33]

Because Smith wrote during the transition from mercantilism to capitalism, confusion over the role of government in the economy is understandable. That role was also a topic of debate among Smith's contemporaries in the United States. Thomas Jefferson shares Smith's commitment to limited government intervention. In his first inaugural, Jefferson said, "a wise and frugal government . . . shall restrain men from injuring one another, . . . shall leave them otherwise free to regulate their own pursuits of industry and improvement."[34] Alexander Hamilton's broad construction of the "general welfare" and "necessary and proper" clauses in the Constitution appalled Jefferson. Hamilton, a mercantilist, interpreted "necessary" as everything applicable to or useful for achieving governmental purposes. This included not only "internal improvements" but also tariff policies, a bounty system, and a national bank. As to the purposes of government, Hamilton confidently stated that "there seems to be no room for a doubt that whatever concerns the general interests of *Learning,* of *Agriculture,* of *Manufactures,* and of *Commerce,* are within the sphere of the national Councils *as far as regards an application of money.*"[35]

Jefferson had grave doubts. Following his election in 1800, he tried to dismantle the Federalists' economic programs, including the national bank. He argued that Americans must choose between economy and liberty *or* profusion and servitude. Jefferson feared that government intervention in the economy would enslave future generations to a huge national debt. Instead, he envisioned a simple society of politically active yeoman farmers. Jefferson thought landownership, public education, and town government would give citizens an interest in politics and moderate their desires. Ultimately, his ideas are closer in spirit to Aristotle than to Smith. Moral community, not capitalist development, was Jefferson's central concern. He refused to believe that "14 out of 15 men were rogues," but he admitted that those numbers might fit "the higher orders and ... those who, rising above the swinish multitude, always contrive to nestle themselves into the places of power and profit."[36] Capitalism raised the specter of corruption, even when guided by an invisible hand.

James Madison, a Federalist and Jefferson's contemporary, offers a defense of limited government closer to Smith's intentions. Unlike Smith, however, Madison extends market principles to government institutions themselves. In *Federalist* No. 10, Madison addresses the problem of factions or groups whose shared interests are contrary to the public interest. According to Madison, the seeds of faction are rooted in human nature. People have different abilities and earn different amounts of property. As a result, they develop opposing class interests and organize themselves in competing groups. Majority factions, composed of the more numerous and less wealthy members of society, are most likely to pursue "improper and wicked project[s]," including "an equal division of property."[37] The problem of democracy is how "to secure the public good and private rights against the danger of such a faction, and at the same time to preserve the spirit and the form of popular government."[38]

According to Madison, the U.S. Constitution solves this problem by applying an economic model to political institutions. As Madison says, "ambition must be made to counteract ambition"—in politics *and* economics. A large republic, a diverse citizenry, a complex federal system, the separation of different branches, a system of checks and balances, the residual power of the people—these constitutional mechanisms create a self-regulating political system. For Madison, the parallels between economic, political, and other interactions are obvious: "this policy of supplying, by opposite and rival interests, the defect of better motives, might be traced through the whole system of human affairs, private as well as public."[39] In politics, it ensures that "a coalition of a majority of the whole society could seldom take place on any other principles than those of justice and the general good."[40] For Madison, institutionalizing competing interests provided the best guarantee of limited government.

Later liberals who transferred Smith's economic theory to politics were less faithful to his intentions. Smith's "potentially extensive" third duty of government almost invites misinterpretation. After all, governments, like markets, might be a good thing because many groups benefit from their various programs. Milton Friedman parodies the misuse of Smith's theory by quoting the Dodo from *Alice in Wonderland*:

"*everybody* has won, and *all* must have prizes."[41] According to Friedman, the political marketplace "operates in precisely the opposite direction ... from Adam Smith's: an individual who intended only to serve the public interest by fostering government intervention is 'led by an invisible hand to promote' private interests, 'which was no part of his intention....'"[42] Ironically, "the twentieth-century liberal has come to favor a revival of the very politics of state intervention and paternalism against which classical liberalism fought."[43]

As Smith's heir, Friedman and other classical liberals would reverse this process. The desire to return to free markets and limited government has earned them the label (economic) "conservatives." Friedman claims that free markets promote a free society in two ways: "On the one hand, freedom in economic arrangements is itself a component of freedom broadly understood, so economic freedom is an end in itself. In the second place, economic freedom is also an indispensable means toward the achievement of political freedom."[44] Applications of Smith's theory to politics often neglect the second point—at their peril. The invisible hand operates in many non- and semieconomic areas of life, for example, the arts, language, and science. It may even apply to politics when participation is voluntary (e.g., neighborhood associations and town meetings). By definition, however, government has a monopoly on the legitimate use of force. It cannot pursue economic policies with an invisible hand, though it may wear a velvet glove instead of brandishing an iron fist. Economic intervention inevitably increases governmental power, contrary to Smith's intentions. Only a free market separates "economic power from political power and in this way enables the one to offset the other."[45]

Not surprisingly, Friedman proposes abolishing numerous government programs, including agricultural price supports, tariffs and quotas, rent control and public housing, minimum wages, regulation of banking, communications, and interstate commerce, and social security insurance.[46] The "lesson to be drawn from the misuse of Smith's third duty" is that government intervention requires thorough justification. Otherwise, Friedman prefers the "temporarily harsh but ultimately beneficent policy of letting market forces work."[47] Like Smith, he claims that they will work, as long as the state only umpires the game.

According to John Gray, liberals share a strong faith in human progress, which he calls "meliorism."[48] Smith believed that individual differences were small and that the division of labor, by combining talents, would create a "universal opulence which extends itself to the lowest ranks of the people."[49] Less forcefully, Locke argued that "*labour makes* the far greater part of *the value* of things" and improves the common stock, ten or even a hundredfold.[50] Madison is more pessimistic, declaring that the "latent causes of faction are thus sown in the nature of man."[51] He fears the power of the state, especially in the hands of an "adverse majority." In most political extensions of Smith's "system of natural liberty," liberals' optimism triumphs over more pessimistic—and more realistic—strains. To understand why, we return to politics proper and rejoin the struggle to democratize liberalism.

A Question of Utility: Equality and Democracy

"I forego any advantage which could be derived to my argument from the idea of abstract right, as a thing independent of utility. I regard utility as the ultimate appeal on all ethical questions...."[52] With these words, John Stuart Mill placed liberalism on a new foundation. According to L.T. Hobhouse, "in his single person, [Mill] spans the interval between the old and the new Liberalism."[53] Nineteenth-century British politics required a new liberalism. A newly enfranchised working class had begun to use the suffrage to elect representatives who supported social reforms. Mill drew the obvious conclusion: "high wages and universal reading are the two elements of democracy; where they coexist, all government, except the government of public opinion, is impossible."[54] In response, he became the first to adapt liberal ideology to a democratic society.

By forgoing "the idea of abstract right," Mill hopes to give liberalism a stronger foundation. He regards rights-based liberalism as a form of philosophical intuitionism. It posits a natural human faculty (i.e., reason or sense) from which it derives a fictitious social contract. Utilitarians identify another basis for liberal society, "the greatest happiness principle." By this principle "actions are right in proportion as they tend to promote happiness, wrong as they tend to produce the reverse of happiness."[55] Prior to John Stuart Mill, utilitarians argued that utility could be calculated by the quantity of pleasure or pain and action involved. Mill objects to this quantitative measure, which reduces utilitarian philosophy to "the greatest animal happiness principle." He argues that pleasures vary qualitatively and that human beings, at least those who have experienced both, prefer activities that involve their higher faculties. "[It is] better to be Socrates dissatisfied than a fool satisfied," according to Mill.[56] He espouses "utility in the largest sense, grounded on the permanent interests of man as a progressive being."[57]

Whereas the social contract of rights-based liberalism merely requires a limited government to protect individual rights, utilitarian liberalism further extends the duties of the state. Mill agrees that "to have a right ... is ... to have something which society ought to defend me in the possession of."[58] He adds that the doctrine of equal rights implies a principle of distributive justice. For Mill, "the equal claim of everybody to happiness ... involves an equal claim to all the means of happiness, except in so far as the inevitable conditions of human life, and the general interest ... set limits to the maxim."[59] Although Mill sets strict "limits to the maxim," liberalism is nonetheless transformed: justice now requires equal rights and equal opportunity to exercise them.

For Mill, Western history reveals the gradual, continuous democratization of society: "so it has been with the distinction of slaves and freemen, nobles and serfs, patricians and plebeians; and so it will be, and in part already is, with the aristocracies of colour, race, and sex."[60] In the mid-nineteenth century, Mill already fears that egalitarian trends threaten individual liberty. Democratic citizens too easily forget that government is not only their servant, but also their master. Majority rule may be self-government, but "'self-government' ... is not the government of each by himself, but of each by all the rest."[61] To protect minority rights from majority tyranny, Mill proposes the following principle: "the sole end for which mankind are warranted, individually or collectively, in interfering with the liberty of action of any of their number, is self-protection."[62] A democratic government can legitimately prevent its citizens from harming others, but they are otherwise free to live as they choose. (Mill regards failure to perform some duties, for example, military service, as "harmful.")

Having defined liberty as noninterference, Mill defends his position on utilitarian grounds. Echoing Adam Smith, he claims that "the only unfailing and permanent source of improvement is liberty, since by it there are as many possible independent centres of improvement as there are individuals."[63] This is especially true in democratic societies, which tend toward collective mediocrity. To "rise above mediocrity," the mass public must be "guided by the counsels and influence of a more highly gifted and instructed One or Few."[64] Yet the masses, confident in their ignorance, are inclined to suppress the "Truth." Mill presents the executions of Socrates and Christ as horrifying examples of their fallibility. He refuses to assume that truth eventually triumphs over error. Only liberty protects "genius" from the masses, who cannot easily appreciate or understand it. In any case, truth grows stronger when it is defended against error. Mill regards intellectual activity as a higher pleasure well worth cultivating. Human beings should base their opinions on reasoned argument, instead of authority or prejudice. Otherwise, they lack real meaning and become dead dogmas, not living truths. Opinions can also become one-sided, even self-serving, when left unchallenged by opposing ideas:

> Unless opinions favourable to democracy and to aristocracy, to property and to equality, to cooperation and to competition, to luxury and to abstinence, to sociality and individuality, to liberty and discipline, ... are expressed with equal freedom, and enforced and defended with equal talent and energy, there is no chance of both elements obtaining their due; one scale is sure to go up, and the other down.[65]

With every extension of the franchise, the scale tips toward democracy and, for Mill, mediocrity. Freedom of speech, or a "marketplace of ideas," provides a counterweight to public opinion.

Mill also defends representative government on utilitarian grounds. In liberal democracies, citizens' rights are secure because they possess sovereign power. Mill strongly supports universal suffrage. He promotes an active citizenry, since political participation can create social awareness. According to Mill, political apathy threatens democratic government. Nonvoters are more likely to be discontented than satisfied with their representatives. Yet, Mill fears another tendency of democratic publics: popular sovereignty can lead to class politics, as well as collective mediocrity. The poorer majority may support economic policies that place intolerable burdens on wealthier citizens. Mill proposes two measures as counterweights. A system of proportional representation would guarantee minority voters some government seats by combining their votes across electoral districts. A plan for plural voting that allocates votes by merit (i.e., occupation and education) could give better informed voters greater influence on public policy.

As a strong believer in human progress, Mill presents proportional representation and plural voting as temporary strategies. In a passage from his autobiography, written with Harriet Taylor, he reiterates his faith that current tensions between liberty and equality will disappear, though more slowly than they had hoped:

> We were now much less democrats than I had been, because so long as education continues to be so wretchedly imperfect, we dreaded the ignorance and especially the selfishness and brutality of the masses; but our ideal of ultimate improvement went far beyond Democracy, and would class us decidedly under the general designation of Socialists.... The social problem of the future we considered to be, how to unite the greatest individual liberty of action with a common ownership in the raw materi-

als of the globe, and an equal participation of all in the benefits of combined labour.[66]

According to Mill, liberal democracies will eventually create virtuous citizens capable of governing society for the common good. They will do so without sacrificing individual liberty to higher purposes as ancient democracies all too often did.

Contemporary Challenges

Possessive individuals, legitimate inequalities, and limited government—these are Locke's liberal legacy. Add Smith's concept of the invisible hand, whereby private interests promote public goods (or, at least, avoid public bads), and the major themes of liberalism are present. By applying Smith's market principle to questions of political justice, Mill's utilitarianism clears the way for a "potentially expansive" liberalism. Although later liberals offer variations on earlier themes, they do not propose a fundamentally different approach.

In this final section, we examine some recent efforts to balance liberalism and democracy. Many of the authors discussed call themselves "communitarian liberals," a term that suggests that they combine communal aspects of ancient democracies with the individual freedoms of modern societies. A prominent communitarian, Amitai Etzioni, conveys the challenges they face in the following metaphor: "societies, like bicycles, teeter and need continuously to be pulled back to the center lest they lean too far toward anarchy or tyranny." Only by finding the "elusive center" can liberals avoid the "curse of either/or."[67]

Individuality and Community

According to Isaac Kramnick, possessive individuals share certain personality traits: they tend to be ambitious, restless, fearful, competitive, insecure, uneasy people. In Smith's words, these qualities "rouse and keep in continual motion the industry of mankind." Smith and many other liberals portray life as a race with money as the prize. To lose the race is a fate worse than death, since economic success defines the self.[68] An interviewee in *Habits of the Heart* describes the pressure to succeed: "to be a square dude is hard work, man." Another says despairingly, "most people have been sold a bill of goods by our system. I call it the Three C's: cash, convenience, consumerism."[69]

According to Robert Bellah, possessive individuals escape the "race of life" only in their private lives. In economics and politics, they are utilitarian: they calculate the costs and benefits, gains and losses, of their actions. With friends and family, they are more expressive, revealing their genuine desires, emotions, and needs. Both types of interaction rest on individual freedom to choose a "lifestyle." Yet Bellah finds that people cannot fully convey their sense of self in these liberal-capitalist terms. They know we are not "born free as we are born rational." Nor are restraints on others "all that makes existence valuable." In Bellah's words, "a completely empty self that operates out of purely arbitrary choice is theoretically imaginable but performatively impossible."[70]

People's actual lives are shaped by what Bellah calls "communities of memory and hope." Families, churches, towns, neighborhoods —these associations elude the language of choice. The liberals we have discussed occasionally acknowledge these social connections. Locke compares parental authority to swaddling clothes, saying, "Age and Reason as they grow up, loosen them till at length they drop quite off, and leave a Man at his own free Disposal."[71] He insists that society cannot tolerate atheists, since "promises, covenants, and oaths, which are the bonds of human society, can have no hold upon an atheist."[72] Friedman includes paternalism (i.e., care for those who cannot care for themselves) among the functions of government. He prefers to regard "the ultimate operative unit in our society [as] the family, not the individual" (though he claims that "children are responsible individuals in embryo").[73] Against charges that utilitarianism elevates private vices to public virtues, Mill responds that it creates "in the mind of every individual an indissoluble association between his own happiness and the good of the whole."[74]

Yet liberalism does little to sustain community. Current debates about hate speech provide an interesting illustration. How, if at all, should the state respond when a white male student yells, "Shut up, you black water buffaloes.... Go back to the zoo where you belong," from a dormitory window at black female students making noise on the sidewalk below? These insults hardly advance knowledge, but the First Amendment may protect them. According to Mary Ellen Gale, by tolerating hate speech, liberals may unravel a "social fabric of mutual respect."[75] The white male student's subtext is "you are not like us" and "you don't belong here." He would define those who belong to the community by excluding others from it, in this case, from the human race.

Critics of multiculturalism fear that it promotes a "politics of identity" that further fragments American society. As a partial response, Bellah suggests that we distinguish authoritarian groups, ranging from the politically correct to the neo-Nazis, from genuine communities. "What makes [the former] different," he says, "is the shallowness and distortion of their memory and the narrowness of what they hope for."[76] Genuine communities form around deep commitments to shared values. Since liberal individualism cannot easily sustain genuine community, it also cannot easily counter political fragmentation or authoritarian groups. It may even contribute to them. According to Benjamin Barber, "barred from legitimate community by abstract liberty, the universal person may be all too ready to abdicate his actual liberty for the benefits of an illegitimate community."[77] Robert Nisbet succinctly says there is "a fatal affinity of power and individual loneliness."[78]

Both sides in this ongoing debate raise the same question: how should Americans "define the 'we' in 'We the People'?"[79] Separatist strategies can create intergroup hostility; they also develop group members' self-esteem. Many liberals now promote strengthening individuality through community. Diane Ravitch suggests that multiculturalism be interpreted as "pluralism with unity." "Celebrations and recognition of diversity should occur within the context of celebrating and recognizing the common bonds that made these accomplishments possible."[80] Rather than invoke the state, Etzioni proposes nonlegal responses to hate speech. Communities should publicly disapprove of such expressions and renew their commitment to toleration of all their members.

Like other liberals, communitarians seek the point of balance between individuality and community. As Ravitch says, "it is time now to value and nurture a healthy balance between cultural pluralism and the common good."[81] For Etzioni, "communities need to foster civility—a sense of social order and mutual consideration."[82] They resurrect earlier associations of "liberal" with "liberality," that ancient virtue of humanity, generosity, and the open mind. Can they re-create a sense of American community? Or has liberal individualism reached an impasse? Caught between empty selves and authoritarian politics? Between modern freedoms and ancient virtues? Bellah captures the challenge liberals face today:

> What we find hard to see is that it is the extreme fragmentation of the modern world that really threatens our individuation; that what is best in our separation and individuation, our sense of dignity and autonomy as persons, requires a new integration if it is to be sustained.[83]

Politics and Markets[84]

"It takes something of an optimist to believe that such relationships, if left alone, produce nothing but felicity," says Theodore Lowi.[85] He regards Smith's invisible hand, the notion that markets self-correct, as a utopian ideal. Actually, existing capitalism has never been laissez-faire. Liberal states establish the rules of the game and provide public goods, which the market cannot. Classical liberals interpret these functions narrowly, but they are still numerous. For example, Friedman admits that government must provide an economic infrastructure to facilitate communication and transportation; a monetary framework to establish a stable currency; a legal system to define contracts, fraud, property, and regulate monopolies; and public policies to regulate "externalities," like environmental pollution. These activities are supposedly consistent with limited government, since their sole purpose is to allow markets to operate efficiently.

What happens, though, when markets fail to produce prosperity? What becomes of the unemployed and the underemployed—the losers in the "race of life"? Classical liberals' response is often harsh. Friedman says, "Life is not fair. It is tempting to believe that government can rectify what nature has spawned. But it is also important to recognize how much we benefit from the very unfairness we deplore." In any case, "it has proved impossible to define 'fair shares' in a way that is generally acceptable, or to satisfy the members of the community that they are being treated 'fairly.'"[86] When the state tries to fix the "race of life," it too often sacrifices individual liberties in the pursuit of equal outcomes.

Welfare state liberals disagree and, like J.S. Mill, argue that equal rights imply equal means to exercise them. T.H. Green, more than Mill, defines freedom as "a positive power or capacity of doing or enjoying something worth doing or enjoying."[87] According to Vernon Van Dyke, government has a positive duty to promote equal opportunity or to give freedom worth. Franklin D. Roosevelt's New Deal exemplifies this vision of freedom. As FDR expressed it, "true individual freedom cannot exist without economic security and independence. . . . We have accepted, so to speak, a second Bill of Rights under which a new basis of security and prosperity can be established for all—regardless of station, race, or creed."[88] His second Bill of Rights, which addressed the needs of labor and capital, included

the right to a useful and remunerative job; the right to earn enough to cover the costs of adequate food, clothing, and recreation; the right of every farmer to raise and sell his products at a return that provides a decent living; the right of every businessman to freedom from unfair competition and domination by monopolies; the right of every family to a decent home; the right to adequate medical care; the right to adequate protection from the economic fears of old age, sickness, accident, and unemployment; and the right to a good education.[89]

According to Roosevelt, these rights were not a "dole." They gave government a rationale for pursuing economic plans that would enrich the nation. He stressed decent jobs, including government-sponsored ones, and social programs as basic aspects of a planned economy.

Later welfare state liberals make similar arguments. Lyndon Johnson's Great Society, especially the Civil Rights and Voting Rights acts, attempted to admit all citizens to full membership in the national community. Great Society economic programs also tried to make the "race of life" fair. In his defense of affirmative action, Johnson explains:

> You do not take a person, who for years has been hobbled by chains and liberate him, bring him to the starting line of a race and then say "you are free to compete with all the others," and still justly believe that you have been completely fair.[90]

Kramnick uses Johnson's words to illustrate the challenge liberals face in creating a "fair meritocracy." Once liberals' new hierarchy, ostensibly based on merit, replaces a feudal order based on birth, new inequalities become similarly entrenched. According to Kramnick, "a doctrine originally designed to serve the class interests of the talented 'have-nots' against the untalented 'haves' now pits the talented 'haves' against the allegedly untalented 'have-nots.'"[91] As long as liberal society discriminates on the basis of class, gender, and race, it cannot know whether the losers in the "race of life" really are the "untalented." For this reason, a liberal principle of distributive justice may require that government guarantee a "fair race." Contrary to Alice's Dodo, whom Friedman quoted, welfare state liberals still assume that the "race of life" yields winners and losers. Their goal is to render the inequalities that result morally legitimate.

With welfare state liberalism, fear of state power recedes. Friedman argued that when politics imitates markets the result betrays Smith's intentions. According to Lowi, the result is an "invertebrate government" that can neither plan nor achieve justice. In a politics of competing groups, coalitions of organized interests, bureaucratic agencies, and congressional committees supersede constitutional provisions and determine public policy. "Invertebrate government" is not only irresponsible but also irrepressible: it grows larger and larger as the demands upon it multiply. Friedman saw the danger and warned other liberals:

"we have been forgetting the basic truth that the greatest threat to human freedom is the concentration of power, whether in the hands of government or anyone else."[92] By using the state to "neutralize" the market, welfare state liberals created a bureaucratic monster and eroded citizens' sense of social responsibility.[93]

The tensions between politics and markets in liberal ideology also appear in popular concepts of distributive justice. Jennifer Hochschild recently identified a disjunction in the economic and political views of American citizens.[94] She defines a disjunction as "a troublesome distinction drawn between two arenas of life" and argues that disjunctions provide "clues to the ways that ideology papers over cracks in the social edifice."[95] The citizens she interviewed espoused personal and political equality, and economic inequality—and could not integrate them. "When asked to juxtapose their egalitarian and differentiating norms—when asked to think about the *political* consequences of redistributing *economic* holdings—most respondents simply stammered apologetically and changed the subject."[96] On economic issues, these citizens were politically paralyzed.

Equal rights may imply equal means, at least to exercise them, but this principle of liberal justice provides little concrete guidance in distributing economic resources. According to Marx, the utilitarian "assumes that the modern petty bourgeoisie ... is the normal man. Whatever is useful to this particular kind of normal man, and to his world, is useful in and for itself. He applies this yardstick to the past, present, and the future."[97] Liberals who insist that economic values follow from political decisions only beg the question.[98] A politics of interests is ill suited for setting economic priorities or achieving distributive justice, partly because a widening gap between rich and poor undermines citizens' sense of democratic community. Aristotle's second definition of "liberality"—as a mean between prodigality and meanness—seems relevant here. Again, Bellah poses the problem for liberals: "we need to reach common understandings about distributive justice—an appropriate sharing of economic resources—which must in turn be based on conceptions of a substantively just society."[99] Hochschild agrees, saying that the presence of a disjunction indicates a "crucial element[s] of democratic deliberation."

Votes and Values

During the nineteenth and twentieth centuries, liberal democracies vastly expanded the power of government in order to satisfy popular demands. A democratized liberalism was seemingly good for the sovereign people and their elected officials. Still, the process of democratizing liberalism has been costly. American citizens are often ambivalent, at best, about democratic politics. Many regard politics as an unsavory activity. More than 30 percent indicated they would have preferred to vote "none of the above" in the 1992 presidential election. Seventy-one percent would not like their children to pursue a political career. Only 7 percent express a "great deal" of confidence in Congress, 16 percent in the presidency, in contrast with 29 percent in the church and 30 percent in the military. In June 1994, 58 percent thought "quite a few" of those running the government were "a little crooked." Thirty-eight percent expressed similar views in 1972.[100]

For these citizens, a "politics of interest" is not a moral endeavor. According to Bellah, citizens' support for markets is based on the belief that their operations are free and fair. These powerful myths are bolstered by the invisibility of market processes. When transferred to politics, however, invisibility precludes responsibility. As one citizen says, "it's like the blind men examining the elephant, and it's like, 'Will somebody *please* get me the overall picture so we can all work with the same information!'"[101] Though no one sees the whole picture, everyone knows money gains access, influences policy, and wins votes. Not surprisingly, voter turnout is relatively low in American politics. In presidential elections, it ranges from 55 to 65 percent.[102] "Politics has become what politicians do; what citizens do (when they do anything) is vote for politicians."[103] Americans are apathetic and cynical about politics, except in small communities.

Americans find residues of Bellah's "communities of memory and hope" in their groups and towns. Like Milton Friedman, Bellah's interviewees express nostalgia for an earlier era. The town meeting best fits their sense of political community. In contrast, national politics is self-interest writ large. A politics of rights or utility or both may be able to harmonize competing interests. Formal rules may also make a "politics of interest" seem fair or, at least, neutral. But liberal principles cannot adequately convey a citizen's moral values and complex identity. "One man, one vote" is the politics of a "thin" or "empty" self.

Lani Guinier, whom Clinton briefly nominated to head the civil rights administration, confronted the built-in biases of seemingly neutral voting procedures. Guinier questioned the fairness of "one man, one vote," claiming that formally neutral electoral procedures could be politically biased in practice. "In a racially divided society, majority rule may be perceived as majority tyranny."[104] Like Mill, Guinier proposed voting schemes that would give minority voters—a different minority—increased power. Her stated goal was equal opportunity to influence outcomes, not equal or even proportionate representation. By challenging simple majority rule on behalf of a black minority, she created a major controversy.

Among other things, Guinier revealed how electoral strategies control citizens' influence on government. According to Benjamin Ginsberg, elections limit the frequency, scope, and intensity of political participation. The vote, cast at regular intervals for known candidates, gives democratic citizens a nondisruptive vehicle for expressing political preferences. Eighteen-year olds received voting rights, in part, to quell student protests over the Vietnam War. In defense of the measure, Senator William Proxmire said, "the situations on many of our college campuses today, alarming as they are, raise this question: why not allow students the right to make a positive choice as an alternative to a negative protest?"[105] Historically, voter registration requirements have shaped the composition of the electorate, keeping less "desirable" citizens away from the polls. The "motor-voter" bill, which allows citizens to register when applying for driver licenses, permits mail-in registration, and makes registration forms available at public assistance agencies, attempts to reverse this tendency.

Cynical citizens, apathetic voters, fragmented groups, and bureaucratic politics. Is this liberal democracy? Or have liberals lost their balance? Yes, to both questions, according to Benjamin Barber:

> It is almost as if there are two democracies in America: the one defined by national parties and presidential politics and bureaucratic policies, a remote world circumscribed by Washington's beltway, walling in the politicians even as it walls out the citizens; and the other defined by neighborhood and block associations, PTAs and community action groups, an intimate domain no larger than a town or a rural county where women and men gather in small groups to adjudicate differences or plan common tasks.[106]

In national politics, liberal institutions have undone democratic participation. The solution is to revitalize citizenship by reconnecting national politics with group and local values. Barber calls the balance "strong democracy" to distinguish it from ancient democracy and representative government. He asks the crucial question: will either the self-interested or the apathetic citizen participate? His answer is important: "even in a privatistic politics dominated by economic interests, it is only the autonomy of politics and the rights of citizens that give modern women and men the real power to shape their common lives." Most simply, "democracy breeds democracy."[107]

What has democracy become? The opening quote characterizes it best. The remnants of common purpose in modern democracy are found in a "field of temporary coalitions among different interests, skills, and generations." A deeper, richer "community of memory and hope" is untenable today. According to Bernice Johnson Reagon, "we've pretty much come to the end of a time when you can have a space that is 'yours alone'—just for the people you want to be there.... There is nowhere you can go and only be with people who are like you. It's over. Give it up."[108]

We now turn to critics of liberal democracy. Many will argue that liberal democracy cannot sustain itself. Many of their criticisms will be familiar to you. In their pursuit of balance, their search for the center, liberals have already considered them. That may be the greatest tribute to liberal ideology.

Notes

1. C.B. MacPherson, *The Real World of Democracy* (New York: Oxford University Press, 1972), 1.

2. Anthony Arblaster, *Democracy* (Minneapolis: University of Minnesota Press, 1987), 13.

3. Derek Phillips, *Looking Backwards: A Critical Appraisal of Communitarian Thought* (Princeton: Princeton University Press, 1993), 131.

4. John Gray, *Liberalism* (Minneapolis: University of Minnesota Press, 1986), ix.

5. Benjamin Constant, *Ancient and Modern Liberty,* quoted by John Gray in *Liberalism,* 3.

6. MacPherson, *Real World of Democracy,* 7.

7. Isaac Kramnick and Frederick Watkins, *The Age of Ideology: Political Thought, 1750 to the Present,* 2d ed. (Englewood Cliffs, N.J.: Prentice Hall, 1979), 3.

8. Arblaster, *Democracy,* 34–36; and Phillips, *Looking Backwards,* 73–74.

9. Quoted by Frank Reissman, "A New Political Culture," *Social Policy,* Summer 1987, 2–4.

10. Joseph Schumpeter, *Capitalism, Socialism, and Democracy* (New York: Harper & Row, 1950), 269. Schumpeter's definition of classical democracy is "that institutional arrangement for arriving at political decisions which realizes the common good by making the people itself decide issues through the election of individuals who are to assemble in order to carry out its will" (p. 250). This representative model already deviates from participatory definitions of democracy as rule *by* the people themselves, not their elected representatives.

11. MacPherson, *Real World of Democracy,* 11.

12. Robert N. Bellah et al., *Habits of the Heart: Individualism and Commitment in American Life* (Berkeley: University of California Press, 1985), 50.

13. Some scholars claim that Thomas Hobbes was the first liberal. Hobbes did posit a state of nature peopled by self-interested individuals and he based political community on a social contract. Because Hobbes's sovereign authority has absolute power, however, I take Locke's *Second Treatise of Government,* in *Two Treatises of Government,* ed. Peter Laslett (New York: Cambridge University Press, 1960), as the first clear statement of liberal ideas.

14. Locke, *Second Treatise,* nos. 6, 12.

15. Ibid., no. 21.

16. Ibid., no. 27.

17. Ibid., no. 28.

18. Ibid., nos. 34, 128.

19. John Locke, *The Reasonableness of Christianity,* ed. I.T. Ramsey (Stanford, Calif.: Stanford University Press, 1958), 66.

20. Locke, *Second Treatise,* no. 119.

21. Arblaster, *Democracy,* 32–35.

22. Locke, *Second Treatise,* no. 14.

23. Bellah, *Habits of the Heart,* 23.

24. C.B. MacPherson, *The Political Theory of Possessive Individualism: Hobbes to Locke* (New York: Oxford University Press, 1962).

25. Robert Dahl, *Who Governs? Democracy and Power in an American City* (New Haven: Yale University Press, 1961), 279.

26. Adam Smith, *The Wealth of Nations,* ed. Edwin Cannan (New York: Modern Library, 1937), 13.

27. Ibid., 4–5.

28. Ibid., 14.

29. Ibid., 423.

30. Ibid., 11.

31. Ibid., 423.

32. Quoted by Milton Friedman and Rose Friedman, *Free to Choose: A Personal Statement* (New York: Avon Books, 1981), 20.

33. Quoted by Vernon Van Dyke, *Ideology and Political Choice: The Search for Freedom, Justice, and Virtue* (Chatham, N.J.: Chatham House, 1995), 14.

34. Thomas Jefferson, "The First Inaugural," in *The Portable Thomas Jefferson,* ed. Merrill Peterson (New York: Viking Press, 1977), 293.

35. Alexander Hamilton, "Report on Manufactures," in *American Political Thought,* 3d ed., ed. Kenneth M. Dolbeare (Chatham, N.J.: Chatham House, 1996), 170.

36. Quoted by Richard Hofstadter in *The American Political Tradition* (New York: Knopf, 1948), 28.

37. James Madison, *Federalist* No. 10, in *The Federalist Papers,* ed. Clinton Rossiter (New York: Mentor Books, 1961), 84.

38. Ibid., 80.

39. Madison, *Federalist* No. 51, 322.

40. Ibid., 325.

41. Friedman and Friedman, *Free to Choose,* 125.

42. Ibid., xix.

43. Friedman and Friedman, *Capitalism and Freedom* (Chicago: University of Chicago Press, 1962), 5–6.

44. Ibid., 8.

45. Friedman and Friedman, *Free to Choose*, 19–25.

46. Friedman, *Capitalism and Freedom*, 35–36.

47. Friedman and Friedman, *Free to Choose*, 55.

48. Gray, *Liberalism*, x.

49. Smith, *Wealth of Nations*, 11.

50. Locke, *Second Treatise*, no. 40.

51. Madison, *Federalist* No. 10, 79.

52. J.S. Mill, *On Liberty*, in *Utilitarianism, On Liberty, and Considerations on Representative Government*, ed. H.B. Acton (London: J.M. Dent, 1972), 79.

53. Quoted by Gray, *Liberalism*, 30–31.

54. Quoted by Arblaster, *Democracy*, 44. The effects of the various reform acts should not be exaggerated. The Reform Act of 1832, by lowering property qualifications, admitted most middle-class men to the electorate. It was not until 1867 that another reform bill granted small farmers and urban laborers the suffrage, and only in 1884 did most adult males gain the right to vote. Most women would not receive the vote until 1928.

55. Mill, *Utilitarianism*, 7.

56. Ibid., 10.

57. Mill, *On Liberty*, 79.

58. Mill, *Utilitarianism*, 56.

59. Ibid., 65.

60. Ibid., 66.

61. Mill, *On Liberty*, 72.

62. Ibid., 78.

63. Ibid., 138.

64. Ibid., 134.

65. Ibid., 115.

66. Quoted by Sanford Lakoff in *Equality in Political Philosophy* (Cambridge: Harvard University Press, 1964), 130.

67. Amitai Etzioni, ed., *Rights and the Common Good: A Communitarian Perspective* (New York: St. Martin's Press, 1995), iv, 1.

68. Isaac Kramnick, "Equal Opportunity and the 'Race of Life,' " *Dissent* 28, no. 2 (Spring 1981): 178–87.

69. Bellah, *Habits of the Heart*, 148, 158.

70. Robert Bellah, "The Quest for the Self," in Etzioni, *Rights and the Common Good*, 55.

71. Locke, *Second Treatise*, 347.

72. John Locke, *A Letter Concerning Toleration*, ed. Patrick Romanell (Indianapolis: Bobbs-Merrill, 1955), 52.

73. Friedman, *Capitalism and Freedom*, 33.

74. Mill, *On Liberty*, 164, and *Utilitarianism*, 18. Karl Marx, among others, regarded utilitarianism as a rationalization of the bourgeois status quo. Of Bentham he said, "in no time and in no country has the most homespun

manufacturer of commonplaces ever strutted about in so self-satisfied a way."

75. Mary Ellen Gale, "Free Speech, Equal Rights, and Water Buffaloes: University Regulation of Discriminatory Verbal Harassment," in Etzioni, *Rights and the Common Good,* 97.

76. Bellah, *Habits of the Heart,* 162.

77. Benjamin Barber, *Strong Democracy: Participatory Politics for a New Age* (Berkeley: University of California Press, 1984), 101.

78. Quoted in ibid.

79. Diane Ravitch, "Pluralism within Unity: A Communitarian Version of Multiculturalism," in Etzioni, *Rights and the Common Good,* 179.

80. Ibid., 184–85.

81. Ibid., 185.

82. Etzioni, *Rights and the Common Good,* iii.

83. Bellah, *Habits of the Heart,* 286.

84. I borrow this heading from the title of Charles Lindblom's now famous book.

85. Theodore Lowi, *The End of Liberalism: The Second Republic of the United States,* 2d ed. (New York: Norton, 1979), 11.

86. Friedman and Friedman, *Free to Choose,* 126–28.

87. Quoted by Van Dyke, *Ideology and Political Choice,* 80.

88. Quoted in ibid., 33.

89. Ibid., 33–34. It is no coincidence that Friedman also presents his restrictions on government intervention as an economic bill of rights. See appendix B of Friedman and Friedman, *Free to Choose.*

90. Quoted by Kramnick in "Equal Opportunity and the 'Race of Life,' " 178.

91. Ibid., 184–85.

92. Friedman and Friedman, *Free to Choose,* 297.

93. Christopher Lasch, "Communitarianism or Populism?" in Etzioni, *Rights and the Common Good,* 59–66.

94. Jennifer Hochschild, "Disjunction and Ambivalence in Citizens' Political Outlooks," in *Reconsidering the Democratic Public,* ed. George Marcus and Russell Hanson (University Park: Pennsylvania State University Press, 1994), 187–210.

95. Ibid., 189, 204.

96. Ibid., 193.

97. Karl Marx, *Capital,* trans. Ben Fowkes (New York: Random House, 1977), 1: 759.

98. Benjamin Barber takes this position, saying, "in this sense, strong democratic politics neither requires nor corresponds specifically with particular economic systems" (*Strong Democracy,* 252–53). Hochschild agrees and presents the popular disjunction as an opportunity for deliberation.

99. Bellah, *Habits of the Heart,* 26.

100. *The Gallup Poll Monthly,* January 1994, 41; April 1994, 6; June 1994, 30.

101. Quoted by Bellah, *Habits of the Heart,* 132.

102. Frances Fox Piven and Richard Cloward, *Why Americans Don't*

Vote (New York: Pantheon, 1989), 5; Thomas T. Mackie and Richard Rose, *International Almanac of Electoral History,* 3d ed. (Washington, D.C.: CQ Press, 1992), 20–21.

103. Barber, *Strong Democracy,* 187.

104. Lani Guinier, *The Tyranny of the Majority: Fundamental Fairness in Representative Democracy* (New York: Free Press, 1994), 3.

105. Quoted by Benjamin Ginsberg, *The Consequences of Consent: Elections, Citizen Control, and Popular Acquiescence* (Reading, Mass.: Addison-Wesley, 1982), 13.

106. Barber, *Strong Democracy,* ix.

107. Ibid., 265.

108. Bernice Johnson Reagon, "Coalition Politics: Turning the Century," in *Home Girls: A Black Feminist Anthology,* ed. Barbara Smith (Latham, N.Y.: Kitchen Table/Women of Color Press, 1983), 357.

3

Conservatism

I hope and pray that, as time goes by, the twentieth century will shed the odium that clings to its name, that it may crystallize as the century in which ... we learned ... how useless it is, how dangerous it is, to strut about ideologizing the world when we need to know that it was born intractable and will die intractable.

— William F. Buckley Jr.

Conservative Ideology?

"To strut about ideologizing the world"—these words have a familiar ring. They recall Napoleon Bonaparte's attack on the French revolutionary Destutt de Tracy. This is no coincidence. As a neoconservative, William F. Buckley Jr.[1] joins a long line of critics of the democratic legacy of French Enlightenment philosophy, including Edmund Burke, Alexis de Tocqueville, and, more recently, J.R. Talmon. Buckley also echoes Daniel Bell, another neoconservative, in calling for an end to ideology. For most conservatives, "ideology" refers to philosophical abstractions that simplify complex realities, inflame popular passions, and undermine political order. Against ideology, neoconservatives claim that the public interest "may be presumed to be what men [*sic*] would choose if they saw clearly, thought rationally, acted disinterestedly and benevolently."[2] This familiar charge raises obvious questions: Isn't conservatism also an ideology? By attacking ideology, don't conservatives undermine themselves?

Conservatism does differ from other ideologies in several ways.

First, conservatism is commonly defined in relation to changing historical contexts, rather than abstract principles of justice. *Webster's Dictionary,* a source for standard usage, defines "conservative" as "tending to favor the preservation of the existing order and to regard proposals for change with distrust." More humorously, Bierce's *Devil's Dictionary* reads: "a statesman who is enamored of existing evils, as distinguished from the Liberal, who wishes to replace them with others."[3] Juxtapositions of liberal and conservative can mislead, however. According to Charles Kesler, the relationship of conservatism to history suggests that it "is more nearly the antonym of 'progressivism' than of 'liberalism.'"[4] Milton Friedman agrees. He refuses to accept the "conservative" label because his ideas are radical "in the political sense of favoring major changes in social institutions."[5]

Such definitions treat conservatism as a disposition or temperament, rather than a belief system. Michael Oakeshott eloquently describes the personality traits conservatives share:

> To be conservative ... is to prefer the familiar to the unknown, to prefer the tried to the untried, fact to mystery, the actual to the possible, the limited to the unbounded, the near to the distant, the sufficient to the superabundant, the convenient to the perfect, present laughter to utopian bliss.[6]

Most simply, conservatism involves "love of the familiar present." According to Oakeshott, every society has traditions (i.e., beliefs, customs, habits, institutions, laws, and rituals) worth preserving, if only because they constitute its identity. Conservatives do not place their hopes in grand dreams and utopian schemes but in "simple longings," especially "the comforting assurance that continuity is more probable than change."[7]

Oakeshott's perspective suggests a second way conservatism differs from other ideologies: "who is conservative?" is an easier question to answer than "what is conservatism?" A conservative personality is easier to recognize than conservative principles. Since conservatives are deeply rooted in society, the "what" of conservatism changes with history. Even Edmund Burke, a major source of conservative doctrine, claims that "circumstances ... give in reality to every political principle its distinguishing colour, and discriminating effect." He "suspends his congratulations on the new liberty of France" until he sees how it works in context.[8] To further complicate matters, the label "conservative" applies to different positions in different contexts. After outlining neoconservatives' beliefs, Irving Kristol asks, "Is neo-conservatism the right label for this constellation of attitudes? I don't mind it—but then,

if the political spectrum moved rightward, and we should become
'neoliberal' tomorrow, I could accept that too."[9]

A third distinctive feature of conservatism is closely related. If conservatism is a belief system at all, then it is one with many internal tensions. Conservatives' roots are often tangled and twisted, even dead or
dying. Oakeshott argues that modern Europe, roughly the past five
centuries, is not congenial to conservatism. Modern men are "in love
with change" and "careless of identity." In Oakeshott's words, "[they]
are acquisitive to the point of greed; ready to drop the bone [they] have
for its reflection magnified in the mirror of the future."[10] European conservatives have resources for resisting liberal capitalists' tendency to
race through life. They can reinvoke memories of a feudal past. American conservatives face the greater challenge posed by a predominantly
liberal capitalist past. The United States lacks the institutions—an established church, a monarchy, an aristocracy, the common law—that
conservatives revere. Americans' disposition, whether frontier mentality, Yankee ingenuity, or entrepreneurial spirit, is fundamentally progressive. America was also born from a theory, the abstractions of the
Declaration of Independence that "all men are created equal" and "endowed by their creator with unalienable rights to life, liberty, and property." For many conservatives, Jefferson's ideas and America's origins
are all too French.

Since American history offers conservatives little worth preserving,
American conservatism is deeply influenced by European ideas. Nevertheless, American conservatives have some roots in native soil, specifically, in the pessimistic side of liberalism. Peter Steinfels describes conservatives' liberalism as "the harder, more fearful sort":

> Pessimistic about human nature, skeptical about the outcome of political
> innovation, distrustful of direct democracy (the "mob"), it would defend
> the principles and practices of liberalism less as vehicles for betterment
> than as bulwarks against folly.[11]

Conservatives also emphasize the pragmatism of American politics that
began with a very prudent revolution. The Declaration of Independence followed a long train of abuses and many petitions for redress.
The Constitution, they argue, is a document meant to evolve over time,
not a set piece. Yet even a pessimistic, pragmatic liberalism creates
some tensions with conservative principles.

Scholarly efforts to define conservatism distinguish several different
forms. The image of a family tree with its roots, trunk, and branches
clarifies the complex relationships involved. There are two major root

systems, economic and social conservatism. Economic conservatives are the classical liberals, such as Milton Friedman, who support individual rights, free markets, and limited government. Since they were the focus of chapter 2, they receive limited attention here. Social or organic conservatives, our current concern, have European roots. Edmund Burke, a British philosopher, is widely regarded as their founding father.

When the tree reaches out to America, the neoconservatives form one of its major branches. They are an academic elite who combine social conservatism, pessimistic liberalism, and, in some cases, socialist "grafts." As Irving Kristol puts it, neoconservatives are former progressives who were "mugged by reality." Their political allies are another branch, the "old right," represented by the Republican Party, especially during the Reagan years. To build a political base, the "old right" also espouses the economic optimism of classical liberals (or economic conservatives). The tensions between their liberal "grafts" and social conservatism led Charles Krauthammer, a "real" neoconservative, to deny Reagan the "conservative" label altogether, calling him a "radical, populist, utopian."[12] Another major branch, the "new right," which divides into populist conservatives, religious fundamentalists, and middle American radicals, has recently emerged. Its supporters often engage in single-issue politics and have an uneasy relationship with the Republican Party.[13]

A fourth difference between conservatism and other ideologies follows from these internal tensions. Because their philosophical premises differ, conservatives come together around specific issues. The "what" of conservatism can be partly defined by looking at conservatives' policy positions. Kenneth Dolbeare and Linda Medcalf discuss how economic and social conservatives agree that America's economic problems—chronic unemployment and high inflation—result from excessive government spending, taxing, and regulating. Social conservatives would limit government programs from a sense of frugality and humility. Economic injustice is one of Buckley's "intractable" problems; poverty can be alleviated, but it cannot be abolished. Economic conservatives, however, assert that free markets would achieve optimality if government would only cease interfering with them. As these variations imply, conservatives often find "it easier to identify what they are against than what they are for."[14]

Conservatism is clearly difficult to define: It is a disposition; it is rooted in society and history; it is fraught with tensions; it coalesces around issues; it is negative, at least, toward liberal capitalism. But is it an ideology? Milton Friedman also resists the label "conservative" because he knows how hard it is to answer this question. He says that "the term conservatism has come to cover so wide a range of views, and views so incompatible with one another, that we shall no doubt see the growth of hyphenated designations, such as libertarian-conservative and aristocratic-conservative."[15] Buckley is more sanguine, comparing conservatism today to a "freeway" that "remains large, large enough to accommodate very different players with highly different prejudices and techniques."[16] A family tree better fits conservatives' organic worldview and leads to the same conclusion. Conservatism is an ideology only if ideology includes what falls between "an attitude of mind" and "a series of all-fulfilling formulae."[17] Buckley sets up this dichotomy and, like most conservatives, he confines ideology to the latter with its negative connotations. Another conservative, Samuel Huntington, tries to find a middle ground when he treats conservatism as a "nonideational ideology." Conservatism is not a system of ideas, but it has substantive content. Huntington defines it as "the articulate, systematic, theoretical resistance to change."[18] Russell Kirk offers a richer sense of the essence of conservatism: "preservation of the ancient moral traditions of humanity."[19] A prolonged crisis of the hearts and minds of the Western world has placed those traditions at risk.

The Conservative Canon

According to Kirk, conservatives share at least six basic principles.[20] The writings of Edmund Burke, the founder of conservatism, illustrate them well. His *Reflections on the Revolution in France,* written before the Revolution became the Terror, might be called "the conservative bible."

First, conservatives believe that a higher moral or spiritual order rules over nature and society. Compared to this higher wisdom, human reason is small and frail. Only arrogance could lead revolutionaries to try to wipe the historical slate clean and write a completely new constitution. Regarding the French Revolution, Burke says, "the very idea of the fabrication of a new government, is enough to fill us with disgust and horror."[21] Revolutionary schemes are immodest, unnatural, and irresponsible. "A conscientious man would be cautious how he dealt in blood. . . . It is no excuse for presumptuous ignorance, that it is directed by insolent passion."[22] What wisdom the human species has emerged from experience accumulated over generations. Individuals are only "the temporary possessors and life-renters" of a society received from their ancestors and returned to posterity. With too frequent changes in society, "the whole chain and continuity of the commonwealth would be broken. No one generation could link with the other. Men would become little better than the flies of a summer."[23] It is to avoid "inconstancy" that Burke consecrates the state and urges citizens to "approach to the faults of the state as to the wounds of a father, with pious awe and trembling solicitude."[24] His Christian allusions reveal the religious character of much conservative thought.

Second, conservatives have great affection, even reverence, for the complexity and mystery of tradition. People are not born free and equal in a state of nature, nor do they form a social contract to secure their natural rights, as some liberals suggest. The social contract (conservatives do use the term) involves far more than the protection of rights and the pursuit of self-interest. According to conservatives, people are born to a family in a society with a history. Social customs, habits, rituals, and symbols are the sources of moral, political, and spiritual authority. These "authorities" are inseparable in practice. As Burke puts it:

> The state ought not to be considered as nothing better than a partnership agreement in a trade of pepper and coffee ... to be taken up for a little temporary interest.... It is to be looked on with other reverence; ... it is a partnership in all science; a partnership in all art; a partnership in every virtue, and in all perfection.[25]

The "ancient opinions and rule of life" give society its moral compass. "Each contract of each particular state is but a clause in the great primæval contract of eternal society."

The state does exist to protect individual rights, but that is only one of its purposes. Liberty must be carefully balanced with other moral goods, among them, duty, order, and sacrifice. A social contract based on natural rights alone misses the intricacy of human relationships and the complexity of social institutions. So do utilitarian schemes, which organize society by mathematical formulae (i.e., cost/benefit analyses). Liberalism only inflames citizens' passions: "by having a right to every thing they want every thing."[26] When citizens are "free to choose," the result is not liberty, but license. True liberty exists only when other moral goods balance individual rights. Burke sometimes puts this point paradoxically, as when he refers to restraint as a right. What he means is that "men have no right to what is not reasonable, and to what is not for their benefit."[27] Neither abstract principle nor public opinion is a good guide to what is reasonable. Only a statesman, a person of greater wisdom and higher virtue, can discern the proper balance of moral goods in social context.

Third, as this implies, there is a hierarchy of orders and classes in every society. Conservatives claim that men have equal rights, but not to equal things. "Real" rights, as opposed to "natural" ones, are "prescriptive." People have a right to what they already own and to what they truly need, more precisely, to dignity and security in their station in life. According to Burke, "happiness ... is to be found by virtue in all conditions; in which consists the true moral equality of mankind." Unhappiness arises when men entertain "false ideas" and "vain expectations" of improving their condition. Economic dreams only "aggravate and imbitter that real inequality, which [they] never can remove."[28]

Political rights are also unequal, and for a related reason. The characteristics that qualify people for political service are unequally distributed. Conservatives claim that human capacities vary naturally from birth. They also argue that a certain (i.e., a cultured and civilized) lifestyle promotes wisdom and virtue. According to Burke, every rightly constituted society produces a natural aristocracy with the virtues of diligence, order, constancy, and regularity. These natural aristocrats have "legitimate presumptions" to instruct, to rule, and thereby to benefit the rest of the people. They are the statesmen, referred to above, which democracies sorely need. "The levellers," those who support greater equality, "only change and pervert the natural order of things, ... setting up in the air what the solidity of the structure requires to be on the ground."[29]

Fourth, property and freedom are inextricably intertwined. In the pursuit of material equality, "levellers" remove restraints on selfish interests and make governments serve them. The likely result—Burke is prophetic—is political instability, followed by anarchy, tyranny, or both. Burke refers to the French *philosophes* when he says, "against these rights of men let no government look for security in the length of its continuance, or in the justice and lenity of its administration."[30] To restrain popular influences, conservatives propose that the separate branches of government represent different social classes. (This is distinct from the American separation of powers in which the branches have different functions, that is, executive, judicial, and legislative. John Adams's conservative interpretation of the U.S. Constitution, in which the presidency represents monarchy, the Senate aristocracy, and the House democracy, was widely regarded as a misinterpretation.) In balanced or mixed government, natural aristocrats counter democratic influences in the name of justice. They mold a "disbanded race of disserters and vagabonds" into a disciplined citizenry.[31]

Fifth, citizens are attached to a government only when it engages their moral imagination. As Burke puts it, "to make us love our country, our country ought to be lovely."[32] Abstract rights and utilitarian schemes cannot accomplish this task. "Old prejudices and unreasoned habits" evoke citizens' emotions and inspire their loyalty. "No cold relation is a zealous citizen," according to Burke.[33] Citizens love the state as family, as neighborhood, as city—as their home. Burke says, "To be attached to the subdivision, to love the little platoon we belong to in society, is the first principle ... of public affections. It is the first link in the series by which we proceed towards a love to our country and to mankind."[34]

Carefully constructed symbols of power bolster political affections. When exposed to the light of reason, politics looks like a shabby affair, an unseemly undertaking. The French revolutionaries' "rights of man" make this mistake:

> All the decent drapery of life is to be rudely torn off. All the super-added ideas, furnished from the wardrobe of a moral imagination, which the heart owns, and the understanding ratifies, as necessary to cover the defects of our naked shivering nature, and to raise it to dignity in our own estimation, are to be exploded as a ridiculous, absurd, and antiquated fashion.[35]

A small step leads from the demystification of politics to the decapitation of the queen, according to Burke. He describes the descending logic of liberal democracy: "on this scheme of things, a king is but a man, a queen is but a woman; a woman is but an animal; and an animal not of the highest order."[36] For Burke, and some neoconservatives, the presence of chivalry indicates the level of civilization in a society. Among the "pleasing illusions" that make "power gentle, and obedience liberal" is women's image as "the fairer sex."[37] Without such illusions, power finds worse means of support, most likely terror and violence.

Sixth, conservatives recognize that every society eventually undergoes changes, but they prefer that change be gradual. They support evolutionary transformations, not revolutionary ones. According to Burke, this is how the Glorious Revolution of 1688 differs from the French Revolution. By offering the Crown to William of Orange, the husband of a member of the royal family, the British maintained the line of succession. Some additional adjustments in royal prerogatives and parliamentary rights preserved the structure of government. Burke says, "There is a middle. There is something else than the mere alternative of absolute destruction, or unreformed existence." Burke's statesmen combine "a disposition to preserve, and an ability to improve." He claims that "every thing else is vulgar in the conception, perilous in the execution."[38] The stateman's moderate and practical wisdom replaces the metaphysical abstractions of liberal ideology.

Moral and spiritual order, reverence for tradition, social hierarchy, property reinforced by freedom (and vice versa), moral imagination, and evolutionary change—these six ideas form the core of conservatism. Burke elaborates them against a relatively stable British background with the chaos of the French Revolution as his foil. Where does the American Revolution fit into this conservative picture? Like Burke, most conservatives place America's pragmatic politics between British precedent and French metaphysics.[39] Even in America, liberal democratic from birth, conservatism has found some roots.

Conservatism in America

"The liberals must be the conservatives in America today ... the greatest need is not so much the creation of more liberal institutions as the successful defense of those which already exist."[40] Samuel Huntington wrote these words in 1957, but they apply equally well to America's founding period. For the conservative Whigs who stayed after the Revolutionary War (many loyalists did not), the Articles of Confederation failed to protect liberal government from the dangers of faction. The factions they feared most were popular majorities whose egalitarian schemes included "a rage for paper money, for an abolition of debts, for an equal division of property, or for any other improper or wicked project."[41] As Peter Steinfels said, the Federalists stressed a cautious, pessimistic liberalism "less as [a] vehicle for betterment than as [a] bulwark against folly."[42]

From a conservative perspective, folly triumphed in the 1800 election of Thomas Jefferson. According to the High Federalist Fisher Ames, "they are certainly blind who do not see, that we are descending from a supposed orderly and stable republican government into a licentious democracy, with a progress that baffles all means to resist, and scarcely leaves leisure to deplore its celerity."[43] America was quickly going the way of the French. Only the South, influenced by its "peculiar institution" of slavery, would remain a bastion of conservatism. Not until the 1964 campaign of Barry Goldwater did conservatism begin to move into the mainstream of national politics. Whether its new presence will persist long after the Reagan era remains to be seen. Among the American branches of the conservative tree, we focus on the neoconservatives and their political allies. But by briefly exploring the roots of conservatism in America we can better understand their ideas.

Early American Conservatism

In order to defend liberalism against democracy, the Federalists sought institutional arrangements that could compensate for what they lacked in social customs. In *A Defense of the Constitutions of the United States,* John Adams provides the most striking example of their approach. Like Burke, Adams opposes the French revolutionaries' concept of equality as sameness. Although "every being has a right to his own, as clear, as moral, as sacred, as any other being has," this hardly suggests that "all men are born with equal powers and faculties, to equal influence in society, to equal property and advantages through life."[44] Ironically, attempts to level society often exacerbate inequalities and increase conflicts between social classes. The Americans and the French can eliminate hereditary titles, but they cannot prevent distinctions of rank. Nor should they try to do so. In a moving passage, Adams describes the various infants he saw in a Hospital of Foundlings: "Some had every sign of grief, sorrow, and despair; others had joy and gayety in their faces. Some were sinking in the arms of death; others looked as if they might live to fourscore. Some were as ugly and others as beautiful, as children or adults ever are; these were stupid; those sensible." All had equal rights, but they would achieve unequal results. Adams's aristocrats must do more than "go to the trouble of being born," but he also knows innate abilities make a difference. Adams defends an aristocracy that is a meritocracy: "Real merit should govern the world; ... men ought to be respected only in proportion to their talents, virtues, and services. But the question always has been how shall this arrangement be accomplished?"[45]

According to Adams, a balanced or mixed government such as the U.S. Constitution is the answer to this question. Unlike Burke, who exempts natural aristocrats, Adams argues that every social class runs the risk of corruption: "my opinion is ... that absolute power intoxicates alike despots, monarchs, aristocrats, and democrats, and jacobins, and *sans culottes*."[46] Separation of powers provides a structural solution to the problem of power. The U.S. government consists of "three different orders of men bound by their interest to watch over each other, and stand the guardians of the laws."[47] A democratic House balances aristocratic despotism, an aristocratic Senate balances democratic licentiousness, and a quasi-monarchical Executive can veto both Houses of Congress. Adams images this arrangement as a balance composed of "the two scales and the hand that holds it." His critics charged that he misconstrued the fundamentally democratic character of American political institutions: "a jack which represented the machinery of government, controlled by a weight which was the people, the power from which the motion of all parts originates" was a better analogy.[48] The image of a jack suggests that separation of powers limits government authority dividing (and conquering) popular majorities, not by balancing classes to prevent corruption.

Did Adams misunderstand the fundamentally democratic character of American society? Its implications for American conservatives are disturbing. In 1821 Adams lamented to Benjamin Rush, another Federalist, "from the year 1761, now more than 50 years, I have constantly lived in an enemies [sic] country."[49] Adams had realized how difficult it is to sustain a natural aristocracy without appropriate social traditions. Fisher Ames's despair over American democracy flowed from the same source. Ames concluded America could not avoid the dangers of democracy, since its materials for a government were all democratic.[50]

Ames defines a democracy as "a government by the passions of the multitude, or, no less correctly, according to the vices and ambition of their leaders."[51] Institutional arrangements could not solve these problems; the U.S. Constitution could not replicate British mixed government. Ames asks, "What could make such a monarchy?" and answers, "Not parchment—we are beginning to be cured of the insane belief, that an engrossing clerk can make a constitution. Mere words, though on parchment, though sworn to, are wind, and worse than wind, because they are perjury."[52] According to Ames, the Federalists mistakenly relied on the civic virtue of the American people without creating a society capable of sustaining it.[53] Once democratic politicians replaced "the good, the rich, [and] the well-born," the pursuit of self-interest would undermine the value of self-sacrifice. Jefferson's election convinced Ames that "the [American] revolution will proceed in exactly the same way, but not with so rapid a pace, as that of France."[54]

To avoid the excesses of democracy in America, the Federalists combined conservative themes with a more pessimistic liberalism. Natural aristocrats must earn their status; no social order has a monopoly on virtue; institutional arrangements stand in for traditional authorities; and mechanical analogies largely replace organic metaphors. Only in the South, where slavery challenged America's commitment to liberty and equality, did liberal influences recede somewhat. To defend their way of life, southern writers invoke another conservative theme: the little platoon. Their defense of community retains a distinctly American cast, however. "Love of the familiar present" is transmuted into the doctrine of states' rights.

John C. Calhoun, a South Carolinian who served as vice-president under John Quincy Adams and Andrew Jackson, developed the doctrine of states' rights to protect the institution of slavery. Calhoun bases his defense of slavery on prescription. White supremacy is a social right, similar to other inequalities of property, for example, between labor and capital. Calhoun adds that slavery is "instead of an evil, a good—a positive good."[55] Slavemasters, including himself, serve as guardians to their slaves, providing them with better conditions than inmates of European poorhouses. Northern abolitionists interfere with an inevitable hierarchy manifest in a successful institution. Calhoun sees their interference as unjust and unwise.

According to Calhoun, the United States is composed of equal states, not equal individuals: "instead of a nation we are in reality an assemblage of nations, or peoples ... united in their sovereign character immediately and directly by their own act, but without losing their separate and independent existence."[56] Simple majority rule violates this social contract because the majority of the population resides in the northern states. To restore equality of the sections, Calhoun defends a state's right to nullify (i.e., to declare void) federal laws. To make nullification unnecessary, Calhoun suggests that rule by "concurrent majorities" replace the votes of "a metaphysical 'people.'" To reach "concurrence," he proposes dividing the nation by section, taking the views of its separate parts and harmonizing them into a unified voice. A dual executive with southern and northern presidents would facilitate this process. Their mutual agreement would be required to ratify legislation.

Although his proposals failed, Calhoun's arguments are brilliant and prophetic. He claims that the South is "the balance of the system; the great conservative power, which prevents other portions, less fortunately constituted, from rushing into conflict."[57] Slavery is the key to stability in the South, and it makes the South a stabilizing influence on the nation. Slavery minimizes social conflict because "every plantation is a little community, with the master at its head, who concentrates in himself the united interests of capital and labor, of which he is the common representative."[58] Northerners, who attack slavery, destabilize the nation and threaten the security of their own property. Like Burke, Calhoun portrays liberal ideology as a slippery slope: Once masters and slaves have equal rights, why not capital and labor next? Northern and southern interests converge over preserving the South's "peculiar institution" of slavery.

Long after the South lost the Civil War, a conservative alliance between southern Democrats and northern Republicans influenced American national politics. With the rise of the new South, sectional arguments began to lose force. Yet conservatives continue to defend states' rights, local control, or both against national politics. "The little platoons" of American conservatives have recognizably liberal features. Public affections coincide with economic interests, and federalist institutions promote organic communities.

The Neoconservatives

The 1984 reelection of Ronald Reagan is widely regarded as the coming of age of American conservatism. The Reagan presidency moved conservatism to the center of national politics, partly by blurring the lines between classical liberal (or economic conservative) and social conservative policy positions. A series of events, including defeat in Vietnam, a serious Soviet threat, Watergate and Iran-*contra*, stagflation and recession, led Americans in a conservative direction. While capitalizing on these events, neoconservatives prefer to explain their political success by emphasizing "the cumulative inadequacies of liberalism." According to Michael Oakeshott, the young—citizens and nations—are ill suited for politics: "everybody's young days are a dream, a delightful insanity, a sweet solipsism."[59] Whether the War of Independence, the Civil War, or the New Deal is America's birthdate, conservatives claim that liberalism loses quality with age.

Irving Kristol, a prominent neoconservative, explores Americans' rightward movement with the question: "if the traditional economics of socialism has been discredited, why has not the traditional economics of capitalism been vindicated?"[60] According to Kristol, the answer lies in liberal capitalists' tendency to "think economically." He concedes to classical liberals that such thinking may be appropriate in economics. But it does not transfer well to other areas, especially to politics and morals. To think economically is to accept "the revolutionary premise that there is no superior, authoritative information available about the good life or the true nature of human happiness."[61] It is to choose moral values like breakfast cereals, athletic shoes, and other products, that is, by personal preference. Two social groups are prone to such thinking: (1) the "me generation," a self-indulgent mass public, often children of the 1960s; and (2) the "new class," a self-satisfied group of intellectuals-cum-politicians who support a massive welfare state. The former group worships and the latter group preaches a false god of material equality. (Ames's fear that democracies combine licentiousness and demagoguery resurfaces here.)

Many of America's current problems are the long-term effects of "thinking economically." Kristol discusses three ways a liberal capitalist mentality undermines the ethical foundations required for a healthy society. First, a secular society can neither resign citizens to their fates nor restrain them with promises of heaven. Without the solace of religion, citizens tend to make excessive demands on the state for material gratification. As Kristol puts it, "liberal civilization finds itself having spiritually expropriated the masses of its citizenry, whose demands for material compensation gradually become as infinite as the infinity they have lost."[62] When the state fails to meet citizens' material needs, it loses authority and legitimacy in their eyes.

Second, and closely related, because the state is merely the servant of private interests, liberal democracies cannot compel sufficient political loyalty from their citizens. Citizens who have not learned to act with regard for the public good "will come to blame all social shortcomings on the agency of collective considerations, the government, and will absolve themselves."[63] More important, natural rights to life, liberty, and property are insufficient bases for political obligation. As Kristol puts it, "no merely utilitarian definition of civic loyalty is going to convince anyone that it makes sense for him to die for his country."[64] Nationalism has filled this void, giving liberal democrats a reason to make sacrifices for the state, while threatening conservatives' principle of temperate liberty. History provides many examples of national fervor overpowering individual freedom (e.g, Japanese Americans' internment during World War II, the "Red Scare" of Eugene McCarthy, even current "anti-PC" campaigns).

Third, the doctrine of laissez-faire gradually undermines even the bourgeois virtues—"honesty, sobriety, diligence, and thrift"—required to achieve economic prosperity. The law of supply and demand says "anything to make a buck." It does not make moral distinctions between economic activities (e.g., pornography and artistry) or economic actors (e.g., speculators and entrepreneurs). According to Kristol, liberals underestimate the importance of such distinctions because they have too limited an imagination when it comes to vice. They blithely assume, with Adam Smith, that private vice promotes public virtue because they do not believe in "destructive vices" or, more strongly, the power of evil. In a fair meritocracy success is the result of genuine ability, honest effort, and a little luck. It is on the basis of this belief that citizens willingly work hard and accept existing inequalities as what they deserve. Contemporary liberalism lacks a concept of distributive justice that could replace this rapidly fading Protestant ethic.

Kristol concludes that "bourgeois society was living off the accumulated moral capital of traditional religion and traditional moral philosophy, and that once this capital was depleted, bourgeois society would find its legitimacy ever more questionable."[65] He asks, "what medicine does one prescribe for a social order that is sick because it has lost its soul?"[66] Some conservatives respond with pessimism and despair, rivaling even Fisher Ames. Andrew Hacker writes, "the United States is about to join other nations of the world which were once prepossessing and are now little more than plots of bounded terrain."[67] Fortunately, others argue that conservatism offers not only a diagnosis of America's sickness but also a cure for it. Conservatives' previously unpopular and unpersuasive arguments have recently become sources of hope.[68] What medicine do they prescribe? To answer this question, we turn to the policy positions around which contemporary conservatives converge.

Contemporary Conservatives and Public Policy

In another article, Kristol outlines the "vague consensus" on political issues that is neoconservatives' prescription for an ailing America.[69] Although Kristol's stated focus is neoconservatism, the five features he identifies are so general that they also apply to the "old right" and the "new right." We might see them as the trunk of American conservatives' family tree. In discussing each feature, I include several contemporary conservatives and identify major tensions within conservatism.

> **Feature 1.** "Neo-conservatism is not at all hostile to the ideas of a welfare state, but it is critical of the Great Society version of this welfare state."

As we saw, Kristol fears the long-term effects of "thinking economically," including its effect on economic policy. According to conservatives, the political analogue to market failure is government failure. It results when government becomes overloaded due to the excessive demands of an unrestrained public. Conservatives argue that the pursuit of individual self-interest does not lead to the common good in politics any more than in economics. Liberals, who claim otherwise, assume "an entirely separate account of human nature for political as opposed to economic man," an obvious absurdity.[70] How, conservatives ask, could liberals miss so simple a point?

We have seen that all ideologies, in different ways and to varying extents, blind people to some aspects of reality. According to George Will, ideological capitalists, such as Milton Friedman, cannot see that to choose an economic system is also to make an ethical and political choice. Will and other conservatives argue that the state is never a neutral umpire in the free market. A meritocracy, like any economic system, rewards some behaviors over others. Will refers not only to the bourgeois virtues (i.e., honesty, sobriety, diligence, and thrift) whose passing liberals also lament. Capitalist economies and liberal democracies also reward unlimited acquisition of private property. The resulting inequalities are justifiable only if—to use a favorite liberal metaphor —the "race of life" is fair. But government cannot guarantee a "fair race" or even adequately compensate the losers without experiencing overload. If classical liberals could recognize this, then they would join other conservatives in supporting a welfare state.

Will defends welfare programs on principled and pragmatic grounds. First, he proposes a new principle of distributive justice: in a just society, "inequalities are reasonably related to reasonable social goals."[71] Social Security, unemployment insurance, national health insurance, a family assistance plan serve the social goal of providing citizens with a minimum level of comfort and security. The moral equality of human beings justifies these entitlement programs. Nevertheless, Will also argues that welfare programs serve pragmatic goals. They give the poorest citizens a stake in the government and urge rich and poor alike to moderate their demands upon it. As Charles Kesler puts the point: "the Welfare State was . . . a prudent adaptation . . . a way to conserve the blessings of liberty in the face of challenges from the radical Left and Right, to temper the materialism of our civilization, to promote a sense of common good among the citizenry."[72] As conservatism comes of age, these authors ask it to "wear a kindly face," but not a paternalistic, bureaucratic one, which brings us to Kristol's second point.

> Feature 2. "Neo-conservatism has great respect . . . for the power of the market to respond efficiently to economic realities while preserving the maximum degree of individual freedom."

According to conservatives, the liberal state not only oversees but also plays the capitalist market. Indeed, with its fiscal and monetary policies, regulations and subsidies, investments and purchases, the state is a major economic player. As a result of Keynesian economic policies, it is in danger of going bankrupt. Simply put, Keynesian economics assumes that economic prosperity (i.e., gross national product and [un]employment levels) is determined by aggregate demand or total spending. In other words, production levels are a function of private and government spending combined. Since citizens can (and Keynesians assume will) spend savings and income, government can bolster a failing economy by increasing taxes and spending the revenues, by increasing deficits, or both.

Conservatives, especially economic conservatives, argue instead for focusing fiscal policy on how changes in supply affect production levels.[73] Tax increases, they claim, are counterincentives for a prosperous economy. Citizens' eventual response will be to work less, whether through absenteeism, longer vacations, lowered productivity, or other strategies, and to invest less because potential returns are not worth the risk. According to supply-side economists, Keynesianism may serve the short-term interests of bureaucrats and politicians by expanding government programs and enlarging their constituencies. In the long-term, only supply-side policies can finance a welfare state and maintain a healthy economy.

To minimize bureaucratic controls further, conservatives prefer welfare programs that rig the market. For example, they favor rent vouchers over housing projects, or food stamps over soup kitchens, or workfare programs over social assistance. Direct payments are less paternalistic forms of government support. Such programs, conservatives claim, are more likely to succeed because they do not increase recipients' dependency on the state. According to Charles Murray, President Johnson's well-intentioned Great Society programs failed tragically because they reinforced the very conditions they set out to alleviate. Murray acknowledges that any government program intended to change behavior may have this unintended consequence simply because it must offer incentives to attract participants (i.e., only the poor qualify for welfare, so to qualify one must become and remain poor). But the more complex and subtle effect of Great Society programs was to homogenize the poor as victims of the system. This undermined distinctions between the hard-working and the nonworking poor. As Murray puts it, "self-sufficiency was no longer taken to be an intrinsic *obligation* of healthy adults."[74] Eventually, the stigma associated with "being on welfare" disappeared, since "to see some as better was perceived as denying that the failures were victims."[75] Murray concludes that the costs of welfare to the self-esteem and well-being of participants in Great Society programs were high. He proposes constraints on government helping out of respect for victims' responsibility for the quality of their lives.

> **Feature 3.** "Neo-conservatism tends to be respectful of traditional values and institutions: religion, the family, the 'high culture' of Western civilization."

Paralleling Burke's attack on the French Revolution, conservatives defend traditional authorities against a specific political target: the counterculture of the 1960s. The 1960s' ethos of liberation has contributed to the moral and spiritual decay of American society. Conservatives reassert the trio—religion, family, culture—in response to several seemingly distinct social issues.

First, and most controversial among these issues, is a woman's right to an abortion. Conservatives treat the pro-choice position as part of a broader trend toward sexual explicitness and licentiousness. Charles Sobran links abortion and pornography, saying, "You can't cheapen (or, if you will, 'liberate') sex without cheapening life itself. Sell the one, and you soon buy the other. 'Sexual freedom' has come to mean freedom from consequences, from loyalty, from moral responsibility."[76] Moral irresponsibility, originally fostered by the disestablishment of religion, is further promoted by its recent segregation to the private sphere. Sobran challenges Supreme Court decisions that preclude voluntary school prayer and tax credits for parochial schools. How, he asks, can these decisions be reconciled with others that permit schools to offer classes in sex education and allow government to fund abortions for poor women? Such decisions reflect neither government neutrality nor a reluctance to legislate morality. Instead, they are examples of double standards. (Like other conservatives, Sobran sees neutrality as an impossibility in any case.)

According to Sobran, conservatives should draw on America's founding documents to oppose its disturbing trend toward a secular society. He argues that the Founders never intended the First Amendment to undermine religion, only to make it more free. The separation of church and state was meant to allow more forms of religion to flourish. In an amazing passage, Sobran links the Declaration of Independence and the First Amendment, claiming that together they protect the God-given right to life of the unborn, who cannot yet speak. Abortion, he concludes, is un-American. The courts, the media, and the academics, who constitute a triangle of cultural power, pose a serious threat to the Constitution. Sobran calls on families and schools to (re)instill moral values in American children. He defends local school boards' efforts to control curricula and state legislatures' attempts to criminalize abortion.

Underlying Sobran's arguments is a traditional concept of the family that other conservatives make explicit. According to Phyllis Schlafly, "the Divine Architect" created differences between men and women, and the "positive woman" rejoices in her unique creative capacities. Schlafly refers to women's biological capacity to give birth and their psychological need to "love something alive."[77] Women's liberationists, who regard these capacities as handicaps, mistakenly try to "neuterize" society. Schlafly treats campaigns for women's rights as broader efforts to promote neutrality "between morality and immorality, and ... between the institution of the family and alternate lifestyles."[78] They represent a "mandate of 'equality' at the expense of justice" and reflect women's selfish desires for money and power. As a southern new right leader puts it:

> Leaving aside the whole question of inequality of ability, let us consider equal opportunity's effect on the family, when a mother decides that the family income and her own "self-fulfillment" take precedence over her maternal duties. Whatever a woman's reasons for going to work—economic necessity, greed, selfishness—.... When men and women are free to choose their own "life styles," and to decide what image of humanity they wish to represent, their children must be left increasingly to the protection of the State....[79]

According to conservatives, the decline of the family is a direct result of women's liberation. It, in turn, creates a profound confusion about sexual identity that potentially leads many Americans to despair. Schlafly concludes that "it is no gain for women, for children, for families, or for America to propel us into a unisex society."[80] Like Sobran, Schlafly turns to the schools for redress, claiming that parents have "not only the right, but the obligation, to set minimum standards of moral conduct at the local level."[81]

Unfortunately, egalitarian tendencies increasingly pervade educational institutions, particularly colleges and universities. Many conservatives fear that institutions of higher education, the remaining centers of culture in Western democracies, are now at risk. Allan Bloom's *The Closing of the American Mind* is the most famous source of this argument.[82] Bloom argues that universities are especially vulnerable in democracies because they are aristocratic institutions, committed to nonmarket standards of excellence, including knowledge about the good life. This commitment runs counter to the egalitarian and relativistic tendencies of society at large. According to Bloom, the vulgar common attitudes of democratic societies have begun to threaten the aristocratic character of American universities. Concrete results appear in proposals for student evaluations, open admissions, grade inflation, and a more "relevant" curriculum. Kristol's critique of "thinking economically" echoes in Bloom's description of the demise of the university:

It was precisely to provide a shelter from the suffrages of the economic system and the popular will they represent that universities were founded. Now that the student right to judge has become dogma, the universities have become democracies in which the students are the constituencies to which the professors are responsible; the professors no longer look upward toward the gods but downward toward the people, or, rather, *vox populi* has become *vox dei*. A whole new race of charlatans or pastry chefs has come into being who act as the tribunes of the people.[83]

Bloom's greatest fear is that when universities can no longer preserve knowledge of cultural traditions, including the authority of natural aristocrats, liberal democracies will succumb to nihilism. Nihilism is the "belief" that "nothing means anything and everything is permitted." It reflects the moral chaos of the democratic soul, and undermines even liberal democrats' ability to defend their own principles. Nihilism frightens Bloom, since "if neither reason nor tradition can bring about consensus, then the force of the first man resourceful and committed enough must needs do so."[84] Democratic societies sorely need the liberal university, their highest form of culture.

> **Feature 4.** "Neo-conservatism affirms the traditional American idea of equality, but rejects egalitarianism—the equality of condition for all citizens—as a proper goal for government to pursue."

Unlike equality of condition, equality of opportunity includes the right to become unequal not only in education, as Bloom argues, but also in income and occupation. Thomas Sowell's critique of affirmative action provides the best and possibly most famous illustration of this position. Sowell discusses how supporters of early civil rights legislation (e.g., *Brown* v. *Board of Education*) "felt betrayed as the original concept of equal individual *opportunity* evolved toward the concept of equal group *results*."[85] He argues that the cause-and-effect vision underlying civil rights furthered this degeneration by suggesting that "statistical disparities in incomes, occupations, education, etc., represent moral inequities, and are caused by 'society.'"[86] Sowell questions whether group differences result from structural discrimination, genetic differences, or both. More precisely, he argues that group differences have a variety of complex origins that are not captured in the statistics courts use to establish discrimination. For example, people from different cultures have different ways of working and value different kinds of work. Asian American children may perform better in school and test higher in mathematics because their families prize education, especially math skills. Since a calculus background often improves employment prospects, more Asian Americans may find decent jobs. Sowell refuses to dismiss such differences as cultural stereotypes: "what is at issue is whether statistical differences mean discrimination, or whether there are innumerable demographic, cultural, and geographic differences that make this crucial automatic inference highly questionable."[87] If it is questionable, then statistics alone do not establish the presence of discrimination. Court decisions in discrimination cases also often turn on the level of aggregation used in compiling the statistics. Findings of discrimination may depend on how the pool of qualified workers is defined. Supporters of affirmative action, whether or not they speak of goals or quotas, prefer "very general levels of aggregation." The thrust of Sowell's argument is that Americans lack the statistical data necessary to claim that discrimination is structural. It is time to abandon affirmative action programs and support civil rights legislation that was meant to give everyone an equal opportunity by prosecuting discrimination against individuals.

> **Feature 5.** "Neo-conservatism believes that American democracy is not likely to survive for long in a world that is overwhelmingly hostile to American values. . . ."

Anticommunism was a central principle of conservatives' foreign policy. According to James Burnham, twentieth-century history involved a protracted struggle between East and West for control of the world.[88] From this perspective, the so-called Cold War was in effect the Third World War. The rhetoric of peaceful coexistence and later détente, along with the assumption that world war must be a distinct future event, have long obscured conflicts with communists around the globe. Major sites included Vietnam and the "dominoes" of southeast Asia; Latin America and the Middle East, where insurgents destabilized U.S. allies; and eastern Europe, where containment was crucial for NATO security.[89] Agreeing on the dangers of communist expansionism, conservatives opposed post-Vietnam American isolationism. They regarded Carter administration policy as especially naive, citing Carter's belief that a liberal democracy would succeed the shah as a tragic example.

In an increasingly interdependent post-Soviet world, conservatives' anticommunist arguments are primarily of historical interest. The general theme that informs them remains important, however. U.S. foreign policy, like other policy areas, requires a moral foundation. For conservatives, communism exemplified the dangers of ideology. Charles Niemeyer describes "the communist mind" as follows: "Tempted by visions of fancy, bribed by a pseudoscientism, they come to believe the reality of dreams, submerge themselves in a world of their own intellectual making, and pretend to be masters of creation. As long as such people are effectively organized for political action, the world can have no peace."[90] The West has been hard-pressed to defeat a worldview that offered mankind "heaven on earth." According to Whittaker Chambers, a loss of faith prompts communists (and other ideologues) to assume divine powers: "The mind which has rejected the soul, and marched alone, has brought the age to the brink of disaster."[91] To return to Kristol, this is a problem liberalism has failed to solve. Without a communist foe to sustain liberals' sense of morality, they can expect a crisis of self-definition, even spiritual desolation.

Taking Our Medicine

So far, most Americans have not followed conservatives' prescription for social health. When Ronald Reagan failed to make his revolution permanent by creating an electoral realignment or even capturing the Republican Party majority, conservatism again assumed the margins of American electoral politics. There are many possible explanations for his failure. Perhaps conservatism is ultimately a European import, American in temperament but foreign in principles. Perhaps conservatism requires a charismatic leader to obscure the tensions between its economic and social roots. Otherwise, an oppositional stance may be the only viable option. Or perhaps conservatives have yet to create the American synthesis that could mobilize and sustain national majorities. According to Charles Kesler, until conservatives learn the art of "democratic statesmanship," they will remain a social movement, not a political party. Kesler recognizes that mobilizing popular majorities runs counter to conservatives' aristocratic ethos: "politics as the art of the democratic statesman was either impossible or unnecessary, depending on whether conservatism was in an elite or a majoritarian mode."[92] Nevertheless, he claims that virtue, wisdom, and consent meet in the American founding. He urges conservatives to debate public policies drawing on American principles of justice elaborated in the Declaration of Independence and the Constitution. It is this "American vernacular" that conservatives have not yet mastered.

Whether or not conservatives adopt Kesler's political strategy (many will find it distasteful), the Republican sweep of Congress in the 1994 election shows that they will remain a force in contemporary politics. In a time of national (re)definition, conservatives attend to the moral and spiritual principles at the core of American public life. With their emphasis on community, history, ritual, and tradition, conservatives provide a source of hope. Real hope, they argue, cannot be found in an ideology. In the words of Russell Kirk,

> Having lost the spirit of consecration, the modern masses are without expectation of anything better than a bigger slice of what they possess already. Dante tells us that damnation is a terribly simple state: the deprivation of hope.... How to restore a living faith to the routine of existence among the lonely crowd, how to remind men that life has ends—this conundrum the thinking conservative has to face.[93]

Notes

1. William F. Buckley Jr., "Did You Ever See a Dream Walking?" in *Keeping the Tablets: Modern American Conservative Thought*, ed. William F. Buckley Jr. and Charles R. Kesler (New York: Harper & Row, 1988), 36.

2. Quoted by Peter Steinfels, *The Neo-Conservatives: The Men Who Are Changing America's Politics* (New York: Simon and Schuster, 1979), 43.

3. Quoted by Russell Kirk, *The Conservative Mind: From Burke to Santayana* (Chicago: Henry Regnery, 1953), 551.

4. Kesler, introduction to Buckley and Kesler, *Keeping the Tablets*, 14.

5. Milton Friedman, *Capitalism and Freedom* (Chicago: University of Chicago Press, 1962), 6.

6. Michael Oakeshott, "On Being Conservative," in *The Portable Conservative Reader*, ed. Russell Kirk (New York: Viking Penguin, 1982), 569.

7. Kirk, *Conservative Mind*, 543.

8. Edmund Burke, *Reflections on the Revolution in France*, ed. Conor Cruise O'Brien (New York: Penguin, 1982), 90.

9. Irving Kristol, "What Is a Neo-Conservative?" *Newsweek* 87 (19 January 1976): 17.

10. Oakeshott, "On Being Conservative," 575.

11. Steinfels, *Neo-Conservatives*, 19.

12. Charles Krauthammer, "Is Reagan Conservative?" *New Republic* 197, no. 4 (27 July 1987).

13. These categories are suggested by Kenneth Dolbeare and Linda Medcalf in *American Ideologies Today: Shaping the New Politics of the 1990s*, 2d ed. (New York: McGraw-Hill, 1993).

14. Kesler, introduction, 11.

15. Friedman, *Capitalism and Freedom*, 6.

16. Buckley, "Did You Ever See a Dream Walking?" 31.

17. Ibid., 22–23.

18. Samuel Huntington, "Conservatism as an Ideology," *American Political Science Review* 51 (June 1957): 461.

19. Kirk, *Conservative Mind,* 6.

20. Ibid., introduction.

21. Burke, *Reflections,* 117.

22. Burke, "Letter to the Sheriffs of Bristol," in Kirk, *Portable Conservative Reader,* 3.

23. Burke, *Reflections,* 193.

24. Ibid., 194.

25. Ibid.

26. Ibid., 151.

27. Ibid., 154.

28. Ibid., 124.

29. Ibid., 138.

30. Ibid., 149.

31. Burke, "Who Speaks for the People?" in Kirk, *Portable Conservative Reader,* 46.

32. Burke, *Reflections,* 172.

33. Ibid., 315.

34. Ibid., 135.

35. Ibid., 171.

36. Ibid.

37. Ibid.

38. Ibid., 266–67.

39. Charles Kesler suggests this comparison in his introduction to *Keeping the Tablets.*

40. Huntington, "Conservatism as an Ideology," 461.

41. Madison, *Federalist* No. 10, in *The Federalist Papers,* ed. Clinton Rossiter (New York: Mentor Books, 1961), 84.

42. Steinfels, *Neo-Conservatives,* 19.

43. Fisher Ames, "The Dangers of American Liberty," in Kirk, *Portable Conservative Reader,* 103.

44. John Adams, "Letter to John Taylor of Carolina, April 15, 1814," in Kirk, *Portable Conservative Reader,* 69.

45. Adams, quoted by Kirk, *Conservative Mind,* 111.

46. Ibid., 125.

47. Quoted by Gordon S. Wood, *The Creation of the American Republic: 1776–1787* (New York: Norton, 1969), 575.

48. Ibid., 584.

49. Ibid., 592.

50. Ames, "Dangers of American Liberty," 89.

51. Ibid., 103–4.

52. Ibid., 100.

53. Ibid., 101–2.

54. Ibid., 112.

55. John C. Calhoun, quoted by Richard Hofstadter in *The American Political Tradition* (New York: Knopf, 1948), 79.

56. John C. Calhoun, "On the Veto Power," in Kirk, *Portable Conservative Reader,* 161–62.

57. Calhoun, quoted by Hofstadter in *American Political Tradition,* 83.
58. Ibid.
59. Oakeshott, "On Being Conservative," 599.
60. Irving Kristol, "Capitalism, Socialism, Nihilism," in Kirk, *Portable Conservative Reader,* 629.
61. Ibid., 633.
62. Ibid., 637.
63. George Will, *Statecraft and Soulcraft,* quoted by Dolbeare and Medcalf in *American Ideologies Today,* 159.
64. Kristol, "Capitalism, Socialism, Nihilism," 637.
65. Ibid., 639.
66. Ibid., 644.
67. Andrew Hacker, quoted by Linda Medcalf and Kenneth Dolbeare in *Neopolitics: American Political Ideas in the 1980's* (Philadelphia: Temple University Press, 1985), 159.
68. Charles Kesler makes this point in his introduction to *Keeping the Tablets.*
69. Kristol, "What Is a Neo-Conservative?" 17. Peter Steinfels says Kristol's outline "at once says too much and too little" (*Neo-Conservatives,* 53). I hope by elaborating on each point to find a better balance.
70. Kesler, "Introduction to Part Four," in Buckley and Kesler, *Keeping the Tablets,* 217.
71. George Will, "A Conservative Welfare State," in Buckley and Kesler, *Keeping the Tablets,* 239.
72. Kesler, "Introduction to Part Four," 218.
73. Paul Craig Roberts, "The Breakdown of the Keynesian Model," in Buckley and Kesler, *Keeping the Tablets,* 220–31.
74. Charles Murray, "The Constraints of Helping," in Buckley and Kesler, *Keeping the Tablets,* 244.
75. Ibid., 247.
76. Joseph Sobran, "The Abortion Culture," in Buckley and Kesler, *Keeping the Tablets,* 330.
77. Phyllis Schlafly, "The Power of the Positive Woman," in *Women Leaders in American Politics,* ed. James David Barber and Barbara Kellerman (Englewood Cliffs, N.J.: Prentice Hall, 1986), 158.
78. Ibid., 163.
79. Thomas Fleming, quoted by Medcalf and Dolbeare in *Neopolitics.*
80. Schlafly, "Power of the Positive Woman," 164.
81. Ibid., 163.
82. Allan Bloom, *The Closing of the American Mind* (New York: Simon and Schuster, 1987).
83. Allan Bloom, "The Democratization of the University," in *How Democratic Is America?* ed. Robert A. Goldwin (Chicago: Rand McNally, 1971), 119.
84. Ibid., 134.
85. Thomas Sowell, "The Civil Rights Vision: From Equal Opportunity to 'Affirmative Action,' " in Buckley and Kesler, *Keeping the Tablets,* 310.

86. Ibid., 309.

87. Ibid., 317.

88. James Burnham, "Communism: The Struggle for the World," in Buckley and Kesler, *Keeping the Tablets,* 353–78.

89. Jeane Kirkpatrick, "Dictatorships and Double Standards," in Buckley and Kesler, *Keeping the Tablets,* 392–414.

90. Gerhart Niemeyer, "The Communist Mind," in Buckley and Kesler, *Keeping the Tablets,* 352.

91. Whittaker Chambers, "The Direct Glance," in Buckley and Kesler, *Keeping the Tablets,* 430.

92. Kesler, introduction, 15.

93. Kirk, *Conservative Mind,* 542–43.

4

Socialism

I see no reason to accept the political invitation of the "death of socialism" rhetoric. To do so would be profoundly unhistorical. Such a verdict persuades only if we accept the sufficiency of the crude Cold War opposition between East European state socialism and West European Keynesian–welfare statist social democracy, as if "between them, Stalinism and Neil Kinnock exhaust the whole of human history."

— Geoff Eley

Reassessing Socialism

To declare socialism dead following the demise of the Soviet Union, the fall of the Berlin Wall, and other upheavals in Eastern Europe is to misunderstand the significance of these events. The Cold War is over, and that provides an opportunity to expand our political imaginations, to explore the complexity and variety of socialist ideas. In doing so, our attention shifts and our focus widens. The Russian Revolution becomes one of many socialist experiments, not the paradigmatic case of actually existing socialism. It may even represent a narrowing of socialist possibilities. It was preceded by religious and secular socialist utopias, accompanied by anarchosyndicalist and social-democratic movements, and followed by anticolonial or national liberation struggles. Placed in historical context, the death of socialism in its Bolshevik guise frees the left to reassess its rich history. This is one reason to study socialism today.

A second reason is the continued importance of class conflict in contemporary politics. The working class Marx described, a revolutionary proletariat representing the universal interests of mankind, never emerged. Tensions remain between the "haves" and the "have-nots" in advanced industrial societies and between the First and the Third Worlds. The victory of liberal capitalism—the other side in the Cold War—is as doubtful as the death of socialism. Yet some conservatives have declared victory, and others continue to fight for it. In her discussion of Thatcher government policy, Ellen Meiksins Wood quotes "one of the Right's most popular journalistic spokesmen: 'Old fashioned Tories say there isn't any class war. New Tories make no bones about it: we are class warriors and we expect to be victorious.'"[1] In *The New Class War*, Frances Fox Piven and Richard Cloward present a similar analysis of Reagan administration attempts to dismantle the welfare state and disorganize the working class.[2] Despite the complexity of class relations (Do workers now wear white, pink, and blue collars?) and political identities (How do gender, race, and sexuality intersect with class?) today, economic and political power remain intertwined. Class analysis helps disentangle the relationships between them and may serve as a model for examining other forms of oppression.

A third reason why socialist ideas remain relevant is the vision of human fulfillment that they offer. According to Joseph Chytry, Marx's greatest contribution was neither his critique of capitalism nor his theory of revolution. It was the recognition that "to be at home for a human [being] means to contemplate himself in a world he or she has created."[3] For Marx, human creativity was primarily expressed, and under capitalism denied, in the production of material objects. Marx's materialist argument has aesthetic and spiritual origins in German Idealism and Romanticism. At a deeper level, Marx tries to sustain the hope that human beings can live meaningful lives. Eric Hobsbawm fears that this hope may be the greatest loss if socialism is declared dead: "the fall of the Soviet-type system, about which all illusion had long gone, is less significant than the apparent end of the dream of which it was the nightmare version."[4] More dangerous dreams, for example, ethnic nationalisms, may fill the ensuing vacuum.

A fourth and, for now, final reason for studying socialism is to distinguish what is Marxian (Marx's actual ideas) from what is Marxist (ideas espoused in his name).[5] Interpreting Marx has long been a high-stakes game of politics. The result is a "string of doctrinal continuities" resulting in the hyphenated and hypothetical person: Marx-Lenin-Stalin. Many factors have contributed to such misrepresentations, including Marx's insistence that theory be related to practice and Engels's simplifications of Marx's ideas. My present point is simply that much of what we know is a "straw-Marxism." As Paul Thomas puts it: "if by 'the reception of Marx' we mean the accurate, disinterested appraisal of his ideas, we can conclude that the reception of Marx has still to be achieved."[6]

Such an appraisal is worth the effort. A commitment to intellectual integrity regarding the history of socialism frees us to reconsider the meaning of human creativity, to reassess class as a political force, and, most important, to expand our political imaginations.

The Origins of Socialism

The origins of the term *socialism* are obscure. Some claim it was first used in 1835 to refer to the utopian community, New Lanark, founded by the English industrialist Robert Owen. In mid-nineteenth-century usage, socialism referred to a "tribal state," "Christian socialism," "great demons in morals and politics," "the real nature of man," and "fairy tales." As introduced by Owen (and Fourier, another utopian socialist), "socialism ... proposed that a society living together should share all the wealth produced."[7] Albert Fried offers a more comprehensive definition that identifies socialists' common themes: "their conviction that each person's obligation to society as a whole was the absolute condition of his equality, that society was a brotherhood, not a collection of strangers drawn together by interest (the usual interpretation of the contract), that the individual derived his highest fulfillment from his solidarity with others, not from the pursuit of advantage and power."[8]

The concept of socialism predates the term. The utopian schemes proposed in Plato's *Republic* and Christ's "Sermon on the Mount" are arguably socialist.[9] Engels describes early matriarchal societies, like the Iroquois Confederacy, as forms of primitive communism. Standard histories of socialism usually begin in mid-nineteenth-century America and Europe. During this period, many religious and secular socialist utopias were founded. According to George Bernard Shaw, America in the 1840s had more socialist communities than anywhere else in the world.[10] These early examples continued to guide the resurgence of communal living that accompanied New Left politics in the 1960s.

A comprehensive history of socialism is beyond the scope of this chapter. The ideas of Karl Marx, founder of modern socialism, are the major emphasis here. Historians identify three major influences on the development of his philosophy: (1) the utopian socialists, (2) Hegel and the Left Hegelians, and (3) the British political economists. While exploring these influences on Marx, we also consider aspects of the socialism(s) that preceded him.

Utopian Socialism

Although Marx learned from their ideas, he was quite critical of the utopian socialists. He portrays them as naive, even dangerous, because they are oblivious to the laws of class struggle and the need for violent revolution; instead, they advocate peaceful change. They believe that all of society—rich and poor—will voluntarily join socialist utopias after observing how they operate. Charles Fourier's fund-raising efforts for his model communities, called phalansteries, exemplify their innocent optimism. After placing an advertisment in a Paris newspaper, Fourier waited at a café for contributions from wealthy donors. No one came, leaving him, according to one source, to wonder how people could fail to see that phalansteries represented the highest form of human existence.

Those who did form utopian communities were often members of an educated, wealthy elite. Despite their good intentions and detailed plans, most of the communities they founded were short-lived. They failed for a variety of reasons, including their members' limited practical skills, internal conflicts, and financial bankruptcy. A religious society, "The United Society of Believers," or the Shakers, proves to be an exception to the rule. Led from England to the United States by Mother Ann Lee, they founded their first community, Niskeyuna, in 1776 near Albany, New York. By the 1850s, eighteen Shaker colonies, composed of 150 to 600 members, ranged from New England west to Kentucky and Ohio. Today, the remaining Shakers continue to accept new members at their community in Sabbathday Lake, Maine.

According to the Shakers, Ann Lee represented God's second coming in the form of a woman; she would redeem the sins of Eve. Their communities were organized as celibate "families" of brothers and sisters. They combined strict sexual taboos (when together, men and women stayed five feet apart and women were not to whisper, wink, or cross their legs) with sexual equality in government. Elders and Eldresses governed Shaker "families," several of which joined together to form a larger community. It was led, in turn, by a Holy Anointed Mother and Father. The Shakers stressed simplicity in all aspects of daily life. They worked prosperous farms and used modern technology, but the purpose of their efforts was not to acquire wealth. They wanted to be self-sufficient and to perfect themselves. Their goal was to create the Kingdom of God on Earth—a New Eden.

A discussion of religious utopianism may seem inappropriate here, since Marx, a self-proclaimed atheist, condemned religion as the "opium of the people." Nevertheless, religious movements are often socialist (liberation theology is a good example), and spiritual themes are common in Marx's supposedly secular writings. Marx regarded religion, especially Christianity, as politically conservative primarily because it surrenders human destiny to divine powers. Denys Turner poses the problem as follows: "insofar as Christianity is true to itself as religion, it must be alienating politically, and insofar as it engages genuinely with the revolutionary critical program of socialism, it must cease to be genuinely religious."[11] Marx's account of labor under capitalism nonetheless parallels the human condition after the Fall. In both cases, humans are separated from essential aspects of their being, other people, and their God. Socialism represents a reunion of sorts, a return to full humanity, which is not unlike Paradise.[12] Joseph Schumpeter describes Marx as a secular prophet who espouses socialism as the millennium.[13]

The secular utopias of the British industrialist Robert Owen and the French philosopher Charles Fourier are closer to Marx's self-understanding. At New Lanark, the largest textile factory in Scotland, Owen tried to demonstrate that efficiency and equality were compatible goals in industrial production. He provided affordable housing, decent wages, and good schools for his employees. To encourage worker productivity, he took a fixed return on investments and returned additional profits to the enterprise. The conviction that many evils result from the effects of a harsh environment on human character fueled his efforts. Against the Protestant Ethic, Owen claimed that by blaming the poor for their fate, the rich escaped their own social responsibilities. In 1824, under attack from the Anglican church and the Tory Party, Owen moved to the relatively uncorrupted and undeveloped United States. He established an Owenite community in New Harmony, Indiana.

Charles Fourier, another utopian socialist, probably had the greatest influence on Marx. His major concept is passionate attraction. Fourier criticizes philosophers who treat human passions as sources of social discord that must be thoroughly controlled. Like Owen, Fourier argues that the passions pose problems only in badly organized societies. To create harmony, society should work with the passions, not against them. They are God's gift to humanity, and God rules by attraction, according to Fourier. Fourier's plans for his phalansteries are often bizarre. For example, the little hordes, young boys who love to get dirty, collect the garbage, and "filth ... become[s] their path to glory."[14] The butterfly principle guides amorous relationships. Individuals "flit" from partner to partner, since monogamy is unnatural.

Writing in Victorian England, Marx shied away from Fourier's sexual schemes. He espoused monogamous heterosexuality as the natural form of sex love, though he attacked the accompanying dependence of women on men. But Fourier's proposals for adapting industrial production to human inclinations (e.g., by varying tasks and forming work groups) shaped Marx's critique of capitalism. More generally, secular utopians helped Marx reformulate social relationships between human beings. Many of the tensions liberals struggle to resolve (e.g., between individual and community, liberty and equality, property and justice) are not universal "laws of nature." According to Marx, the very idea that social life requires these "tradeoffs" is the product of a specific —modern bourgeois—society.

Hegel and the Left Hegelians

A second influence on Marx, Hegel and the Left Hegelians, illuminates his theory of history. Marx uses two words to describe history: it is dialectical and materialist. In the following passage, he suggests how they are related and describes his relationship to Hegel: "With him [Hegel] it [the dialectic] is standing on its head. It must be turned right side up again, if you would discover the rational kernel within the mystical shell."[15] By inverting Hegel's dialectic, Marx reveals the "secret"—the materialist basis—of history. According to Marx, Hegel's greatest contribution was the concept of history as a process of man's self-creation through the activity of labor.[16] The term *dialectics* refers to that self-creative historical process. The familiar formula—thesis versus antithesis equals synthesis—fails adequately to capture its meaning. Engels provides a fuller, richer definition: "dialectics ... comprehends things and their representations, ideas, in their essential connection, concatenation, motion, origin, and ending."[17] A dialectician sees the internal relationships between things, the continuous motion of events, and the general patterns of historical change.

Engels says that Marx adopts the "revolutionary side" of Hegel's "dialectical method."[18] Nevertheless, Hegel sees human creations as vehicles for a higher power—a self-manifesting and self-knowing Idea —to assume historical form. According to Marx, this is upside down. To turn Hegel right side up, he draws on the materialism of Ludwig Feuerbach, a Left Hegelian. Feuerbach argues that Hegel, by portraying humanity as a manifestation of "spirit," denies humans real, material, sensuous existence. For Feuerbach, "spirit," if it exists at all, is a human creation, more precisely, a projection. "Spirit" embodies man's hopes of a better world, one without conflict and pain, without evil and death. The problem, Feuerbach argues, is that by projecting these qualities elsewhere, humans deprive themselves of them, that is, humanity becomes not-spirit, dependent, inferior, and passive beings.

Feuerbach claims instead that the essence of humanity or our species-being appears in our relationships with one another in society. Marx agreed: "Feuerbach resolves the religious essence into the human essence, but the human essence is no abstraction inherent in each single individual. In its reality it is the ensemble of social relations."[19]

A reason to study socialism is to sustain the hope that human beings can live meaningful lives. As an aesthetic and spiritual worldview, Marxism bases that hope on humans' self-creative capacities. According to William Adams, Marx traces human creations to the social "foundations of economic life and revolutionary practice," instead of attributing them to an external cause, be it God or Nature.[20] For Marx, "the history of *industry* and the established *objective* existence of industry are the *open* book of *man's essential powers*."[21] The capacity to create consciously distinguishes human labor from the efforts of other animal species to survive. Because they are self-aware, humans can potentially control what they produce and how they produce it. People also can discover and express themselves in their products and productive activities.

What, you might ask, distinguishes this approach to industry from capitalists' praise for entrepreneurial activity and technological innovation? To answer this question, we need to return to the rational kernel Marx would extract from the mystical shell of Hegel's dialectic. At the same time, we consider a third influence on Marx—the political economists.

The Political Economists

Despite the differences between Adam Smith, James Mill, David Ricardo, and others, Marx criticizes political economists en masse for their concept of civil (or liberal capitalist) society. In civil society, "the individual appears detached from ... natural bonds." Worse still, "the various forms of social connectedness confront the individual as a mere means towards his private purposes, as external necessity." According to Marx, political economists "tear apart" the dialectical relationships between individuals, societies, and history. This allows them to achieve "the[ir] aim ... to present production ... as encased in eternal natural laws independent of history, at which opportunity *bourgeois* relations are then quietly smuggled in as the inviolable natural laws on which society in the abstract is founded."[22]

Although the political economists are materialists, their materialism is mechanical, static, or both. (It is only fair to note that Feuerbach made a similar mistake. Marx accused him of talking "too much about nature and too little about politics."[23]) Political economy begins with isolated individuals whose liberty depends on freedom from the interference of other people. Instead, Marx argues that human beings are social animals, who "can only individuate [themselves] in the midst of society."[24] "Production by an isolated individual outside society ... is as much of an absurdity as is the development of language without individuals living *together* and talking to each other."[25] As people interact, they develop their capacity to produce and eventually outgrow their current society. Different societies reflect historical stages—Asiatic, ancient, feudal, modern bourgeois—in the development of man's productive powers.

How does production shape society, according to Marx? Is Marx an economic determinist? Marx's most succinct and famous statement of his theory of history is this:

> In the social production of their life, men enter into definite relations that are indispensable and independent of their will, relations of production which correspond to a definite stage of development of their material productive forces. The sum total of these relations of production constitutes the economic structure of society, the real foundation, on which rises a legal and political superstructure and to which correspond definite forms of social consciousness. The mode of production of material life conditions the social, political, and intellectual life process in general.[26]

Marx's basic distinction is between economic structure and superstructure, but the latter is further divided into legal, political, and intellectual life. Although Marx says that the superstructure "rises" on the economic base, he also says they "correspond" to and "condition" each other. This suggests an interactive relationship, rather than a causal one. Engels clarifies that relationship when he says that "the *ultimately* determining element in history is the production and reproduction of real life."[27] According to G.A. Cohen, the relationship between structure and superstructure is functional, rather than causal.[28] Specific relations of production require certain class relations, state institutions and laws, and dominant ideas to sustain and to stimulate further development. As productive capacities continue to develop, what once was functional becomes dysfunctional, resulting in economic crises, political unrest, and eventually social change. This interpretation captures the complexity of historical processes better than a simple cause-effect relationship can. It also creates a greater role for human activity in historical development. Although Marx says social relations are independent of human will, he does not mean that people cannot affect them, only that they act within a context that limits their options.

In such a brief overview, we can only scratch the surface of Marx's theory of history. Among the many topics that remain, the role of class conflict in historical change is especially important. In *The Communist Manifesto*, Marx declares that "the history of all hitherto existing society is the history of class struggles."[29] To assess this claim, we turn to Marx's critique of capitalism, the focus of his most important work, *Capital*.

Class, Capitalism, and Consciousness

Classes are defined by relationships to the productive forces (raw materials, labor-power, machinery, etc.) of a society. It is important to understand what does not constitute a class for Marx.[30] The amount of property people own, the kind of property they have, whether they sell or buy commodities—these features do not suffice to determine class membership. Only the structural relationship between its members and the mode of production establishes a class. Class relationships are conflictual, not symbiotic, because a dominant class systematically controls the labor (and the products) of a subordinate class. For example, the classes in conflict under capitalism are the bourgeoisie (those who own means of production and purchase labor) and the proletariat (those who lack means of production and must sell their labor to live). Marx recognizes that conflict occurs not only between classes but also within them. He also acknowledges that multiple classes exist simultaneously in a society. Yet he maintains that in every society, a dominant class relation corresponds to its relations of production.

Marx defines classes by objective relationships that are empirically verifiable. We can determine who owns the factories, who works for wages, and so on, in a society. Marx also uses class in another sense. He distinguishes between a class *in itself* (objective) and a class *for itself* (subjective).[31] With his subjective concept of class, Marx raises the question of class consciousness: how does a class, especially the proletariat, become a revolutionary force? Recent studies of Marxism often focus on the problem of class consciousness in modern societies. The emergence of a service sector, the separation of stockholders from management, the development of multi- and transnational corporations, and so forth, make it much more difficult to define classes by relationships of ownership and control. Classes are also divided by cultural, gender, and racial differences, and new movements representing these identities are politically powerful today. Was Marx's concept of a revolutionary proletariat a utopian vision? Or, in conservatives' terms, a metaphysical abstraction? Did he assume too close a connection between economic relationships and political revolution? If classes *for themselves* have not emerged spontaneously, what role, if any, should class analysis play in socialist politics today? Wood argues that "class organization [is] a political task ... simply because the translation of *common interests* into *concerted action* requires organization and coordination." She sees the absence of class consciousness as a problem of logistics.[32] We return to her argument after examining Marx's account of how class consciousness develops in capitalist society.

According to Marx, capitalist societies have four major problems; each contributes to the creation of a revolutionary proletariat. They are (1) contradictions, (2) exploitation, (3) alienation, and (4) fetishism. Marx's theory of history suggests that every society becomes obsolete when its productive forces outgrow its relations of production. In Marx's terms, the latter begin to "fetter" or to "contradict" the former, preventing people from using them fully and developing them further. In capitalist society, the very means the bourgeoisie use to increase profits result in their eventual demise.[33] According to Marx, capitalists' profits do not originate in the market, that is, from buying low and selling high. Instead, workers create "surplus value" for the capitalist during the production process. Marx argues that every commodity has a value equivalent to the values of the other commodities—labor power, raw materials, and instruments of production—involved in producing it. This is also how the value of workers' labor power is calculated. A "fair" wage is determined by the amount of money a worker needs to feed, clothe, shelter, and educate himself and his family at the current standard of living in his society. Labor power—the workers' commodity—has a peculiar property: it can produce more than its value.

Marx gives the example of a worker who sells his labor power for a daily wage of three shillings, enough to meet his needs for a day.[34] However, this worker produces three shillings' worth of products in six hours. This means that any products produced during a longer day become surplus value (i.e., value above costs) for the capitalist. Capitalists, Marx argues, pursue a number of strategies to increase their surplus value. Obviously, it is in their interest to lengthen the working day. They also can increase productivity by speeding up and/or mechanizing the production process, and they can introduce incentives, like piecework, to motivate workers. Mechanization has the added advantage of decreasing labor costs. By creating unemployment, it increases competition for jobs and drives wages down. Mass production techniques also lower prices, allowing workers to live better for less.

Capitalists pursue these strategies to compete effectively with one another (i.e., to survive financially). They are subject to economic laws too, though self-interested ones. Marx says, "I paint the capitalist . . . in no sense *couleur de rose*. But here individuals are dealt with only in so far as they are the personifications of economic categories, embodiments of particular class-relations and class-interests."[35] Marx argues that capitalists exploit workers, whether or not they pay a fair wage (i.e., the full value of their labor power) because they do not make a reciprocal contribution to production. Marx does not recognize investing money, organizing factories, managing production, inventing technology, and the like, as labor. These activities are important, but they do not create value. Marx knows that this does not square with capitalists' self-understanding: they think they work. Yet Marx insists that capitalists are parasites, feeding on the bodies of dead and dying laborers.

Eventually, capitalism outdoes—and undoes—itself. Marx points to periodic crises of overproduction and underconsumption when an all-too-productive economy slows down or even stops due to limited markets. Although surplus value originates in production, it is realized only through exchange in the marketplace. In their efforts to increase surplus value, capitalists decrease the purchasing power of the workers who buy their products. Of course, by internationalizing production (i.e., by taking jobs and goods overseas) capitalists can postpone the big crash. But only temporarily. Eventually, "The development of Modern Industry, . . . cuts from under its feet the very foundation on which the bourgeoisie produces and appropriates products. What the bourgeoisie, therefore, produces, above all, is its own gravediggers."[36]

The revolutionary proletariat, the agents of social change, are its gravediggers. In developing industry, capitalists bring workers together in factories and build communication and transportation networks between them. With every crisis, more small and medium-size businesses fail, more workers are unemployed, and the ranks of the proletariat swell, at least by objective indicators. According to Marx, the subjective conditions for forming a revolutionary class are also present. Marx discusses how capitalism "alienates" workers by robbing their lives of meaning and destroying their sense of self-worth. Alienation takes four specific forms. Under capitalism, workers are alienated from their products, which capitalists appropriate; their productive activity, which becomes tedious and dangerous; their fellow workers, who compete with them for jobs, products, and wages; and their species-being by living less than human lives. The combined effect is that the worker "no longer feels himself to be freely active in any but his animal functions—eating, drinking, procreating, or at most in his dwelling and in dressing-up, etc., and in his human functions he no longer feels himself to be anything but an animal." This is an inversion of the real relationship: "what is animal becomes human and what is human becomes animal."[37]

According to Marx, objective and subjective factors converge to create the conditions for revolution. In other words, their relationship to production gradually teaches workers that they have the collective capacity to change society. This brings us to fetishism, a fourth problem in capitalist societies. Most simply, a fetish is an object to which people impute special powers. Hegel's "spirit," which Feuerbach criticized as a projection, is a philosophical example. In capitalist economies, "the market" becomes a fetish. When Adam Smith refers to an "invisible hand" that guides economic relations by the "laws of supply and demand," he implies that market relations involve processes beyond human control. For Marx, the "mystery of commodities" is that "a definite social relation between men ... assumes, in their eyes, the fantastic form of a relation between things."[38] He concludes that "the life-process of society ... does not strip off its mystical veil until it is treated as production by freely associated men, and is consciously regulated by them in accordance with a settled plan."[39] In other words, socialism attempts to return people to their powers—and their senses.

Communism and Socialism

Following Geoff Eley, I suggested earlier that a "single-minded focus on the Bolshevik experiment as the main measure of revolutionary authenticity" artificially narrows the range of socialist possibilities.[40] Historically, there are at least two major strains of socialism: social democracy and revolutionary communism. In Marx's sketch of the revolution and its aftermath they exist in some tension. Unfortunately, Marx provided only a sketch; on the revolution, he was notoriously brief and vague. This is consistent with his insistence that "we call communism the *real* movement which abolishes the present state of things."[41] Communism can only be described as it is at present emerging from capitalism. This strategy left later revolutionaries considerable room for interpretation.

Marx presents a revolution in two stages. The initial phase, which he calls proletarian dictatorship or crude communism, still carries the birthmarks of capitalist society, and they account for many of its flaws. (Marx is often his own worst critic!) Marx's descriptions of it vary. Sometimes a proletarian parliamentary majority pursues legal reforms within the state; sometimes the Communist Party leads the proletariat in seizing state power. Historical context clearly shapes revolutionary strategy. Marx concedes that electoral success is more likely in America and England, whereas India and Russia probably require violent revolution. Different means also suit different ends. A ten-hour workday can be legislated more easily than the confiscation of private property! This variety suggests to Eley that "the most impressive movements combine both impulses, lending the stability of centrally directed permanent organization to the maximum scope for rank-and-file resurgence."[42]

Marx does not juxtapose dictatorship and democracy, as many liberal democrats would. He harkens back to an earlier concept of democracy as rule of the people and recognizes that even democracy can be and, at times, must be tyrannical. What distinguishes proletarian dictatorship from other class states is that the proletariat acts on behalf of humanity; its state no longer represents class interests. The transition to socialism involves removing all residues of class conflict, including transforming a competitive, individualistic human nature. Marx recognizes that this transition will be a painful process. After the revolution, when expectations are high, production is to be collectivized and distribution is to be equalized. The community, Marx says, becomes a universal capitalist, and every citizen becomes a common laborer.[43] Under these conditions, equal right or bourgeois justice is fully realized. But "*equal* right is an unequal right for unequal labour" and "*therefore, a right of inequality, in its content, like every right.*"[44] Genuine equality requires treating different individuals differently, instead of measuring everyone by the same formal standard (e.g., hours worked). Only with the next transition, from proletarian dictatorship to socialist society, can the bourgeois standard of equal right be replaced by the socialist principle: "from each according to his ability, to each according to his needs!"[45]

Politically, the dictatorship of the proletariat also represents a transitional state. Marx's political theory is relatively undeveloped, perhaps to his peril. His most developed remarks about political institutions after the revolution occur in a discussion of the Paris Commune. There he praises the Communards for pursuing the following measures: (1) replacement of standing armies by the armed people; (2) introduction of universal suffrage, immediate recall, and workers' wages for government officials; (3) integration of executive and legislative powers in a single body to clarify responsibility; (4) separation of church and state; (5) provision for universal public education; and (6) decentralization of power in a federal structure.[46] Such a state, Marx argues, will gradually "wither away." Eventually, it will cease being a political power, an institution seemingly standing above society yet actually ruling for a specific class. As Marx puts it, central authority persists to coordinate society, but the "administration of things" supersedes the "domination of people."[47] This condition fits Marx's definition of freedom: "freedom ... can only consist in socialized man, the associated producers, rationally regulating their interchange with Nature, bringing it under their common control...."[48] Once the state withers, a tremendous blossoming of human potential will follow.

Today, Marx's revolutionary schemes can be regarded only with considerable skepticism. There is much to rethink here, for example, the dangers of violent revolution and the extent of state power, the possibilities of democratic alliances and the formation of class consciousness. The process of revising socialism began during Marx's lifetime, well before the Bolshevik revolution. In the 1870s, debates between democratic socialists, revolutionary communists, and social anarchists undermined Marx's efforts to create an international proletariat.

Revisionism: Social Democracy and Revolutionary Communism

In 1864 Marx gave the inaugural address for the International Workingmen's Association, or the First International. His address praised the growth of cooperatives, like Owen's New Lanark, the expansion of the trade union movement, and the political reforms that accompanied it (e.g., the victory of the Ten-Hours Bill in England). But he stressed that the proletariat cannot rest content with using the bourgeois state; it must ultimately conquer political power. The International serves this end two ways: it combines revolutionary forces, emphasizing the proletariats' strength in numbers; and it encourages opposition to "bourgeois wars," by blurring national boundaries.[49]

Yet trouble quickly arose in the International. In 1872 the General Council, led by Marx, passed a circular condemning the social democrats and the anarchists, whom we discuss in the next chapter. Marx outlines his objections to social democracy in an 1879 "Circular Letter" to Bebel, Liebknecht, and Bracke, leaders of the German Social Democratic Party. In strong language, he accuses them of representing the "petty bourgeoisie":

> Instead of determined political opposition, general mediation; instead of struggle against the government and the bourgeoisie, an attempt to win over and persuade them; instead of defiant resistance to ill treatment from

above, humble submission and confession that the punishment was deserved. Historically necessary conflicts are all interpreted as misunderstandings, and all discussion ends with the assurance that after all we are all agreed on the main point.[50]

Obviously, not. What ideas of the social democrats did Marx regard as mistaken?

Eduard Bernstein is widely regarded as the major theoretician of the German Social Democratic Party (SPD). Bernstein's central concern was the gap between socialist theory and practice, more specifically the tension between revolutionary rhetoric and electoral strategies. In his *Evolutionary Socialism,* Bernstein revises Marxist theory and, some argue, rejects its central concepts. Bernstein argues that history proceeds, not through dialectical contradictions, but through organic evolutionism. Liberal capitalism steadily moves toward democratic socialism. He regarded the SPD's electoral gains (by 1890, they were the largest party in the Reichstag, controlling one-quarter of the total votes) and the success of reform legislation (Germany, under Bismarck, had the most extensive social welfare programs in Europe) as evidence. Marx, Bernstein argues, was too materialist and too deterministic—a "Calvinist without God." Bernstein concludes that it is neither possible nor desirable to give socialism "a purely materialist foundation."[51] Socialism rests on ethical factors; it is a result of conscious human choice.

Bernstein bases his argument on more than the SPD's stunning successes. He claims that the economic contradictions Marx anticipated have not emerged. Marx envisioned increasing polarization of classes as a result of increasingly frequent and severe economic crises. Bernstein identifies opposing factors: the presence of small and medium-size businesses alongside large monopolies, the dispersal of property through joint-stock companies, a general improvement in standards of living, the fluidity, diversity, and increased cooperation of classes. In addition, capitalism has created counterweights, for example, flexible credit, a world market, cartels and monopolies, communication and transportation networks, to manage and stabilize economic markets. What Marx saw as economic crises, Bernstein portrays as trade cycles. Periods of overproduction and underconsumption are mechanisms by which the market adjusts to socioeconomic changes. They do not indicate fatal flaws in the basic structure of capitalist economies.

Many of Bernstein's critics sustained Marx's theory by arguing that the "big crash" simply had not happened yet. Bernstein responded that Marx meant his theory to describe his own times. Since capitalism had not collapsed and socialism had not triumphed, it was time to admit that Marx had been mistaken. Bernstein claimed that changing events compelled a consistent historical materialist to rethink Marx's theory. (This argument supports a plurality of Marxisms with a fuzzy line between what is Marxist and Marxian.) To this pragmatic argument, Bernstein added a more principled one. He insisted that socialism must occur through democratic means—or not at all. Revolutionary rhetoric not only alienated bourgeois allies and falsified historical events but it also denied workers' real needs:

> We cannot demand from a class, the great majority of whose members live under crowded conditions, are badly educated, and have an uncertain and insufficient income, the high intellectual and moral standard which the organization and existence of a socialist community presupposes. We will, therefore, not ascribe it to them by fiction.[52]

For all these reasons, Bernstein concluded that "a greater security for lasting success lies in a steady advance than in the possibilities offered by a catastrophic crash."[53]

Many of Bernstein's critics have argued that subsequent events (e.g., the SPD's support for the German war effort and its failure to govern under the Weimar Republic) disprove his theory. In Germany, class collaboration led to fascism, not socialism—a topic to which we return in a later chapter. Lenin's critique of social democracy also contributed to the eclipse of Bernstein's ideas. In 1903 Lenin declared, "The Economists have gone to one extreme. To straighten matters out somebody had to pull in the other direction—and that is what I have done."[54] His *What Is to Be Done?* written during Russia's 1905 revolution, provides a program for organizing a revolutionary socialist party. In comparing Bernstein and Lenin, it is important to remember their different historical contexts. At the turn of the century, Russia's economy was primarily agricultural and roughly 80 percent of the populace were peasants. These were hardly the preconditions Marx outlined for a socialist revolution. Late in his life, Marx began to study Russia to explore the possibility of skipping a historical stage by transforming feudal villages directly into socialist communes. Lenin's efforts took a different form. He focused on the Communist Party, more specifically, its revolutionary vanguard, as the mechanism for transforming society during an extended dictatorship of the proletariat.

Lenin distinguishes two forms of proletarian consciousness. Of its own accord or spontaneously, the proletariat can only develop trade union consciousness, a form of bourgeois ideology that limits its demands to bread-and-butter reforms. The task of the Communist Party is to bring revolutionary consciousness to the proletariat from without, to lend the economic struggle a political form. According to Lenin, the Communist Party cannot be a broad democracy without making itself vulnerable to suppression. A party vanguard, a small, secret, conspiratorial band of professional revolutionaries, connected to the masses by a series of transmission belts (e.g., unions, cooperatives, soviets, youth groups), is a more realistic organizational strategy.[55] Lenin refers to this as democratic centralism, but the stress is on centralism. Although Lenin vehemently opposed personality cults, his organizational scheme is easily abused by a powerful leader. Leon Trotsky, a Menshevik (the name of the Russian social democrats), identified the danger early: "In inner-party politics, these methods lead, as we shall yet see, to this: the party organization substitutes itself for the party, the central committee substitutes itself for the [party] organization, and, finally, a 'dictator' substitutes himself for the central committee."[56]

Lenin's rationale for a party vanguard appears in his *State and Revolution,* written in 1917 at the height of the Bolshevik revolution. Although he is committed to revolution "with people as they are now," he recognizes that means "people who cannot dispense with subordination, control, and 'foremen and accountants.'"[57] During the dictatorship of the proletariat, the party uses the state as a special repressive force to transform society. It simultaneously destroys feudal and capitalist values in order to develop an advanced industrial economy. Paradoxically, only after the revolution, through the rule of a party state, does Russia realize the preconditions for socialism. Only then does the proletarian dictatorship "wither away." A society that approximates Marx's vision of socialism replaces it.

Late in life, Lenin wrote about the failure of his plans. He recognized that a small popular base forced repression of opposition parties and soviets, that his nationalization program created a "bureaucratic swamp," and that workers had little voice in the Bolshevik state, though it supposedly represented their interests.[58] Some of these problems are linked to the failure of the international proletariat to support the Russian Revolution. In his theory of imperialism, Lenin argued that revolutions in less developed countries would cut off capitalists' sources of cheap labor, raw materials, and force them to exploit their indigenous proletariat to the breaking point, precipitating the worldwide revolution Marx anticipated. Instead, the Bolsheviks faced the economic and political pressures associated with sustaining socialism in one country.

Another, more serious problem of revolutionary communism is shared by social democrats. Marx and Engels offer some cautionary thoughts on it. In 1879 Marx agreed with the social democrats that the proletariat should work with the bourgeoisie, until the latter wanted to stop the revolution short. Then the proletariat should oppose its previous allies and conquer state power to "make the revolution permanent."[59] In 1895, however, Engels presents violent revolution as an increasingly dangerous strategy, given the layout of modern cities and modern military technology. Using Paris as an example, he describes how a modern army can march down broad boulevards destroying all protesters in their path. Current conditions, he suggests, require workers to arm themselves with votes, to fight via the ballot box, to pursue nonviolent revolution.[60]

It seems that the greater scale and power of the modern state poses problems for social democrats and revolutionary communists. On the one hand, Soviet communism leaves an ugly legacy of a command economy, a corrupt bureaucracy, and a centralized state—of political oppression. On the other hand, the co-optation of social democratic parties makes it difficult to distinguish their reformist policies from welfare state liberalism. I quoted Geoff Eley to the effect that "the most impressive movements combine both impulses [i.e., permanent organization and mass participation]." The question remains whether they suffice, even in tandem. Or, is socialism dead?

Is Socialism Dead?

The best response to this question may be to ask another: in what sense? Certainly, Marx's ideas continue to influence many forms of social critique, far more than we can begin to consider in this final section.[61] Critical theorists, known as the Frankfurt School for their origins in 1920s Germany, contribute greatly to our understanding of mass culture and mass psychology. Their writings range from Theodor Adorno's study of the authoritarian personality, to Walter Benjamin's work on mechanically reproduced artwork, to Jürgen Habermas's efforts to resurrect democratic discourse. In addition, French structuralists and poststructuralists analyze the unique forms power assumes in modern states. Here too is tremendous variety, including Louis Althusser's analysis of ideological state apparatuses; Jacques Derrida's studies of language, identity, and difference; and Michel Foucault's genealogies of carceral institutions such as asylums, factories, and prisons.

Marxist ideas also continue to influence political action, especially in the Third World. Post-Leninist and, in some cases, anti-Leninist adaptations of Marxism to national liberation struggles range from the mass line of Chairman Mao, to Latin American dependency theory and guerrilla warfare, to African tribal strategies. We also cannot forget European and American socialism, especially the New Left of the 1960s. Although it is fashionable to criticize yesterday's hippies as today's yuppies, many student radicals remain political activists. They are often members of new social movements fighting for civil rights, ecology, feminism, and peace, though with a toned-down rhetoric of class struggle.

A stronger criticism of the New Left is that it confused resistance with revolution, that it lacked a coherent program for social change. The broad goals and vague language of such documents as "The Port Huron Statement" seem to support this claim. In *The Agony of the American Left,* Christopher Lasch uses the free speech movement as a case in point:

> At Berkeley the students might have capitalized on their free-speech victory by pressing on to ... other issues. Instead they celebrated the triumph of free speech by proclaiming the stirring political slogan: "Fuck." Why should free speech have issued only in "fuck"? The new slogan could be counted on, presumably, to provoke the administration into reprisals; had that become an end in itself?[62]

Lasch concludes that many of the radicals were so "deeply alienated from American society" that institutions "embody[ing] values transcending the present political system" seemed impossible.[63] Only "nihilistic gestures" and "hysterical militancy" remained as available options.

Hobsbawm's fears about the future of any society without hope resurface here. The Western socialism that, as Lasch puts it, "oscillates between capitulation and a mindless revolutionary militancy based on irrelevant models," has died.[64] Will worse ideals fill the ensuing vacuum? Ironically, the transformation of the former Soviet Union and Eastern Europe may increase this danger. According to Hobsbawm, Stalinism was—more irony here—"good for the West." "All that made Western democracy worth living for its people—social security, the welfare state, a high and rising income for its wage-earners, and its natural consequences, diminution in social inequality and equality of life-changes—was the result of fear."[65] Hobsbawm overstates his case and underestimates capitalists' ingenuity. Nevertheless, it may prove harder to create a gentler and kinder America without a serious Soviet threat.

Perhaps hope is still to be found somewhere in the socialist tradition. But a socialism that styles itself as anticapitalism cannot survive in the post–Cold War era either. Its proponents also need to rethink their ideas. Writing in the shadow of recent events, socialists are questioning their standard dichotomies. They also recognize that stereotypes, such as markets versus plans, democracy versus bureaucracy, even revolution versus reform, ignore or minimize the complexity of modern politics. Although socialist responses to their new context differ, widespread relief accompanies the demise of actually existing socialism. I would like to conclude by discussing three problem areas that socialists are rethinking.

The first is how to reinvigorate the politics of class struggle, absent all claims of a materialist base, even an "ultimately determinant" one. Some scholars, like Ellen Meiksins Wood, argue that class struggle has continued under conservative governments. Many socialists have missed this because they sought a different revolutionary subject, an "idealized" proletariat. In keeping with her stress on logistics, Wood argues that connections between class interests and socialist politics must be carefully developed and nurtured. A new labor movement will be built only by organizing around the "political impulses" already present in working class struggles. Eric Bronner proposes a similar strategy, though from a slightly different perspective. His "socialism unbound . . . rests on little more than an ethical commitment to a set of unrealized ideals."[66] Those ideals include internationalism, political democracy, and economic justice. Although class remains a unifying point under capitalism, Bronner recognizes that identities and oppression take many forms. For him, more than for Wood, the central issue is not what party to join but what values to pursue through any feasible organizing strategy.

A second problem area, and one that the above authors tend to neglect, is state power. Wood tries to reorient socialism from seizing the state to eliminating class conflict, arguing that electoral strategies contribute to capitalist hegemony only when political issues are detached from class relations.[67] Bronner would avoid the dilemma of reform versus revolution by assessing the ability of the system to tolerate reform and pressing it to its limits.[68] Neither approach is worked out in enough detail.

Jürgen Habermas offers a more complex approach to current tensions between economic and political systems. Money and power, respectively, control these systems. That distinguishes them from the lifeworld, the site of civic discourse and the source of civic values, shaped by political discourse. As Habermas sees it, in late capitalist societies politicoeconomic systems increasingly colonize the lifeworld. Communication processes increasingly involve strategically motivated attempts to gain money, power, or both. Nevertheless, Habermas claims that politicoeconomic systems ultimately cannot meet the demands for economic prosperity and equal rights that they generate. Nor can they produce new meanings that they could more successfully satisfy. Habermas concludes that citizens eventually will withdraw their support for the system, resulting in a crisis of legitimacy.

For Habermas, human beings' basic need to communicate with one another generates an alternative to politicoeconomic systems. In his ideal speech situation, Habermas outlines the characteristics of a more humane society. Decisions reached under conditions approximating ideal speech represent an uncoerced consensus. Although politicoeconomic systems persist, the decision-making processes of ideal speech potentially allow citizens to reassert lifeworld control over them. Habermas regards new social movements, which arise at the seam between system and lifeworld, as indications that political transformation remains a realistic possibility.[69]

According to Habermas, these movements "resurrect"—he uses the biblical term—citizens' hopes of living meaningful lives.[70] This brings us to a third problem area, which can be addressed by returning to where we began, the recent revolutions in Eastern Europe. For Vaclav Havel, writing in Czechoslovakia, Habermas's systemic or structural approach to meaning is much too easy, too simple. It misses the internal effects of the tensions between dominant systems and human lives. Havel argues that post-totalitarian states force individuals to split themselves. Publically, to varying extents, citizens accept the system though they sense its falsity: to get along, they willingly "live within the lie." To live in harmony with oneself, to "live within the truth," is to be "thrown" into a dissident role. Dissidence takes many forms, none of them traditional. It includes efforts to make the law real, to develop alternative or parallel institutional structures, to differentiate—as Habermas does—existing structures, creating free spaces betweeen them. For Havel, however, "the most intrinsic and fundamental confrontation between human beings and the system takes place at a level incomparably more profound than that of traditional politics. . . ."[71] It occurs in individual efforts to be honest in our daily lives. Such efforts are not limited to citizens of post-totalitarian states. Of events in Eastern Europe, Havel says, "and do we not in fact stand (although in the eternal measures of civilization, we are far behind) as a kind of warning to the West, revealing to it its own latent tendencies?"[72]

Although Havel would probably be appalled (for him, Bolshevism is socialism), I want to suggest that there is a socialist impulse or intuition in this remark. It is perhaps the socialist tradition's best moment. In a recent essay, Habermas described socialism as the commitment to be more human than one's society allows.[73] Hobsbawm makes a similar point less cryptically: "Socialists are there to remind the world that people and not production come first. That people must not be sacrificed."[74] If socialism in this sense is dead, then we all should share Hobsbawm's fears.

Notes

1. Ellen Meiksins Wood, *The Retreat from Class: A New "True" Socialism* (London: New Left Books, 1986), 182.

2. Frances Fox Piven and Richard Cloward, *The New Class War* (New York: Pantheon, 1982).

3. Joseph Chytry, *The Aesthetic State* (Berkeley: University of California Press, 1992), 244.

4. Eric Hobsbawm, "Lost Horizons," *New Statesman & Society*, 14 September 1990, 16.

5. Terrell Carver makes this distinction in "Reading Marx: Life and Works," in *The Cambridge Companion to Marx*, ed. Terrell Carver (Cambridge, England: Cambridge University Press, 1991), 1–22.

6. Paul Thomas, "Critical Reception: Marx Then and Now," in Carver, *Cambridge Companion*, 32.

7. *The Oxford English Dictionary*, 2d ed., s.v. "socialism."

8. Albert Fried, "The Course of American Socialism: A Synoptic View," in *Socialism in America: From the Shakers to the Third International—A Documentary History*, ed. Albert Fried (New York: Columbia University Press, 1992), 3.

9. I am indebted to Isaac Kramnick with whom I first studied political ideologies for this insight.

10. Eric Hobsbawm, "Out of the Ashes," in *After the Fall: The Failure of Communism and the Future of Socialism*, ed. Robin Blackburn (London: New Left Books, 1991), 316.

11. Denys Turner, "Religion: Illusions and Liberation," in Carver, *Cambridge Companion*, 329.

12. See Dennis Fischman, *Political Discourse in Exile: Karl Marx and the Jewish Question* (Amherst: University of Massachusetts Press, 1991).

13. Joseph Schumpeter, *Capitalism, Socialism, and Democracy*, 3d ed. (New York: Harper, 1950).

14. Charles Fourier, *The Utopian Vision of Charles Fourier*, trans. and ed. Jonathan Beecher and Richard Bienvenu (Boston: Beacon Press, 1971), 320.

15. Karl Marx, *Capital*, vol. 1, in *The Marx-Engels Reader*, 2d ed., ed. Robert C. Tucker (New York: Norton, 1978), 302.

16. Karl Marx, *Economic and Philosophical Manuscripts of 1844*, in Tucker, *Marx-Engels Reader*, 112.

17. Friedrich Engels, "Socialism: Utopian and Scientific," in Tucker, *Marx-Engels Reader*, 696.

18. Friedrich Engels, *Ludwig Feuerbach and the Age of Classical German Philosophy,* in *Karl Marx and Friedrich Engels: Selected Works* (New York: International Publishers, 1968), 610.

19. Karl Marx, "Theses on Feuerbach," in Tucker, *Marx-Engels Reader,* 145.

20. William Adams, "Aesthetics: Liberating the Senses," in Carver, *Cambridge Companion,* 246–74.

21. Marx, *Economic and Philosophical Manuscripts,* 89.

22. Karl Marx, *Grundrisse,* in Tucker, *Marx-Engels Reader,* 223, 225.

23. Karl Marx, "Letter to Ruge (March 13, 1843)," in *Selected Correspondence* (Moscow: Foreign Language Publishers, 1956).

24. Marx, *Grundrisse,* 223.

25. Ibid.

26. Karl Marx, preface to *A Contribution to the Critique of Political Economy,* in Tucker, *Marx-Engels Reader,* 4.

27. Friedrich Engels, "Letter to Bloch" (September 21–22, 1890), in Tucker, *Marx-Engels Reader,* 760.

28. G.A. Cohen, *Karl Marx's Theory of History: A Defense* (Princeton: Princeton University Press, 1978).

29. Karl Marx, *Manifesto of the Communist Party,* in Tucker, *Marx-Engels Reader,* 473.

30. Jon Elster, *Making Sense of Marx* (New York: Cambridge University Press, 1985).

31. Karl Marx, *The Eighteenth Brumaire of Louis Bonaparte,* in Tucker, *Marx-Engels Reader,* 608.

32. Wood, *Retreat from Class,* 196.

33. I use profit and surplus value interchangeably here, bypassing the extensive controversy over how Marx derives prices from values—or the "transformation problem." Although Marx recognizes in volume 3 of *Capital* that supply and demand—or market relations—affect prices, he continues to assume that commodities enter into the production of other commodities at their value. This may invalidate the labor theory of value as a quantitative measure of exploitation under capitalism. I would argue, however, that it continues to illuminate the quality of human relationships in capitalist economies.

34. Marx provides this example in *Capital,* vol. 1, chap. 6.

35. Marx, *Capital,* 1: 297.

36. Marx, *Manifesto of the Communist Party,* 483.

37. Marx, *Economic and Philosophical Manuscripts,* 74.

38. Marx, *Capital,* 321.

39. Ibid., 327.

40. Geoff Eley, "Reviewing the Socialist Tradition," in *The Crises of Socialism in Europe,* ed. Christine Lemke and Gary Marks (Durham, N.C.: Duke University Press, 1992), 34.

41. Karl Marx and Friedrich Engels, *The German Ideology,* in Tucker, *Marx-Engels Reader,* 162.

42. Eley, "Reviewing the Socialist Tradition," 43.

43. Marx, *Economic and Philosophical Manuscripts,* 83.

44. Karl Marx, "Critique of the Gotha Program," in Tucker, *Marx-Engels Reader,* 530.

45. Ibid., 531.

46. Karl Marx, "The Civil War in France," in Tucker, *Marx-Engels Reader,* 627–28.

47. Karl Marx, "After the Revolution: Marx Debates Bakunin," in Tucker, *Marx-Engels Reader,* 545.

48. Marx, *Capital,* 441.

49. Karl Marx, "Inaugural Address of the Working Men's International Association," in Tucker, *Marx-Engels Reader,* 512–19.

50. Karl Marx, "Letter to Bebel, Liebknecht, Bracke," in Tucker, *Marx-Engels Reader,* 553.

51. Eduard Bernstein, *Evolutionary Socialism: A Criticism and Affirmation,* trans. Edith C. Harvey (New York: Stockholm Books, 1961).

52. Ibid., 221.

53. Ibid., xxviii.

54. Quoted by David McLellan, *Marxism after Marx* (Boston: Houghton Mifflin, 1979), 88.

55. V.I. Lenin, *What Is to Be Done?* in *The Lenin Anthology,* ed. Robert C. Tucker (New York: Norton, 1975).

56. Quoted in McLellan, *Marxism after Marx,* 79.

57. V.I. Lenin, *State and Revolution,* in Tucker, *Lenin Anthology,* 344.

58. V.I. Lenin, "Better Fewer, but Better," in Tucker, *Lenin Anthology,* 734–46.

59. Karl Marx, "Address to the Communist League," in Tucker, *Marx-Engels Reader,* 506–11.

60. Friedrich Engels, "The Tactics of Social Democracy," in Tucker, *Marx-Engels Reader,* 556–73.

61. For a basic collection of socialist writings, see *Marxism: Essential Writings,* ed. David McLellan (New York: Oxford University Press, 1988).

62. Christopher Lasch, *The Agony of the American Left* (New York: Knopf, 1967), 185.

63. Ibid., 186.

64. Ibid., 211.

65. Eric Hobsbawm, "Goodbye to All That," in Blackburn, *After the Fall,* 122.

66. Stephen Eric Bronner, *Socialism Unbound* (New York: Routledge, 1990), xxiv.

67. Wood, *Retreat from Class,* 193.

68. Bronner, *Socialism Unbound,* 180.

69. Jürgen Habermas, *Theory of Communicative Action,* vol. 2, *Life-world and System,* trans. Thomas McCarthy (Boston: Beacon Press, 1987), 374–403.

70. Jürgen Habermas, "What Does Socialism Mean Today? The Revolutions of Recuperation and the Need for New Thinking," in Blackburn, *After the Fall,* 25–46.

71. Vaclav Havel, *The Power of the Powerless: Citizens against the State*

in Central-Eastern Europe (Armonk, N.Y.: M.E. Sharpe, 1985), 89.

72. Ibid., 38–39.

73. Habermas, "What Does Socialism Mean Today?" 45.

74. Hobsbawm, "Out of the Ashes," 324.

5
Anarchism

> *What is to be the form of government in the future? I hear some of my younger readers reply: "Why, how can you ask such a question? You are a republican." "A republican! Yes; but that word specifies nothing. Res publica; that is, the public thing. . . . Even kings are republicans." "Well! you are a democrat?" — "No." — "What! you would have a monarchy?" — "No." — "A constitutionalist?" — "God forbid!" — "You are then an aristocrat?" — "Not at all." — "You want a mixed government?" — "Still less." — "What are you, then?" — "I am an anarchist."*

> — Pierre-Joseph Proudhon

What Is Anarchism?

What does anarchy specify? Nothing, according to Proudhon's younger readers. They assume he speaks satirically: "Oh! . . . This is a hit at the government." He says instead, "I have just given you my serious and well-considered profession of faith."[1] Proudhon was the first to use the term *anarchism* to describe a political ideology. Following the Greek *anarchos,* which means "without rule," he defines anarchism as "the absence of a master, of a sovereign." For further clarification, he adds, "the meaning ordinarily attached to the word 'anarchy' is absence of principle, absence of rule; consequently, it has been regarded as synonymous with 'disorder.' "[2] Do anarchists advocate disorder? Yes, according to popular perceptions. Most people associate anarchism with acts of violence or what anarchists called "propaganda by the deed." Alexander Berkman and the McKinley assassination, the Chicago anarchists

95

and Haymarket Square, the Red Army Brigade and international ter-
rorism come to mind when one mentions anarchism. In his classic
study George Woodcock says, "The stereotype of the anarchist is that
of the cold-blooded assassin who attacks with dagger or bomb the
symbolic pillars of established society. Anarchy, in popular parlance, is
malign chaos."[3]

Anarchists have long challenged this stereotype. Proudhon insists
that "although a firm friend of order, I am (in the full force of the term)
an anarchist."[4] Anarchism, as he defines it, has positive connotations. It
refers to a natural harmony among freely associated individuals that
renders political rule superfluous. No wonder anarchism creates confusion. Proudhon acknowledges "the seeming paradox of order in anarchy."[5] To create anew, anarchists must destroy; to promote harmony,
they foment revolution; to reorder society, they free individuals; to realize freedom, they stress moral law. Emma Goldman's definition sums
up the paradox of anarchism: "It is the philosophy of the sovereignty
of the individual. It is the theory of social harmony."[6]

Anarchists would resolve or at least affirm the tension between individual and society. Anarchism reminds Ulrike Heider of "the Roman
god Janus whose two faces are turned in opposite directions."[7] Sometimes the two sides of anarchism's Janus-face split apart. Scholars often
distinguish between individualist and socialist anarchism. The former
extends liberals' principle of individual freedom to its furthest point
where personal integrity supersedes government authority. The latter
refers to nonauthoritarian socialists who refuse to impose a proletarian
dictatorship during the transition from capitalism to socialism. These
anarchist "faces" are not necessarily mutually exclusive. When seen together, they suggest that anarchism offers an alternative to liberal capitalism *and* authoritarian socialism. A century after Proudhon, Heider
anticipates a political future in which anarchism will play a major role.
Radical ecologists, animal rights activists, bohemians, neopagans,
anarchafeminists, anarchosyndicalists, anarchocapitalists, or libertari-
ans are among the anarchist groups that are politically active today.[8]
This diverse list establishes the continuing presence of anarchism in
contemporary politics. Some scholars even suggest that anarchism may
guide international efforts to create a new poststate world order.[9] If so,
it is time to clear up confusion about the meaning of anarchism.

We might begin with a comprehensive definition of the term, one
that emphasizes anarchists' common themes. According to John P.
Clark, confusion about anarchism arises because scholars neglect classical anarchist theory and historical anarchist practice. This leads to in-
complete definitions that present anarchism as merely destructive or, at

best, utopian. Clark's complete definition includes the following four components:

1. a view of an ideal, noncoercive, nonauthoritarian society;
2. a criticism of existing society and its institutions based on this antiauthoritarian ideal;
3. a view of human nature that justifies the hope for significant progress toward the ideal; and
4. a strategy for change, involving immediate institution of noncoercive, nonauthoritarian, and decentralist alternatives.[10]

Before turning to classical anarchism and anarchist practice, we explore these four aspects of anarchist ideology in more detail.

First, "anarchy" is the term anarchists use to refer to their ideal society. They regard it as a natural order, examples of which are easily found in animal species and human history. Anarchists' illustrations range from flocks of geese and packs of wolves to the Iroquois Confederacy and the Spanish Republic. The central feature of these "anarchies" is the absence of coercive authority. This may also mean the absence of government, but not necessarily so. Social anarchists often describe a complex federal system for coordinating local, regional, national, and international politics. Individualist anarchists may accept a limited government to protect natural rights while privatizing most social services (e.g., fire and police, hospitals and schools, mail and roads). Marx's description of the "withering away of the state" clarifies anarchists' view of authority. "Stateless socialism" no longer requires "the domination of people" but continues to provide for "the administration of things." Neither Marx nor the anarchists say where to draw the line between them, though the latter offer a bit more guidance. Anarchists recognize the need for a social mechanism for coordinating action; we might say a functional "government." But they reject the political state as a separate power over and above society. To make their stateless society possible requires far more than Marx's elimination of class conflict and class rule. According to Clark, "economic, social, racial, sexual, and generational equality, mutual aid, cooperation, and communalism" characterize anarchists' noncoercive society.[11]

Second, anarchists question claims that the state rests on moral or natural foundations. Emma Goldman's essay, "Anarchism: What It Really Stands For" illustrates this aspect of anarchist philosophy well.[12] She questions the claim that states, whether liberal capitalist or authoritarian socialist, are based on natural law or right. Nature, she argues, works freely and spontaneously. For example, it is a natural law that human beings need air, food, light, shelter, etc. Since the state requires coercion to sustain its laws, it can only be opposed to nature. Goldman also notes that the state fails to achieve its purpose, that is, law and order. She says, "order derived through submission and maintained by terror is not much of a safe guaranty; yet that is the only 'order' that governments have ever maintained."[13] Indeed, the state itself violates order; it is the greatest of criminals. Taxation and conscription violate citizens' rights to property and liberty, and war threatens their very lives. The state creates other criminals by protecting an economic order that misdirects human energies. Echoing Marx, Goldman argues that states protect the property of nonproducers, who make labor unbearable for everyone else. To arguments that human nature nonetheless requires states, Goldman responds: "Poor human nature, what horrible crimes have been committed in thy name! Every fool . . . presumes to speak authoritatively of human nature. . . . Yet, how can any one speak of it today, with every soul in a prison, with every heart fettered, wounded, and maimed?"[14]

Third, anarchists do speak of human nature; however, they do not base their future hopes on an idealized image of humanity. Anarchists recognize that people are easily corrupted, especially by the prospect of power. According to Proudhon, "Government is by its nature counterrevolutionary. . . . Give power to a Saint Vincent de Paul and he will be a Guizot or a Talleyrand."[15] Mikhail Bakunin similarly argues that Marxists "are enemies of the powers-that-be only because they cannot take their places"; state power contaminates even "the sincerest of socialist revolutionaries."[16] What is this human nature that social conditions can so effectively undermine?

Clark calls it the capacity for voluntaristic action or a libertarian potential. As he puts it, "the problem for anarchists is to create the social conditions under which the libertarian rather than the authoritarian (or, in some cases, the cooperative rather than the competitive) capacities of people are realized."[17] George Crowder provides a slightly different characterization, claiming that anarchists share a commitment to "moral self-direction."[18] In conservatives' now familiar language, anarchists' liberty is not license. Instead of "anything goes," they advocate obedience to conscience. On this point, individualist and socialist anarchists agree, though they disagree over whether conscience is best realized on the outskirts of society or in the midst of it. George Woodcock conveys their common ground in the following passage: "No conception of anarchism is further from the truth than that which regards it as an extreme form of democracy. Democracy advocates the sovereignty of the people. *Anarchism advocates the sovereignty of the person* [emphasis mine]."[19]

Fourth, it is the immediate and, I would add, total commitment to nonauthoritarianism that distinguishes anarchism from other revolutionary strategies. Anarchists consistently refuse to rely on existing institutions (i.e., states and/or markets) to promote change. This precludes liberal democratic politics as well as proletarian dictatorship. Regarding the former, anarchists point out that citizens "choose" representatives only at prescribed intervals under controlled conditions. Suffrage expansion, anarchists argue, is often how governments respond to social unrest. As we saw, eighteen-year-olds were granted voting rights to quell antiwar protests. It is an old anarchist saying that "if voting could change the system, it would be illegal." Regarding proletarian dictatorship, nineteenth-century anarchists anticipated the slippery slope leading from Marxism to Leninism to Stalinism. In the 1870s, Bakunin asked, "can it really be that the entire proletariat will stand at the head of the [new socialist] administration?"[20] Much more remains to be said about anarchists' nonauthoritarian revolution. For now, Emma Goldman's description suffices to counter common stereotypes:

> Anarchism ... stands for direct action, the open defiance of, and resistance to, all laws and restrictions, economic, social, and moral. But defiance and resistance are illegal. Therein lies the salvation of man. Everything illegal necessitates integrity, self-reliance, and courage. In short, it calls for free, independent spirits, for "men who are men, and who have a bone in their backs which you cannot pass your hand through."[21]

For anarchists, revolutionary activities are useful in themselves as forms of personal redemption, if not social transformation.[22]

A noncoercive social order, based on natural or moral laws, upheld by the authority of conscience, and achieved through principled resistance—these are the defining features of anarchism. They are a far cry from popular associations of the term with chaos, disorder, and violence. With these general themes in mind, we can examine classical anarchist theory in greater detail.

Individualist Anarchism: Godwin, Stirner, and Thoreau

According to Daniel Guerin, "one cannot conceive of a libertarian who is not an individualist."[23] Although anarchists' emphases on the indi-

vidual and society vary, their common concern is with individual freedom as "moral self-direction." Individualist anarchists develop this
theme most systematically. George Crowder suggests approaching their
arguments through Isaiah Berlin's distinction between negative and
positive liberty. Negative liberty refers to freedom *from* the interference
of others, or to a legally protected sphere within which individuals can
freely choose their actions and values. Positive liberty refers to freedom
for the realization of a fully human life. It does not preclude and may
even require a social order that prescribes citizens' conduct according
to a rational plan. Berlin's distinction overlaps in interesting ways with
the distinction between ancient and modern democracies we discussed
earlier. Negative liberty is unique to modern democracy. Ancient democracies are examples of positive liberty and, from a modern perspective, may appear to violate negative liberty. Although Berlin occasionally suggests that the two concepts of liberty overlap, he usually
presents them as opposite poles, as in the following passage:

> The former [negative] want to curb authority as such. The latter [positive]
> want it placed in their own hands. That is a cardinal issue. These are not
> two different interpretations of a single concept, but two profoundly di-
> vergent and irreconcilable attitudes to the ends of life.[24]

Since positive liberty opens the door to authoritarianism, anarchism
can only fall on the negative liberty side of Berlin's conceptual dichotomy. But in placing it there, Berlin misconstrues anarchists' position.
Behind anarchists' attack on authority is "the principle of the inviola-
bility of self-direction by the authentic rational and moral will."[25] They
hold a concept of positive liberty for which negative liberty is a necessary precondition and which precludes all authoritarian impulses.

Crowder argues that William Godwin, who never identified himself
as an anarchist, captures their attack on government in his *Inquiry
Concerning Political Justice*.[26] According to Godwin, governments destroy "moral self-direction" in several related ways. First, they protect
inequalities of property that sustain an economically dependent class.
Godwin echoes early liberals when he argues that such dependence undermines moral freedom. Nevertheless, he also regards the wealthy as
dependent. Because they associate worth with wealth, they are especially vulnerable to manipulation and corruption. Second, governmental laws undermine citizens' moral capacities. Like other anarchists,
Godwin emphasizes the motives behind action, and he regards fear of
punishment as a demeaning one. It is ultimately self-defeating, since reflection, not retribution, builds character. Third, when citizens grant

authority to government, they also agree to suspend their judgment. Once established, a government assumes its citizens' obligation to obey and inculcates "confidence" in the decisions it makes. (Godwin anticipates the era of pollsters and spin doctors who manage public opinion.) Citizens ultimately obey out of habit more than conviction. For individualist anarchists, this is a grave problem.

Godwin's ideal individual is subject only to the "coercion" of conscience. For Godwin, individualism is not self-interested or egoistic: "it is just that I should do all the good in my power." Society has a right to require "everything that it is my duty to do" and it, in turn, is bound to do "everything that can contribute to [its members'] welfare."[27] But laws are superfluous, even counterproductive, inducements to virtue. "A virtuous disposition is principally generated by the uncontrolled exercise of private judgment and the rigid conformity of every man to the dictates of his conscience."[28] Godwin is confident that "justice is sufficiently intelligible in its own nature" and that "we are all of us endowed with reason, able to compare, to judge, and to infer."[29] Rational persuasion takes the place of legal codes: "Reason is omnipotent: if my conduct be wrong, a very simple statement, flowing from a clear and comprehensive view, will make it appear to be such."[30] This suffices unless society corrupts reason, obscuring the nature of virtuous action and undermining human motivation to pursue it. To protect himself from corrupting influences, Godwin refused to eat meals in public, to attend the theater, and agreed to marry only late in life!

Max Stirner stresses individual independence to a greater extent, at times even denying any reality beyond the self. Daniel Guerin argues that Stirner anticipates existentialism in passages such as "I start from a hypothesis by taking myself as hypothesis ... I use it solely for my enjoyment and satisfaction ... I exist only because I nourish my Self." Some of Stirner's aphorisms are vehemently antisocial: "The people is dead! Good-day, Self!" and "If it is right for *me*, it is right. It is possible that it is wrong for others: let them take care of themselves!"[31] Stirner's vehemence results from his acute awareness of individuals' internalization of social values. In this, he anticipates another intellectual development: psychoanalysis. According to Stirner, family, church, party, and nation are ghosts that haunt us from birth. All of us fight a lifelong battle to assert ourselves against them. Victory is a return to self, in the words of Stirner's famous title, to *The Ego and His Own*. As he puts it, "ownness knows no commandment of 'faithfulness, adhesion, etc.,' ownness permits everything, even apostasy, defection." "... One must commit *immoral* actions in order to commit his own —i.e., here, that one must break faith, yes even his oath, in order to determine himself instead of being determined by moral considerations."[32]

Although Stirner associated with others, he did so only on his own terms. He opposed socialist parties that, because they could not bear nonpartisanship, became a state within the state. Stirner insists instead, "The individual is *unique,* not a member of the party. He unites freely, and separates freely again."[33] "The party is nothing other than a party in which he takes part."[34] Stirner argues against the state along similar lines. He adopts Proudhon's distinction between "property" as a right to ownership protected by the state and "possession" as a right to use integral to human life. The liberal state claims to secure the "rights of man" but protects instead the property of some from use by others. Even a socialist state only declares property rights, which individuals already possess by virtue of being human, a universal law. Stirner respects neither:

> What man can obtain belongs to him: the world belongs to *me.* Do you say anything else by your opposite proposition, "The world belongs to all"? All are I and again I, etc. But you make out of the "all" a spook, and make it sacred, so that then the "all" becomes the individual's fearful *master.* Then the ghost of "right" places itself on their side.[35]

No state can secure human rights: "Neither God nor Man ('human society') is proprietor, but the individual."[36]

Henry David Thoreau, a third individualist anarchist, is best known for *Walden,* his story of two years spent in relative isolation on the outskirts of Concord, Massachusetts. More important to anarchists is the "Essay on Civil Disobedience," a critique of the Mexican-American War, in which Thoreau attacks organized government *and* organized resistance to it. He begins the essay with the motto "That government is best which governs least." He argues for extending it further to "That government is best which governs not at all."[37] Government is our tool and, as such, it possesses nothing people do not already have and accomplishes nothing people cannot already do. Worse still, it saps our integrity and vitality. Echoing Godwin and Stirner, Thoreau argues that people serve government as machines, not men, with their bodies or, at best, their heads, not their souls. Thoreau uses military examples, but his meaning reaches beyond the literal:

> A common and natural result of an undue respect for law is, that you may see a file of soldiers, colonel, captain, corporal, privates, powder-monkeys, and all, marching in admirable order over hill and dale to the

wars, against their wills, ay, against their common sense and con-
sciences....[38]

When they are not directly serving the state, people continue to support
its authority indirectly through numerous acts of habitual conformity.
Thoreau asks why people obey unjust laws and why they fight to
change them. Instead, he counsels immediate withdrawal of support,
"both in person and in property." Withhold taxes, dodge the draft, refuse to vote—"let your life be a counter friction to stop the machine."[39]
According to Thoreau, "the only obligation which I have a right to assume is to do at any time what I think truly right."[40] That is, to act
from principle. What of democratic procedures? Constitutional amend-
ments? Thoreau says he hasn't the time to follow legal means for social
change. Besides, "any man more right than his neighbors constitutes a
majority of one already."[41]

For Godwin, Stirner, and Thoreau, anarchism provides a way of
life for individuals of conscience. But how will free individuals combine
to form a harmonious society? According to individualist anarchists,
social harmony is part of the natural order accessible to human reason.
Rather than rely on innate moral sentiments, as social anarchists will,
individualist anarchists give moral principles a rational foundation.
Proudhon's views help clarify their shared position. According to
Proudhon, "in a given society, the authority of man over man is in-
versely proportional to the stage of intellectual development which that
society has reached."[42] When citizens, like children, reach the age of
reason, they reject political authority:

> At the moment that man inquires into the motives which govern the will
> of his sovereign—at that moment man revolts. If he obeys no longer be-
> cause the king commands, but because the king demonstrates the wisdom
> of his commands, it may be said that henceforth he will recognize no au-
> thority, and that he has become his own king.[43]

A society of "kings" is possible because " 'justice, equality, equation,
equilibrium, harmony': these are 'all synonymous terms' in which we
find united both 'the law of the universe and the law of humanity.' "[44]
For Proudhon, self-sufficiency is no longer an option for individuals
living in complex modern societies. But "mutualism," a principle of reciprocal respect that bases economic exchanges on equal value, is a viable alternative. It adequately balances individual freedom and natural
or moral law.

Individualist anarchism is itself the child of the French Enlightenment and the French Revolution. The dual legacy of liberals' rights of man and utilitarians' rational calculus undergirds these anarchists' philosophy. Modern scientists doubt that a natural or moral order exists or that, if it does, unassisted human reason can know it with any certainty. If they are correct, then anarchism is less viable today. Before exploring that issue, however, we should consider social anarchists' corresponding claim that moral sentiment leads to social harmony.

Social Anarchism: Bakunin and Kropotkin

In 1901, years after Marx's death, Mikhail Bakunin wrote of their relationship:

> We saw each other fairly often and I very much admired him for his knowledge and for his passionate and earnest devotion to the cause of the proletariat.... But there was never real intimacy between us. Our temperaments did not harmonise. He called me a sentimental idealist; and he was right. I called him vain, treacherous and morose; and I too was right.[45]

In this passage, Bakunin sums up thirty years of intense conflict over revolutionary strategy. His earlier remarks were less balanced. In 1868 he compared Marx to Proudhon, saying that the latter "possessed the authentic instinct of the revolutionary; he respected Satan and proclaimed anarchy.... As a German and a Jew, [Marx] is authoritarian from head to heels."[46] A few years later, in 1872, Marx led a successful effort to expel Bakunin and his anarchist alliance from the First International. The anarchists were charged with "sectarianism" for organizing a secret party with "contrary statutes." Bakunin was personally accused of embezzling a 300 ruble advance for the Russian translation of *Capital*. Marx also described Bakunin as an "ass" whose writings were an "assembled rubbish mishmash."[47]

Serious doctrinal differences lay behind these personal attacks. In his debates with Marx, Bakunin explains why social anarchists oppose authoritarian socialism. They disagree over four related issues: (1) the relationship between politics and economics; (2) the preconditions for revolution; (3) the role of scientific knowledge; and (4) the transition to socialist society. By examining each, we can better understand social anarchism.

First, Bakunin praised Marx's historical materialist method, which he understood as the "principle that all religious, political, and legal developments in history are not the cause but the effects of economic developments."[48] But he feared Marx's related arguments that economic revolution (or the abolition of capital) must precede political revolution and that the proletariat can use the state to transform society. Bakunin portrays a "people's State" as a contradiction in terms. He claims that Marxists implicitly agree by referring to the "withering away of the state." He asks, "if their state is going to be a genuine people's State, why should it then dissolve itself—and if its rule is necessary for the real emancipation of the people, how dare they call it a people's State?"[49] According to Bakunin, for the proletariat "to win political freedom first can signify no other thing but to win this freedom only." Politics and economics are mutually reinforcing and, unless socialists struggle against both simultaneously, political power will recreate economic slavery. Anarchists advocate "complete abstention from all politics" but not because "the state [is] the chief evil," as Engels caricatures their position.[50] They insist that "so long as political power exists, there will be ruler and ruled, masters and slaves, exploiters and exploited."[51]

Second, Bakunin's doubts about a "people's State" should be seen in his Russian context. He asks, "if the proletariat is to be the ruling class, over whom will it rule?" The answer he anticipates is over "the peasant 'rabble.'" Marx's notes on Bakunin's *Statism and Anarchy* confirm his fears. Marx writes that "the proletariat ... must as a government" pursue measures that "win [the peasant] for the revolution" and "facilitate the transition from private to collective property in land."[52] Bakunin suggests instead that peasant societies, specifically, Russian villages, or "artels," have a revolutionary potential that the industrialized proletariat sorely lacks. He envisions a revolution initiated by city workers and supported by the peasantry. He fears that these two classes will dismiss one another as corrupt or savage, respectively.

> The more enlightened, more civilized Socialism of the city workers, a Socialism which because of this very circumstance takes on a somewhat bourgeois character, slights and scorns the primitive, natural, and much more savage Socialism of the villages, and since it distrusts the latter, it always tries to restrain it, to oppress it in the very name of equality and freedom, which naturally makes for dense ignorance about city Socialism on the part of the peasants, who confound this socialism with the bourgeois spirit of the cities.[53]

Marx would later argue that Russia might be able to skip the capitalist stage and move directly from traditional to socialist society, but only if European revolutions complemented its more primitive peasant one.

Third, Bakunin defends the peasantry against "learned Socialists'" claims to superior knowledge. His response to a speech is revealing here: "Marx is still carrying on the same old vain activities, spoiling the workers by making logic-choppers out of them. It's the same old insane theorizing and dissatisfied self-satisfaction."[54] Bakunin places his faith elsewhere—in the people themselves. As he puts it, "revolutionary Socialists believe that there is much more of practical reason and intelligence in the instinctive aspirations and real needs of the masses of people than in the profound minds of all these learned doctors and self-appointed tutors of humanity...."[55] According to Bakunin, scientific theories cannot predict when the revolution will occur. Nor can it be organized from above. Anarchist revolution "arises spontaneously in the hearts of the people"; it comes like "a thief in the night"; it is "often precipitated by apparently trivial causes"; it creates "new forms of free social life which ... arise from the very depths of the soul of the people."[56] Bakunin pointed to the spontaneous, though short-lived, success of the Paris Commune to support his views. Engels saw its rapid demise as evidence that a transitional dictatorship was required to sustain proletarian revolution.

Fourth, Bakunin does not argue that the people can create "anarchy" without any guidance. He is also "a partisan of science," but he wants to "diffuse science ... among the people," not to "impose [it] upon" them.[57] His revolutionary leaders were "invisible pilots" or "the midwives" to the people's "self-liberation," not a Leninist party vanguard. Bakunin says,

> All that individuals can do is to clarify, propagate, and work out ideas corresponding to the popular instinct, and, what is more, to contribute their incessant efforts to revolutionary organization of the natural power of the masses—but nothing else beyond that; the rest can and should be done by the people themselves.[58]

What will the revolutionary masses do? Bakunin anticipates "organizing of a society by means of a free federation from below upward, of workers' associations ... first into a commune, then a federation of communes into regions, of regions into nations, and of nations into an international fraternal association."[59] Only the people can transform "political government" into "a simple administration of common affairs." For Bakunin, "it is necessary ruthlessly to destroy *all* the ... economic, political, and social conditions which produce within individuals [a] tradition of evil"—simultaneously.[60]

At this point, the question of social anarchists' idealism or Romanticism reemerges. Why do they believe in social solidarity given the counterexamples that surround them? The ideas of Petyr Kropotkin, a Russian aristocrat turned anarchist, provide a partial answer. Kropotkin challenges Darwin's view that the evolution of species occurs via the survival of the fittest. He argues that a second principle—mutual aid—is equally if not more important for species survival, even progress. Kropotkin distinguishes mutual aid from altruistic sentiments, describing it instead as a "sociable habit" or "vague instinct" that prompts "mutual support." It is mutual aid, he argues, that made the Industrial Revolution and earlier great examples of human civilization, ancient Greece and medieval Europe, possible.

Kropotkin writes cautiously about the possible origins of mutual aid:

> ... whatever the opinions as to the first origin of the mutual-aid feeling or instinct may be—whether a biological or a supernatural cause is ascribed to it—we must trace its existence as far back as to the lowest stages of the animal world; and from these stages we can follow its uninterrupted evolution, in opposition to a number of contrary agencies, through all degrees of human development, up to the present times.[61]

He is astounded that mutual aid persists, despite attempts by the modern state to destroy it. According to Kropotkin, the modern state destroys "particular bonds" and absorbs "social functions" in order better to control its citizens: "the State alone, and the State's Church, must take care of matters of general interest, while the subjects must ... appeal to the Government each time that they feel a common need."[62] "Unbridled, narrow-minded individualism" is the effect, not the cause, of the modern state. Yet "although the destruction of mutual-aid institutions has been going on in practice and theory, for full three or four hundred years, hundreds of millions of men continue to live under such institutions...."[63] For this reason, Kropotkin concludes that mutual support, not mutual struggle, may play the major part in human evolution.

Kropotkin claims that the ethical principle that makes "anarchy" possible is built into the natural/historical order of things—animal, human, and perhaps divine. George Crowder carefully restates Kropotkin's thesis as follows: "Animals and humans share certain instincts of sympathy and mutual assistance and ... these have a certain significance. Least controversially ... they provide, in both cases, a natural mechanism of association."[64] Is this still too much to claim? Before reaching our conclusion, we should consider how anarchism works in practice.

Anarchist Organization in Practice

Although anarchists practiced "propaganda by the deed" in the late nineteenth and early twentieth centuries, I discuss anarchist organizations instead for several reasons. First, anarchist-inspired terrorist acts are less prominent today, in part because anarchists have recognized their limitations. As early as the 1890s, Kropotkin acknowledged "that one must be with the people, who no longer want isolated acts, but want men of action inside their ranks." He also questioned "the illusion that one can defeat the coalition of exploiters with a few pounds of explosives."[65] Shortly thereafter, anarchists began to organize trade unions on anarchosyndicalist principles, rather than social democratic ones. Most anarchists who advocate direct action today refer to changing daily life, especially work and family relations. One contemporary anarchist says, "the habit of direct action is perhaps identical with being a free person, prepared to live responsibly in a free society."[66]

Second, contrary to popular stereotypes, anarchists still involved in "propaganda by the deed" do not advocate senseless violence. They hope with a dramatic act—a violent "No" to authority—to inspire the masses to revolution. Since even their destructive acts point toward a new society, anarchists' visions of the latter seem most important here.[67] Third, and closely related, stereotypes of anarchism portray it as not only destructive, but also utopian. Examples of anarchists' successful attempts to reorder societies counter this common criticism. The examples I have chosen—the Iroquois Confederacy, the Spanish Civil War, and 1960s anarchafeminism—are diverse enough to convey the richness of anarchist history.

The Iroquois Confederacy

Somewhere between A.D. 1000 and 1400 (accounts vary), five nations —Seneca, Onondaga, Oneida, Mohawk, and Cayuga—formed the Iroquois Confederacy. "The Great Law of Peace," the terms of their agreement, is the oldest living constitution. Among the American Founders, Benjamin Franklin and Thomas Jefferson knew the Great Law well. The Iroquois' anarchist principles influenced the Articles of Confederation. The Great Law later served as a model for the League of Nations and the United Nations.[68] Although Friedrich Engels refers to the Iroquois Confederacy in his *Origin of the Family, Private Property, and the State* as "primitive communism," it is more properly described as an "anarchy."[69] To call it "primitive" is to assume the values of modern "civilization," an assumption anarchists would ask us to question.

Deganawidea, a Huron, proposed the Confederacy to end generations of warfare among the five tribes. Hiawatha, an Onondaga orator (not of Longfellow's poem), negotiated the peace that was transcribed into English around 1880 by Seth Newhouse, a Mohawk. The Great Law begins with the image of the "Tree of the Great Peace," a metaphor for the league's unity. It reads:

> I, Deganawidea, and the Confederated Chiefs, now uproot the tallest pine tree, and into the cavity thereby made we cast all weapons of war. Into the depths of the earth, deep down into the under-earth currents of water flowing to unknown regions, we cast all weapons of strife. We bury them from sight and we plant again the tree. Thus shall the Great Peace be established.[70]

The law establishes a Council of the League to govern the Five Nations. The Council follows a complex process to reach consensus on decisions. Each nation first debates an issue internally, then the "older brothers" (Senecas and Mohawks) and the "younger brothers" (Cayugas and Oneidas) agree among themselves. If these two groups disagree, the Onondaga break the tie or send the issue back for further debate. If they agree, the Onondaga affirm the decision. Consensus means that all agree "without unwarrantable dissent," not that they are unanimous. If those opposed to a decision cannot "go with" the Council, then each tribe retains its right to independent action.

Each nation is represented on the Great Council. The Iroquois are a gynocratic society; women are seen as progenitors of the nations. Council members are chosen by the matrons of their clans and, for some seats, because of their special qualities. Although women do not serve on the Council, they can recall any member who "has not in mind the welfare of the people, or disobeys the rules of the Great Law." The description of Council members conveys the social responsibilities expected of them:

> The chiefs of the League of Five Nations shall be mentors of the people for all time.... Their hearts shall be full of peace and good will and their minds filled with a yearning for the welfare of the people of the League.... Neither anger nor fury shall find lodging in their minds and all their words and actions shall be marked by calm deliberation.[71]

The Great Law also mandates openness to all races (some colonists held dual citizenship), religious freedom, procedures for redress from the Council, national self-determination for peaceful non-Iroquois, and other rights.

As interactions with Europeans made painfully clear, the Iroquois rejected the notion of private property, especially ownership of the land. Nature's bounty is given to all creatures to use as they need it. According to Franklin and Jefferson, communal property preserved the "natural simplicity" of Iroquois society. Franklin's description of Iroquois "economics" parallels Proudhon's distinction between property and possession:

> All the property that is necessary to a man is his natural Right, which none may justly deprive him of, but all Property superfluous to such Purposes is the property of the Public who, by their Laws have created it and who may, by other Laws dispose of it.[72]

Private property only creates artificial needs and social conflicts. Franklin recognized that "European conditions" horrified the Iroquois:

> The Care and Labour of providing for Artificial and fashionable Wants, the sight of so many Rich wallowing in superfluous plenty, whereby so many are kept poor and distress'd for Want, the Insolence of Office ... and the restraints of Custom, all contrive to disgust them [Indians] with what we call civil Society.[73]

The Iroquois "marveled" that the poor endured "such an injustice and that they took not the others by the throte, or set fire on their houses."[74]

The Great Law beautifully illustrates anarchists' ideal of a nonauthoritarian society. As Paula Gunn-Allen describes it, "the success of their systems depended on complementary institutions and organized relationships among all sectors of their world."[75] Clans, genders, needs, tribes—all parts are balanced in the whole. The American colonists also marveled. The Iroquois, it seemed, were a living example of "enlightened liberty." In Franklin's words: "all their Government is by Counsel of the Sages; there is no Force, there are no Prisons, no officers to compel Obedience or inflict Punishment."[76] Jefferson exclaimed, "public opinion is in the place of law, and restrains morals as powerfully as laws ever did anywhere."[77] As Deganawidea said: "We bind ourselves together, for many purposes ... so that our people and grandchildren shall remain in the circle of security, peace, and happiness. Our strength shall be in union and our way the way of reason, righteousness, and peace."[78] Despite U.S. government and Christian missionaries' attempts to eradicate Native American cultures, the Iroquois today still follow the Great Law of Peace.

The Spanish Anarchists

In 1910 Spanish anarchists founded the CNT (Spanish National Confederation of Labor), a trade union association. Organized on syndicalist principles, it combined workers by factory or town and managed operations through members' efforts. In 1924 the FAI, an underground party committed to countering reformism, became its revolutionary companion and conscience. According to George Woodcock, the CNT/FAI alliance is "the only time in the history of anarchism [that] Bakunin's plan of a secret elite of devoted militants controlling a public mass organization of partially converted workers came into being."[79] Our focus is a small part of that history: the Spanish Civil War from 1936 to 1939.

In the Spanish elections of 1936, a Popular Front coalition of socialists, republicans, anarchists, communists, and syndicalists defeated a right-wing regime composed of monarchists, clericals, army officers, fascists, and their supporters. Francisco Franco, an army general, responded with a military insurrection against the new republic. The civil war that ensued quickly became a social revolution. Peasants and workers, many familiar with anarchism, took control of cities, farms, and industries throughout Spain. The anarchists euphemistically described this absence of authority as "organized indiscipline." For three years, republican forces fought Franco's army until, in 1939, he successfully imposed a fascist government on Spain. On the eve of their defeat, Emma Goldman declared that "the collectivization of land and industry shines out as the greatest achievement of any revolutionary period. Even if Franco were to win and the Spanish anarchists were to be exterminated, the idea they have launched will live on."[80] George Woodcock also maintains that, despite their eventual defeat, the Spanish anarchists "cannot be ignored in a final assessment of . . . anarchist claims to have discovered a way to live in free and peaceful community."[81] What were their successes and failures?

The anarchists led wartime efforts to reorganize Spanish industry and agriculture. In Catalonia, an industrialized region, revolutionary workers' committees took over factories whose owners fled Spain after the republican government was elected. A 1936 trade union conference in Barcelona established guidelines for worker self-management, which the Catalan government later ratified. Factories with more than one hundred workers were collectivized, as were those whose owners were declared "subversive" and whose products were vitally important. Collectivized factories were run by management committees of five to fifteen members who represented the different trades and services involved. The assembled workers nominated committee members and could recall them. The management committee selected a factory manager, also subject to recall, who planned workloads, set fixed wages, and distributed profits.

Assessments of the collectivized factories vary, but they suggest that self-management generally succeeded. Franz Borkenau, an eyewitness, describes a bus factory in Barcelona three weeks after the revolution:

> ... it seems to run as smoothly as if nothing had happened. I visited the men at their machines. The rooms looked tidy, the work was done in a regular manner.... It is a large factory, and things could not have been made to look nice for the benefit of a visitor, had they really been in a bad muddle.... It is an extraordinary achievement for a group of workers to take over one factory, under however favourable conditions, and within a few days to make it run with complete regularity.[82]

Conditions were hardly favorable. Barcelona was newly, and barely, under anarchist control. George Orwell gives an eyewitness account: "Every shop and cafe had an inscription saying that it had been collectivized.... Waiters and shop-walkers looked you in the face and treated you as an equal.... The revolutionary posters were everywhere, flaming from the walls in clear reds and blues.... Crowds of people streamed constantly to and fro...."[83] Under these conditions, the anarchists managed the city, like its factories, with little disruption and without state support. According to Vernon Richards, a British libertarian, telephone, gas, light, and train services were restored forty-eight hours after the revolution, and, as long as they had flour, the bakers' collective provided bread for all who needed it. Richards concludes, "it speaks highly of their organising capacities and intelligence that the Catalan workers were able to take over the railways and resume services with a minimum of delay."[84]

In the Spanish countryside, collectivization varied by region, and was extensive: 500 collectives in the Levant, 400 in Aragon, 230 in parts of Castile, and in Andalusia every "republican" village. As many as 3 million people voluntarily joined the rural collective movement. Yields increased from 30 to 50 percent with collectivization, partly because private ownership had been so unproductive. Rather than support independent farmers or pay higher wages, many wealthy landowners had previously left their land uncultivated. The new collectives confiscated, combined, and cultivated these farms. Along with agricultural planning to diversify and irrigate crops, this meant that "for the first time within living memory in many parts of rural Spain, there was work and food, if not luxury, for all."[85]

Spain's rural character and village structure made it an ideal site for anarchism. The Spanish peasants brought a strong sense of social solidarity to anarchist endeavors. Fenner Brockway, a British Labor Party observer, described the Segorbe collective: "the spirit of the peasants, their enthusiasm, and the way they contribute to the common effort and the pride which they take in it, are all admirable."[86] Rural organization closely paralleled that of the cities and factories. A general assembly of peasants elected a management committee whose members continued to perform manual labor. All goods, except personal items for family use, were put into the common stock. Peasants formed work groups with designated areas to cultivate or tasks to perform. Wages were based on effort and need, and consisted of special *pesatas* to be used at communal shops; any extra was converted into personal spending money. Those peasants who remained outside the collectives could help with communal work efforts and sell their produce in communal shops, but they did not receive communal services and benefits. The pressure of public opinion—according to Woodcock, "that great anarchist substitute for overt authority,"—the advantages of membership, and the tradition of village life, led as many as 90 percent of the peasants to join.[87]

Industry and agriculture were not only similarly organized, but they also experienced similar problems. Each collective enterprise tended to focus on its internal concerns. This made coordinating distribution and production difficult at best. The chaos of wartime and the governing coalition's resistance to anarchist methods made conditions even worse. By late 1936, the anarchists agreed to join a coalition government, partly to sustain their now prolonged war effort. Some commentators argue that by compromising their antigovernment principles, the anarchists contributed to their eventual demise. But given lack of international support for the republican forces, Soviet military aid for the communists, and German and Italian assistance to the fascists, it is hard to see how the anarchists could have survived otherwise.

Is there a lesson here regarding the limits of anarchism in practice? Woodcock thinks so. As he puts it, "strong in spontaneous impulse, [the anarchists] were incapable of the kind of tenacity necessary to hold whatever they gained."[88] George Orwell's description of the anarchist front, on which he served, reinforces the point:

> We had no tin hats, no bayonets, hardly any revolvers or pistols, and not more than one bomb between five or ten men.... And apart from weapons there was a shortage of all the minor necessities of war.... As time went on, and the desultory rifle-fire rattled among the hills, I began to

wonder with increasing scepticism whether anything would ever happen to bring a bit of life, or rather a bit of death, into this cock-eyed war.[89]

Engels's sarcastic question, "Have these men ever seen a revolution? It is the most authoritarian thing there is. It is when one part of the population masters another by violent means," seems apt.[90] Woodcock more respectfully suggests that "given the situation, the problem seems to have been insoluble in anarchist terms."[91]

What, finally, is the legacy of anarchist efforts during the Spanish Civil War? Woodcock's assessment is most balanced:

> In the arts of war the Spanish anarchists failed miserably, and their organization and following were virtually destroyed as a result of their failure.... But in the arts of peace they showed that their faith in the organizing powers of workers and peasants, in the natural social virtues of ordinary people, had not been misplaced.[92]

Anarchafeminism from the Sixties

The history of American feminism, discussed in a later chapter, reveals two distinct women's "movements."[93] One consists of large, formal organizations, like the National Woman Suffrage Association and the National Organization for Women, dedicated to achieving political rights. The other includes a variety of small, informal groups, ranging from benevolent associations to the settlement movement to consciousness-raising groups. The latter movement has more radical goals and is more skeptical about political strategies, liberal reformist and socialist revolutionary. Many of its members left mainstream politics behind rather than compromise their moral principles.

This was especially true in the 1960s when many feminists became exasperated with the New Left. All too often women's issues were dismissed as "petit-bourgeois" or "counterrevolutionary," even as women members were cast as "housewives to the revolution." Carol Ehrlich argues that the 1960s' feminists who rejected traditional socialist organizations were "unconscious anarchists." They were "skeptical of any social theory that comes with a built-in set of leaders and followers, no matter how 'democratic' this centralized structure is supposed to be." They saw that an inclusive politics requires alternative organizations and that "non-hierarchical structures are essential to feminist practice."[94]

The experiences of small-group feminists further expand our understanding of anarchist concepts of power and freedom. For most political scientists, "A has power over B to the extent that he can get B to do something that B would not otherwise do."[95] In other words, power is defined as control over other people. In *The Feminist Case against Bureaucracy*, Kathy Ferguson claims that a concept of power as control over reinforces the notion that to be efficient, organizations must be hierarchically administered. She argues that this theory of organization reflects its social context, one of unequal relations between classes, races, and sexes. "Bureaucracy, as the 'scientific organization of inequality,' serves as a filter for these other forms of domination, projecting them into an institutional arena that both rationalizes and maintains them."[96] From subordinate positions inside and outside the bureaucratic system (e.g., as secretaries and/or housewives), women have developed alternatives to hierarchical administration. Indeed, Ferguson claims that

> the feminist case against bureaucracy goes beyond the other critiques in that it constructs its alternative out of concrete and shared experiences of women, rather than out of a romantic vision of precapitalist life or an abstract ideal of "human nature."[97]

Anarchafeminists' case against bureaucracy rests on a concept of power that differs significantly from political scientists' dominant one. Power is the capacity, energy, or potential to engage in meaningful actions as individuals or in groups—or empowerment. Ferguson defines empowerment not as "the ability to make people do what they would not otherwise do, but the ability to enable people to do what they could not otherwise do."[98] Empowerment involves the freedom to control our own lives. Its meaning is expressed in the following anarchist slogan: "Power to no one and to everyone: To each the power over his/her own life, and no others."[99] The creation of nonhierarchical organizations is inseparable from the "reinvention of everyday life." This anarchist notion of direct action closely parallels feminists' more familiar phrase "the personal is political." Anarchafeminists hardly fit their stereotype as "the ladies' auxiliary of male bomb-throwers."[100]

In *Decisions without Hierarchy*, Kathleen Iannello provides case studies of two anarchafeminist organizations, a peace group and a health collective, which further develop Ferguson's case. Iannello argues that both groups manage to avoid two dangers often associated with alternative—socialist and anarchist—organizations. The first is the "iron law of oligarchy" or the presumably inevitable tendency of nonhierarchical organizations gradually to (re)develop a bureaucratic structure, including distinctions of rank. The second is the "tyranny of structurelessness" or the similarly inevitable tendency of some members to become leaders, to assume powers more insidious because they are unacknowledged and hence unassailable. The anarchafeminists Iannello studies avoid both dangers not by rejecting structure but by addressing it. Their explicit goal is to "eradicate all the structural factors that create and maintain leaders and followers."[101] Consensus, empowerment, and emerging leadership are the major issues their organizations face.

Consensus, "defined as participation by all members 'in a collective formulation of problems and negotiation of decisions,'" is the operating procedure of the peace group. Although consensus formation is time-consuming, members see the win/win situation that results as well worth the effort involved. As one puts it, "satisfaction lies in the fact that every person ends up being committed to the decision we make and so when the decision gets made, people are much better able to live with it and there is satisfaction in knowing we all support it."[102] Nevertheless, Iannello notes that the peace group, a volunteer organization, faces few external pressures to survive.

In contrast, the health collective, a business that must operate efficiently, follows a more modified consensual organization. Although consensus still means that "each individual agrees with the decision on a group level," only critical decisions about the direction of the collective are made by its full staff.[103] Routine decisions are delegated horizontally to coordinators or committees. Only when a routine decision becomes a critical issue is it brought back to the group as a whole. Although the health collective is a "semistructured business," no one "runs" it or the more "collectively organized" peace group. As one member of the latter says, "I don't see any vertical to it." Another adds, "decision-making is a continuing process."[104]

Members of both groups associate empowerment with the rotation of roles so that everyone gains expertise in a variety of areas. A peace group member explicitly links "rigidity of roles" to the "risk of power-dominated situations."[105] The health collective also faces the greater challenge here, since its members want secure positions with appropriate salaries. Still, they maintain "selective rotation" based on organizational necessities. In both groups, leadership involves developing individual capacities, including one's own. One peace group member, a self-described "leadership-type person," says:

> the organization is real conscious of process. If I am facilitating the meetings too much, I make sure that others do it. The group allows me to do what I am good at and what I like, but without it infringing on others in the group.... Each member comes into the group with different skills and

we utilize that without involving egos.... Each person carries responsibility, so I monitor myself as does everyone.[106]

In the health collective's modified structure, delegated trust "stands in" for group process. A member explains: "We trust the people who sit in those [coordinator] roles. They represent us, they make recommendations to us, yet they are part of us. They can't change the direction of the collective politically, financially, or medically."[107]

The paradox of anarchy—how to reconcile social order with individual freedom—with which we began this chapter reemerges in these passages. Anarchafeminist organizations avoid power as domination only by continually "re-solving" that paradox.

The Future of Anarchism

Common themes run through these examples from anarchist organizations. They illustrate the complexity of society and the importance of balancing its many parts. They reveal deep respect for all aspects of life. They reinforce mutual respect through example and opinion, not rules and laws. The Iroquois tribal chiefs are the people's mentors, not their sovereigns. Members of the health collective delegate their trust, not their power, to the coordinators. Consensual decision making combines mutual support with mutual respect. In these organizations, all members agree to "go with" a decision, or it is not adopted. They reject the zero-sum and top-down approaches of liberal democratic and authoritarian socialist politics. The Spanish case reveals their vulnerability to external pressures. Waging war and selling goods pose major challenges for "anarchy" in practice. Yet the Iroquois' federated structure provided the basis for a long-lasting peace, and anarchafeminists' "modified consensual" structure partially addresses the problem of economic efficiency. Under some circumstances, it seems that nonhierarchical organizations can persist alongside authoritarian institutions. Perhaps, anarchism is neither so destructive nor so utopian as its critics suggest.

According to George Crowder, we should shift the terms of the debate, in any case. He says, "if such an ideal is really unattainable, we ought to ask why that is so rather than merely take existing institutions for granted."[108] This is not to say that the future is anarchist, however. At least, not in nineteenth-century anarchist terms. Crowder argues that classical anarchism rests on two questionable supports: (1) a teleological account of human nature; and (2) a naturalist account of ethics.

They converge in anarchists' perfectionist idea of human freedom. As he puts it,

> Beneath the perfectionist idea of freedom lies the assumption that virtue, attained by reason, is not merely distinctive of man but the end to which he tends naturally, in the sense that it is a constitutive feature of his personality when fully developed.[109]

In an era of modern science, it is difficult to sustain such a concept of human nature. Since many now doubt the correspondence of human reason and moral virtue, as well as the progress of history to any predetermined purpose, Crowder claims that anarchism requires redefinition.

A concept of "Humanity" is also inconsistent with another anarchist principle. Anarchists, we have seen, oppose the very idea of representation. What, then, of anarchists' attempts to represent people to themselves? How can anarchists tell people who they really are? Including how they can be free?[110] According to Todd May, classical anarchists' claims about human nature exemplify the problem of representation. Anarchists' own principles require that no one speak or act for anyone else, let alone "Mankind." May identifies poststructuralism as both the completion of anarchism and an alternative to representation. That argument lies beyond the scope of this chapter, though we revisit it in chapter 6. For now, we might consider another question. If anarchists give up philosophical as well as political authority, what remains? Does anarchism require the firm foundations that claims to represent "Humanity" provide?

The meaning of *an-archy* (i.e., without rule) suggests a partial answer. A ruler is that person(s) whom citizens accept as the "author" of their common actions.[111] Authority, as traditionally defined, involves some form of representation. To construe anarchy only as its opposite (i.e., as antirepresentation), misses another kind of "authorship." In *Compassionate Authority*, Kathleen Jones traces "authority" to its origins in the Latin *augere* ("to augment"). It "connotes an activity of growth. . . . In the public arena, authority expresses our connection with others as an augmentation of ourselves, rather than an obstacle to self-fulfillment."[112] This definition of authority avoids the coercive/noncoercive dichotomy with which anarchists and their critics struggle. Construing authority as "growth" conveys anarchists' continual efforts to represent themselves as free individuals in harmony with society. As an ongoing process of growth, "authority" acknowledges the ambiguous, tenuous future of any anarchy.

Notes

1. Pierre-Joseph Proudhon, *What Is Property? An Inquiry into the Principle of Right and of Government,* ed. George Woodcock (New York: Dover, 1970), 272.

2. Ibid., 277, n. 1.

3. George Woodcock, *Anarchism: A History of Libertarian Ideas and Movements* (New York: World, 1972), 10.

4. Proudhon, *What Is Property?* 272.

5. Quoted by Woodcock, *Anarchism,* 12.

6. Emma Goldman, "Anarchism: What It Really Stands For," in *Anarchism and Other Essays* (New York: Dover, 1969), 67.

7. Ulrike Heider, *Anarchism: Left, Right, and Green,* trans. Danny Lewis and Ulrike Bode (San Francisco: City Lights Books, 1994), 1.

8. Ibid. While these anarchist organizations are primarily issue-oriented, some scholars further subdivide types of social anarchism. They use the following terms: mutualism, the federated social order described by Proudhon; anarchocommunalism, the all-encompassing socialist vision outlined by Bakunin; and anarchosyndicalism, the worker-managed and -owned industrial organizations associated with the Italian and Spanish anarchists. I have not included anarchocapitalists, like Murray Rothbard, among individualist anarchists. They differ from anarchists in their emphasis on individual rights to some extent independent of duty or virtue. Anarchocapitalism lacks the individualist and socialist anarchists' vision of moral perfection.

9. Richard A. Falk, "Anarchism and World Order," in *Anarchism,* ed. J. Roland Pennock and John W. Chapman (New York: New York University Press, 1978), 63–87.

10. John P. Clark, "What Is Anarchism?" in Pennock and Chapman, *Anarchism,* 13.

11. Ibid., 14.

12. Goldman, "Anarchism: What It Really Stands For," 47–67.

13. Ibid., 59.

14. Ibid., 61–62.

15. Quoted by Daniel Guerin, *Anarchism* (New York: Monthly Review Press, 1970), 22.

16. Mikhail Bakunin, *The Political Philosophy of Bakunin, Scientific Anarchism,* ed. G.P. Maximoff (Glencoe, Ill.: Free Press, 1953), 284.

17. Clark, "What Is Anarchism?" 16–17.

18. George Crowder, *Classical Anarchist Theory* (New York: Oxford University Press, 1994).

19. Woodcock, *Anarchism,* 33.

20. Quoted in Alvin Gouldner, "Marx's Last Battle: Bakunin and the First International," *Theory and Society* 11 (1982): 865.

21. Goldman, "Anarchism: What It Really Stands For," 65.

22. Irving Horowitz makes this distinction in his introduction to *The Anarchists,* ed. Irving Horowitz (New York: Dell, 1964), 56.

23. Guerin, *Anarchism,* 27.

24. Isaiah Berlin, "Two Concepts of Liberty," in *Four Essays on Liberty* (New York: Oxford University Press, 1969), 166.

25. Crowder, *Classical Anarchist Theory,* 53.

26. Ibid., chap. 2. My interpretation of Godwin is influenced by Crowder's ideas.

27. William Godwin, "The Rights of Man and the Principles of Society," from *Political Justice,* in Horowitz, *Anarchists,* 111, 113.

28. Ibid., 118.

29. Ibid., 119.

30. Godwin, quoted by Crowder, *Classical Anarchist Theory,* 71.

31. Quoted by Guerin, *Anarchism,* 29.

32. Max Stirner, "The Ego and His Own," in Horowitz, *Anarchists,* 298.

33. Ibid., 297.

34. Ibid., 299.

35. Ibid., 311.

36. Ibid.

37. Henry David Thoreau, "Essay on Civil Disobedience," in Horowitz, *Anarchists,* 312.

38. Ibid., 314.

39. Ibid., 321.

40. Ibid., 314.

41. Ibid., 321.

42. Proudhon, *What Is Property?* 277.

43. Ibid., 275.

44. Pierre-Joseph Proudhon, "Letter to Bergman, 15 November 1861," quoted by Crowder, *Classical Anarchist Theory,* 82.

45. Quoted by David McLellan in *Karl Marx: His Life and Thought* (New York: Harper & Row, 1973), 455.

46. Quoted in Franz Mehring, *Karl Marx: The Story of His Life,* trans. Edward Fitzgerald (Atlantic Highlands, N.J.: Humanities Press, 1966), 405.

47. Mehring provides an account of the proceedings in ibid., 491.

48. Quoted by Mehring, in ibid., 404.

49. Bakunin, *Political Philosophy,* 288.

50. Friedrich Engels, "Versus the Anarchists," in *The Marx-Engels Reader,* ed. Robert C. Tucker (New York: Norton, 1978), 728.

51. Bakunin, *Political Philosophy,* 297.

52. Quoted by McLellan, *Karl Marx,* 440.

53. Bakunin, *Political Philosophy,* 394.

54. Quoted by Mehring, *Marx,* 146–47.

55. Bakunin, *Political Philosophy,* 300.

56. Quoted by Guerin, *Anarchism,* 34–35.

57. Bakunin, *Political Philosophy,* 300.

58. Ibid., 298.

59. Ibid.

60. Quoted in Gouldner, "Marx's Last Battle," 874.

61. Petyr Kropotkin, *Mutual Aid: A Factor in Evolution* (1914; reprint Boston: Porter Sargent, 1976), 298–99.

62. Ibid., 227.

63. Ibid., 229.

64. Crowder, *Classical Anarchist Theory*, 164.

65. Quoted by Guerin, *Anarchism*, 78.

66. David Wieck, "The Habit of Direct Action," in Howard Ehrlich, Carol Ehrlich, David De Leon, and Glenda Morris, eds., *Reinventing Anarchy: What Are Anarchists Thinking These Days?* (Boston: Routledge and Kegan Paul, 1979), 332.

67. See Clark's "What Is Anarchism?" for a more extensive discussion of this second criticism.

68. Bruce E. Johansen, *Forgotten Founders: How the American Indian Helped Shape Democracy* (Cambridge: Harvard University Press, 1982), introduction, chap. 4.

69. Friedrich Engels, *The Origin of the Family, Private Property, and the State* (New York: International Publishers, 1972), 113.

70. Quoted by Sharon O'Brien, *American Indian Tribal Governments* (Norman: University of Oklahoma Press, 1989), 18.

71. Quoted by Johansen, *Forgotten Founders*, 27.

72. Quoted in ibid., 105.

73. Quoted in ibid., 94.

74. Quoted by Paula Gunn-Allen in *The Sacred Hoop: Recovering the Feminine in American Indian Traditions* (Boston: Beacon Press, 1986), 219.

75. Ibid., 31.

76. Quoted by Johansen, *Forgotten Founders*, 87.

77. Quoted in ibid., 103.

78. Quoted by O'Brien, *American Indian Tribal Governments*, 113.

79. Woodcock, *Anarchism*, 380.

80. Quoted in Guerin, *Anarchism*, 142.

81. Woodcock, *Anarchism*, 398.

82. Quoted in ibid., 395–96.

83. George Orwell, *Homage to Catalonia* (New York: Harcourt Brace Jovanovich, 1952), 4–5.

84. Quoted in Woodcock, *Anarchism*, 394.

85. Ibid., 397.

86. Quoted in Guerin, *Anarchism*, 135.

87. Woodcock, *Anarchism*, 397.

88. Ibid., 390.

89. Orwell, *Homage to Catalonia*, 34–35.

90. Friedrich Engels, "On Authority," in Tucker, *Marx-Engels Reader*, 733.

91. Woodcock, *Anarchism*, 393.

92. Ibid., 398.

93. Jo Freeman suggests this distinction in *The Politics of Women's Liberation: A Case Study of an Emerging Social Movement and Its Relation to the Policy Process* (New York: Longman, 1975).

94. Carol Ehrlich, "Socialism, Anarchism, Feminism," in Ehrlich et al., *Reinventing Anarchy*, 263, 266.

95. Robert Dahl, "The Concept of Power," *Behavioral Science* 2, no. 3 (July 1966): 202–3.

96. Kathy E. Ferguson, *The Feminist Case against Bureaucracy* (Philadelphia: Temple University Press, 1984), 8.

97. Ibid., 27.

98. Kathy E. Ferguson, "Male-Ordered Politics," in *Idioms of Inquiry: Critique and Renewal in Political Science,* ed. Terence Ball (Albany, N.Y.: SUNY Press, 1987), 221.

99. Quoted in Ehrlich, "Socialism," 265.

100. Ibid., 261.

101. Kathleen P. Iannello, *Decisions without Hierarchy: Feminist Interventions in Organization Theory and Practice* (New York: Routledge, 1992), 42.

102. Ibid., 64.

103. Ibid., 81.

104. Ibid., 64, 69.

105. Ibid., 66.

106. Ibid., 67.

107. Ibid., 94.

108. Crowder, *Classical Anarchist Theory,* 196.

109. Ibid., 181.

110. Todd May, *The Political Philosophy of Poststructuralist Anarchism* (University Park: Pennsylvania State University Press, 1994), chaps. 4, 6.

111. Thomas Hobbes, *Leviathan: Or The Matter, Forme, and Power of a Commonwealth, Ecclesiastical and Civil,* ed. Michael Oakeshott (New York: Collier Books, 1962), chap. 16.

112. Kathleen Jones, *Compassionate Authority: Democracy and the Representation of Women* (New York: Routledge, 1993), 21–22.

6

Fascism

Evil is banal because human beings are placed in situations in which many will predictably yield to the temptation to justify themselves by blaming others and, sometimes, to hurt, torture, or kill them. The state repeatedly reflects these impulses, harming human beings in the name of the people.

— Murray Edelman

Nationalism, Patriotism, and Superpatriotism

Nationalism, defined as "a state of mind, in which the supreme loyalty of the individual is felt to be due the nation-state," is a relatively recent phenomenon.[1] The notion that nationalities should be organized as states arose only in the late eighteenth century. Prior to this, heredity, language, custom, tradition, religion, even territory—the marks of a nation—did not require a state. Other forms of social and political organization (e.g., clans, guilds, kingdoms, manors, sects) were sufficient. With the gradual entry of the masses into politics after the American and French revolutions this situation changed. Neither an emerging capitalist economy nor an increasingly secular culture could create the sense of political obligation that a democracy required from its citizens. The nation-state filled the void, uniting individuals around a common cause and a higher purpose.

Both aspects of the term, nation and state, are important. According to Max Weber, a state is distinguished from other political forms by its claim to a *"monopoly of the legitimate use of physical force within a given territory."*[2] Coercive power backs up political authority even in democratic states. But the state as a military and police power can be

further distinguished from the government as a legislative and adminis-
trative body, though anarchists note the common root of the terms *policy* and *police*. Both state and government are distinct from the nation.
Nationalism refers first and foremost to a people's "living and active
corporate will," to their felt sense of community.[3] This subjective factor
is more important in defining a nation than the objective characteristics
its people share.

At its origins, nationalism was not necessarily exclusionary or imperialist. Eighteenth-century nationalism in America and France espoused the universal rights of man. A nationalist could be an internationalist, at least in theory. In the war-torn twentieth century, the idea
that nationalism could be a positive force in international politics may
seem naive. Yet Michael Parenti presents the International Brigade that
fought Franco's fascist forces in the Spanish Civil War as an example of
"international patriotism." He recounts Charles Nusser's story of his
visit to Guernica, Spain, in June 1985, shortly after President Reagan's
trip to Bitberg, Germany. Unlike Reagan, who laid a wreath "on the
graves of the Nazi criminals," Nusser paid homage to "the *victims* of
the fascist murderers." The organizer of the gathering described Nusser
and a friend as "Patriots of the World." Nusser concluded that "there
have always been too many patriots in various countries straining to
get at the throats of patriots in other countries."[4]

Parenti argues that Nusser captures the difference between superpatriotism and real patriotism. Superpatriotism involves "the tendency
to place nationalistic pride and supremacy above every other public
consideration, the readiness to follow our leaders uncritically in their
dealings with other nations, especially confrontations involving the use
of ... military force and violence."[5] In contrast, real patriots "feel a
special attachment to their own country but not in some competitive
way that pits the United States against other powers." As international-
ists, "they love the people of all nations, seeing them as different representations of the same human family."[6] Superpatriotism is nationalism
gone terribly wrong.

This chapter examines Italian Fascism and German National Socialism as examples of superpatriotism. Fascism began in Italy with
Mussolini's successful 1922 "March on Rome." *Fasci,* the small, armed
groups that formed throughout Italy during World War I, were Mussolini's "organs of creation and agitation." The word comes from the
Latin *fasces* and evokes the symbol of Roman justice, a bundle of rods
from which an ax protrudes.[7] According to Mussolini, Fascism was the
negation of socialism, democracy, and liberalism. Inspired by the Italian example, Fascist parties gradually spread across central, eastern,

and southern Europe. Following the March on Rome, Hermann Esser, one of Hitler's associates, proclaimed: "What has been done in Italy by a handful of courageous men is not impossible. *In Bavaria too we have Italy's Mussolini [sic]. His name is Adolf Hitler....*"[8] In 1933, only nine years later, Adolf Hitler would assume total power over the German nation. In 1934, Joseph Goebbels, Hitler's minister of propaganda, said that "the march on Rome was a signal, a sign of storm for liberal democracy."[9] Mussolini had declared that "Fascism as an idea, a doctrine, a realization, is universal; it is Italian in its particular institutions, but it is universal by reason of its nature."[10] To understand its nature, we require the additional conceptual tools that are the focus of the next section.

An Aesthetic(ized) Politics

According to Murray Edelman, political scientists' standard definition of politics as "who gets what, where, when, and how" is one-sided. In emphasizing resource allocation, it neglects the symbolic functions of politics, the myriad ways the state arouses and addresses citizens' hopes and fears. For Edelman, politics is "obsessional, mythical, and emotional," as well as rational and strategic. "Political forms ... come to symbolize what large masses of men need to believe about the state to reassure themselves. It is the needs, the hopes, and the anxieties of men that determine the meanings. But political forms also convey goods, services, and power to specific groups of men."[11]

To analyze political symbols Edelman employs a number of psychological concepts. Psychologists identify two basic types of symbols: referential symbols and condensation symbols. Referential symbols represent "the objective elements in objects or situations: the elements identified in the same way by different people."[12] "Condensation symbols evoke the emotions associated with the situation." They frequently "condense into one symbolic event, sign, or act patriotic pride, anxieties, remembrances of past glories or humiliations, promises of future greatness: some one of these or all of them."[13]

Each type of symbol serves a different function for the personality. By accurately identifying objects, referential symbols help individuals know and control external reality. Condensation symbols help individuals adjust to society and address their ambivalence about politics. They perform the latter function by allowing citizens to externalize their "unresolved inner problems," that is, to displace and/or project their fears and hopes on other objects.[14] In performing their functions, condensation symbols may or may not reflect empirical realities.

Edelman illustrates these symbols' different functions with the distinction between an adversary and an enemy. Adversaries are legitimate opponents with whom we engage in limited struggles over tactical issues (e.g., an opposing candidate in an electoral contest). To defeat an adversary, we require the relatively accurate information that referential symbols provide. Enemies serve the far more complex sociopsychological function of overcoming citizens' ambivalence about politics. An enemy is fundamentally flawed, a morally depraved person or persons (e.g., a leader, nation, or race) who poses a continuing threat to the survival of our state. In opposing an enemy, "we" unite against "them." As condensation symbols, enemies create complex coalitions; for example, Mussolini's *fasci* fought socialism, democracy, and liberalism. Enemies also serve as convenient targets for citizens' fear and anger. In scapegoating and victim blaming, "evil" traits are displaced or projected on an Other. The characteristics ascribed to political enemies often have historical roots; they are drawn from a "stockpool" of stereotypes. These imputed traits obscure and override empirical reality.[15]

Although referential and condensation symbols are analytically distinct, symbolic politics often includes aspects of both. Edelman focuses on two symbolic forms that pervade politics: ritual and myth. He defines ritual as a "motor activity that involves its participants symbolically in a common enterprise, calling their attention to their relatedness and joint interests in a compelling way. It thereby both promotes conformity and evokes satisfaction and joy in conformity."[16] For example, the so-called rational voter not only casts a ballot but also performs a ritual. When elections are seen as rituals, it is easier to understand why voters express satisfaction regardless of the outcome. Whether or not their candidate wins, they have reaffirmed their role as democratic citizens. Myth reinforces ritual, and vice versa. Edelman quotes Malinowski, an anthropologist, to suggest that myth functions "to account for extraordinary privileges or duties, for great social inequalities, for severe burdens of rank, in short for 'sociological strain.'"[17] He includes "the rational character of the voting act, the reality of the controls elections exert over governmental policy directions, [etc.]" among the myths of democratic politics.[18] Elections reduce the "strain" of unequal power and wealth by displacing citizens' resentment onto constitutional mechanisms. Edelman concludes that "the most conspicuously 'democratic' institutions are largely symbolic and expressive in function."[19]

As myth and ritual, symbolic politics takes on aesthetic qualities that increase as empirical reality fades. According to Edelman, condensation symbols are art forms, and vice versa. The expressive power of artistic creations depends on their distance from ordinary experience.

At its most extreme, art is self-referential, that is, "art for art's sake." Walter Benjamin refers to the transcendent quality of a work of art as its "aura."[20] Aura connotes a mystical element—the eternal, the unique —that evokes a sense of awe, a cult-like feeling in viewers. The development of techniques for mechanically reproducing artwork, which made it available for mass consumption, destroyed its aura. Art became another commodity for exhibit and sale; it too was transitory, ordinary, and easily replaced.

At first glance, the symbolic politics of modern democracies seemingly follows the same trend. The aura that surrounded gods and kings has been replaced by the "selling of the president." A politics of "sound bites" and "spin doctors" may also be remote from citizens' everyday experience, but in a very different way. In Marx's terms, political candidates have become commodity fetishes, largely without aura. Yet auratic remnants persist in mass democracies. The sovereign people of a liberal democracy worship themselves in the form of a nation-state. As Edelman puts it, "in their obsession with the state, men are of course obsessed with themselves ... ; man and politics [are] reflections of each other."[21] For example, as "head of state," the president embodies the nation and retains aura in his ceremonial functions. Political leaders also create aura by constructing adversaries as enemies (e.g., Reagan's reference to the former Soviet Union as an "evil empire"). In modern democracies, aura is used to shape public opinion for a variety of purposes (i.e., to gain reelection, to maintain legitimacy, to reaffirm loyalties, and so on). Yet auratic art in its pure form has no external goal; it is an end in itself.

According to Simonetta Falasca-Zamponi, Benjamin regarded fascist politics as a modern adaptation of aura in its purest sense. Under fascism "the principle of *l'art pour l'art* [has] been transferred to politics."[22] Aesthetics is no longer a tool of politics but has become its cultural frame. As Zamponi puts it, "symbols, myths and rituals [are treated] not just as functional appendixes to power, but as the elements through which a governmental power, in this case fascism, defines its goals and shapes its political identity."[23] Within this aesthetic frame, the nation-state is a self-defining and self-justifying creative force. Michael Parenti describes superpatriotism in similar terms:

> The nation-state is transformed into something more than an instrumental value whose function is to protect other social values. For the superpatriot, the nation becomes an end in itself, a powerfully abstracted symbol that claims our ultimate loyalty, an entity whose existence is taken as morally self-justifying.[24]

To understand fascism we need to consider not only the traditional politics of resource allocation but also the symbolic politics of meaning creation. Concepts from psychology—ambivalence, condensation, displacement, and projection—reveal the functions of symbolic politics. Aura, an aesthetic quality, suggests that the fascist state is a form of pure art. Nationalism, we might surmise, goes terribly wrong when symbolic politics abandons reality and becomes an end in itself.

Symbols of Class, Race, and Nation

The roots of Italian Fascist and German National Socialist propaganda are found in late-nineteenth- and early-twentieth-century radical right-wing movements. According to F.L. Carsten, these movements supported national extremism, anti-Semitism, and mass democracy.[25] Mussolini and Hitler combined these elements differently, and their propaganda reflected their historical contexts. Mussolini placed a greater emphasis on class in his myth of Italian unity, whereas Hitler stressed the purity of the Aryan race.

In *Mein Kampf,* Hitler discusses the purpose of propaganda. Although he refers specifically to German "war propaganda," his references should be construed more generally: life is war. As he put it in a 1929 speech, "If men wish to live, then they are forced to kill others.... As long as there are peoples on this earth there will be nations against nations.... There is in reality no distinction between peace and war.... One is either the hammer or the anvil. We confess that it is our purpose to prepare the German people again for the role of the hammer."[26] Propaganda is a means to national survival and, as such, is beyond criteria of truth and falsity, good and evil. Lies that motivate action, including violence, are justified when they help create a superior humanity. Hitler romanticizes the horrors of war, giving them a spiritual meaning. Violence without a "firm, spiritual base," a "fanatical outlook," cannot be sustained. It is a "blood sacrifice" that "strikes the best part of the people, since every persecution which occurs without a spiritual basis seems morally unjustified."[27] The art of propaganda involves "finding, through a psychologically correct form, the way to the attention and thence to the heart of the broad masses." Since the masses know little and retain less, effective propaganda cannot be complex. "A very few points" to "harp on ... in slogans" suffice.[28] Most important, a leader must concentrate the people's attention "upon a single foe."[29]

In National Socialist propaganda "the Jew" is the enemy of the German people. Germany's history of anti-Semitism made the Jewish people a likely target. Prominent nineteenth-century academics such as Karl Marx, Heinrich Treitschke, and Eugen Dühring had presented the Jews as greedy capitalists, crass materialists, and an "inferior race." Houston Stewart Chamberlain, an Englishman who resided in Germany, had the most direct influence on Adolf Hitler. Chamberlain portrayed the "intellectual and moral history of Europe" as a "struggle between ... Germanic sentiment and anti-Germanic disposition." He feared the "infection" of Indo-Europeans by Jewish blood. If it continued "there would be only one people of pure race left in Europe, that of the Jews, all the rest would be a herd of pseudo-Hebraic mestizos, a people beyond all doubt degenerate physically, mentally, and morally."[30]

Anti-Semitism was also common in German politics long before Nazi rule. In 1878 Adolf Stoecker founded the first right-wing extremist party, "The Christian Social Worker's Party," in Berlin. His goal was "to demonstrate to the people the roots of its misery, the power of finance, the spirit of mammon and the stock exchange" in the Jews.[31] He was the first of many politicians to propose laws banning Jews from certain occupations. In the 1890s, anti-Semites gained their first Reichstag seats, but their numbers in Germany remained small. Anti-Semitism was a stronger force in Austrian politics, especially in Vienna, where the Jews dominated trade and industry. Two Austrians, Georg Schönerer, leader of the Pan-German movement, and Karl Lueger, mayor of Vienna, greatly influenced Hitler's political tactics. Schönerer called on all Germans to fight the Jews and the Slavs (Czechs, Hungarians, Poles, Serbs, and Croats) as corrupters of the Germanic race. He portrayed the Jews as "international speculators without a fatherland" and "a symptom of the general economic disease."[32] Lueger focused more on socioeconomic issues crucial to the "little man." On his death, a socialist newspaper praised him as "the first bourgeois politician who reckoned with the masses, moved the masses, and sank the roots of his power deeply into the soil."[33] Hitler, who described his Viennese period as formative, would later bring nationalism and socialism together against their common enemy: the Jews.

In *Mein Kampf,* Hitler recounts the history of how Jewish parasites took over their German hosts.[34] As he tells it: After coming to Germany as foreign merchants, the Jews became money-lenders to the German Court and by increasing the distance between kings, princes, and the people caused their downfall; with the rise of liberalism, the Jews began to seek civil rights, especially religious freedom, and to support democratic ideas; then, as class conflict arose, the Jews joined the proletariat and established Marxism; socialist internationalism helped the

Jews destroy nation, race, personality, and, hence, "all human culture." Now, "the essential obstacle is removed to the domination of the inferior being—and this is the Jew."

In Hitler's myth, the Jews perform the multiple functions of a condensation symbol. Criticisms of monarchism, liberalism, and socialism are redirected against them, creating new possibilities for political coalitions. His Jewish target also addresses citizens' ambivalence toward the nation-state as a result of postwar economic decline and political instability. An internal parasite, not government policy, becomes the source of Germany's current disease (dis-ease?). The masses can project their fear and anger on "the Jews" and reserve their courage and faith for a new Germany. The National Socialists, unlike other parties, offer "new hope of a good life" to the "little people." The aura of racial nationalism sometimes supported Nazi social policy in especially disturbing ways. One of the Nazis whom Milton Mayer interviewed recounts this story, which shows how myth reduces the "strain" of inequality:

> I was sitting in a cinema with a Jewish friend and her daughter of thirteen, while a Nazi parade went across the screen, and the girl caught her mother's arm and whispered, "Oh, Mother, Mother, if I weren't a Jew, I think I'd be a Nazi!"[35]

Anti-Semitism was a minor theme in Italian Fascism, again due to historical context. There were relatively few Jews in Italy, and they did not possess great wealth or status. Italy's major problems were poverty and apathy, especially in the less developed south. These circumstances suggested class war as a political strategy. Mussolini gave it a new focus by combining class and nation, by portraying the Italians, not the proletariat, as "the oppressed." In doing so, he reinforced doubts about the Italian socialists' patriotism (they had initially declared neutrality in World War I). In late 1914 Mussolini left the Socialist Party, abandoning proletarian internationalism for Italian nationalism. His reasons are obscure: perhaps he anticipated a postwar Fascist government, or maybe he was frustrated by the socialists' inactivity. Following the war, local *fasci* seized many regions, often with support from the army, the police, major landowners and industrialists, all of whom feared socialist control more.

Mussolini organized local *fasci* into a political party, the Popolo d'Italia, with a clear objective: "Our programme is simple: we want to rule Italy."[36] In October 1922 the Fascist threat of a "March on Rome" led the king to form a new government with Mussolini as prime minister.[37] As Mussolini gradually absorbed and suppressed opposition parties, he also tried to transform Italy into a "block of granite," into "a monolith." According to Alfredo Rocco, Mussolini's minister of justice, "Unlimited and unrestrained class self-defence ... inevitably leads to anarchy.... Having reduced the problem to these terms, only one solution is possible: the realization of justice among the classes by and through the state...."[38]

Since we discuss Mussolini's corporatist state later, our focus here is the aura of Italian Fascism. Like Hitler, Mussolini portrayed Fascists' "tendency to empire" as "spiritual and ethical" and as a "manifestation of their vitality": "peoples who rise or rearise are imperialist; renunciation is characteristic of dying peoples."[39] According to Walter Benjamin, in a technological age aesthetic politics can only lead to total war. He quotes Marinetti's poetic account of the Italian's Ethiopian war as an example of modern aura: "War is beautiful because it initiates the dreamt-of metalization of the human body. War is beautiful because it enriches a flowering meadow with the fiery orchids of machine guns...."[40] Like the National Socialists, the Italian Fascists used myth to motivate action. As Mussolini puts it, "We have created our myth. The myth is a faith, it is a passion. It is not necessary that it be a reality. It is a reality by the fact that it is a goal, a hope, a faith...."[41] In their myth "a state of permanent war between bourgeoisie and proletariat" would "generate new energies, new moral values, new men who will be close to ancient heroes."[42]

According to Mussolini, Fascism gives Italians a "new style," which he defined as "first of all work, second discipline, then disinterest, then probity of life, then loyalty, openness, courage."[43] As in Germany, myth and ritual worked in tandem to create the "new Italian." The Roman salute is an Italian Fascist ritual that Falasci-Zamponi discusses at length. In 1925 Mussolini began to require civil administrators to substitute it for the "bourgeois shaking hands." Falasca-Zamponi claims that "the regime defined itself as anti-bourgeois through the Roman salute. Bourgeois meant inefficiency, slowness and ... ugliness. Fascism was efficient, dynamic, and harmonic." Mussolini declared it "more hygienic, more aesthetic and shorter!" Over time, rules for the salute multiplied, and proper performance of it began to identify the "real Fascist." A note that read "devoted to shaking hands" placed in a personnel file indicated "a lesser fascist spirit." Falasci concludes that "the means had become ends as if the gesture itself, in the case of the Roman salute, could bring a change in character in the Italians."[44] From merely symbolizing membership, ritual began actually to constitute it. With this shift, aura superseded function, and politics became art.

History gave Hitler and Mussolini powerful symbols—"the Jews" and "the bourgeois"—which they used to mobilize their respective nations. In using them, they crossed the line between fantasy and reality, making aesthetics their end, as well as their means to power. What, we might ask, renders democratic citizens vulnerable to fascist propaganda? In the next two sections, we shift our focus from aesthetic politics to resource allocation, a more traditional political concern. But symbolic and material politics remain intertwined. Only by considering both can we begin to identify when nationalism is prone to excess.

Masses, Leaders, and the State

Many historically specific factors played a role in the ascendancy of Italian Fascism and German National Socialism. Two were international in scope: World War I, especially the Versailles Treaty, which imposed harsh reparations on Germany and dashed Italy's hopes for territorial gains; and the Great Depression, which caused high inflation and unemployment throughout Europe. Others were specific to Italy and Germany: the absence of a civic culture to support constitutional government; the strain of late, rapid, state-supported economic modernization; political fragmentation, complicated by weak middle-class parties and strong right- and left-wing opposition; proportional representation electoral systems resulting in coalition governments; and, in Germany, a constitutional provision for emergency powers.

According to some scholars, these historical conditions explain why fascism took hold in Italy and Germany. Both countries needed strong leadership to overcome political conflict and restore economic prosperity. Although historically accurate, this explanation tells only part of the story. It suggests that fascism is a relatively unique phenomena, restricted to several European countries in the interwar years. Yet we have already seen that fascism responds to more general human needs, deep-seated psychological ones. We now turn to fascists' alternative to the trio "Liberalism, Democracy, and Socialism."

The Masses

Hitler and Mussolini came to power by legal means through a series of appointments and elections. From 1928 to March 1933, the National Socialists increased their party membership from 100,000 to 1.5 million, electoral support from 2.6 percent to 43.9 percent, and Reichstag seats from 12 to 230, making them its largest single party, though not yet a majority one. Aggregate statistics suggest that the Nazis drew voters primarily from the middle-class parties, which lost a full 80 percent of their supporters, compared to the Marxists (down 10 percent), the

Catholics (held steady), and the conservatives, especially nationalists (down 40 percent). According to Seymour Martin Lipset, "the ideal-typical Nazi voter in 1932 was a middle-class self-employed Protestant who lived either on a farm or in a small community, and who had previously voted for a centrist or regionalist political party strongly opposed to the power and influence of big business and big labor."[45] In March 1933 the newly elected Reichstag accepted Hitler's declaration of a national emergency and granted him dictatorial powers.[46] In the next election (November 1933), the National Socialists prevented opposition parties from competing. They received 92 percent of the vote, 661 Reichstag seats, and took control.

Mussolini's rise to power was similarly legal. Parliamentary government had been introduced in 1861 when Italy was unified. It was followed by universal manhood suffrage (1913) and proportional representation (1917). In Italy's first postwar election (1919), the newly formed Fascist Party did not receive any seats in the Chamber of Deputies. In 1921, however, it earned 35 seats (out of 500) and 19.6 percent of the total vote. The Fascists' self-portrait as the party of "law and order" had gained them the support of civil servants, army officers, business and industrial leaders, and skilled tradesmen. Following the "March on Rome" and Mussolini's appointment as chancellor, the Chamber of Deputies granted him emergency powers (limited to one year). Mussolini used his power to modify electoral laws in order to guarantee the party that received the most votes in an election two-thirds of the legislative seats. In 1924, the Fascists received more than three-fifths of the total vote, rendering the new law irrelevant. The 1924 election marked the end of parliamentary democracy. Mussolini soon neutralized the Council of Deputies by outlawing all other parties and curtailing universal suffrage. In the 1930s he replaced the Council with a Chamber of Fasces and Corporations. It was an economic—not a democratic —"parliament."

The Leaders: The Führer and *Il Duce*
Hitler and Mussolini offered charismatic leadership as an escape from liberal democracy. In *Mein Kampf,* Hitler expresses contempt for "parliamentarism."[47] After observing the Austrian parliament, he describes the delegates as absent, bored, ignorant, asleep, lazy, inarticulate, and opportunistic. Most important, they are irresponsible, except in election years, when they miraculously change form, appearing among the masses full of promises they cannot keep. The people, in turn, can neither recognize nor appreciate genius. As Hitler puts it, "The revulsion of the masses for every outstanding genius is positively

instinctive. Sooner will a camel pass through a needle's eye than a great man be 'discovered' by an election."[48] He concludes that "majority rule sins against the basic aristocratic principle."[49]

The *Führerstaat* is Hitler's alternative: "In it there is no majority vote on individual questions, but only the decision of an individual [the Führer] who must answer with his fortune and his life for his choice."[50] The Führer represents the people by who he is, by his innate character, his intuitive sense, and ultimately, his personal will:

> The Führer is no "representative" of a particular group whose wishes he must carry out. He is no "organ" of the state in the sense of a mere executive agent. He is rather the bearer of the collective will of the people. In his will the will of the people is realized. He transforms the mere feelings of the people into a conscious will.[51]

In aesthetic terms, the Führer embodies the essence of the people. In his person, the individual, the nation, and the race converge.

The *Führerstaat* transcends liberals' social contract based on individual rights. It has more spiritual goals: *"The highest purpose of a folkish state is concern for the preservation of those original racial elements which bestow culture and create the beauty and dignity of a higher mankind."*[52] Its deepest roots lie in the blood and soil of the nation. In such a state, liberty takes on a positive meaning; it involves self-sacrifice, not self-interest. According to Hitler, *Pflichterfüllung* (fulfillment of duty), "magnificently designates this kind of activity.... It means not to be self-sufficient but to serve the community." He adds, "The basic attitude from which such activity arises, we call—to distinguish it from egoism and selfishness—idealism. By this we understand only the individual's capacity to make sacrifices for the community, for his fellow men."[53]

Mussolini also argues that liberalism wrongly subordinates the state power to the individual. He says,

> if liberty is to be the attribute of living men and not that of abstract dummies invented by individualistic Liberalism, then Fascism stands for liberty and for the only liberty worth having, the liberty of the State and of the individual within the State.[54]

His slogans convey a similar spirit of leadership: "Everything within the state; everything for the state; nothing outside the state"; "Fascism is Mussolinism"; "Mussolini is always right." (*Il Duce*, like the *Führer*, means leader.)[55] However, the Italian state is not based in a preexisting

nation or *volk* rooted in blood and soil. Instead, the Fascist state creates the nation, forming its many parts into an organic whole. Mussolini's Fascist state is "an unique and original creation. It is not reaction-
ary but revolutionary."[56] As creator, the leader is an artist, a poet, a
sculptor. In a chilling passage, Mussolini describes his creative experience:

> When I feel the masses in my hands, since they believe in me, or when I
> mingle with them, and they almost crush me, then I feel like one with the
> masses. However, there is at the same time a little aversion, like the poet
> feels against the material he works with. Does not the sculptor sometimes
> break the marble out of rage, because it does not precisely mould in his
> hands according to his vision?[57]

He reiterates more succinctly, "everything depends on that: to dominate the masses as an artist."[58]

Gleichschaltung and Corporatism

To rule a complex society, even by charismatic authority, requires state
structures, especially coordinating mechanisms. *Gleichschaltung,* or
synchronization, was the Nazis' term for their top-down penetration of
all aspects of society. Hitler's well-known slogan was "responsibility
towards above, authority towards below."[59] The Führer led the party,
the party led the state, and all three represented the will of the people.
This hierarchy addressed popular ambivalence toward the state. The
average citizen could idealize the "Führer," identify with the "party,"
and dominate the "Jews." Little was left to chance. Hitler established
special shock troops, the SA and the SS, alongside the German army.
The Nazis also had many front organizations, for example, the Hitler
Youth, Hitler Student League, Officers' League, Women's League, Labor Front, and other occupational groups. The Nazi Party became a
"state within the state" and a part of citizens' daily lives.

Milton Mayer's interviewees capture this aspect of National Socialist rule well. Most were not "fanatikers," but "March violets." They
joined the Nazi Party late, in March 1933, largely because " 'everybody'
was doing it." As Mayer puts it, "in a nation of seventy million, they
were the sixty-nine million plus."[60] They joined to get or to keep their
jobs, for the "good fellowship" at party gatherings, for the various programs, like "Strength through Joy" subsidized vacations, and simply to
be part of something "bigger" than themselves. The Führer had been a
"little man" too, and his was the party of "we little men." To them,
Gleichschaltung was "always for the better, in bread and butter, in

housing, health, and hope, wherever the New Order touched them."[61] Of the death camps and the genocide, they "knew" little—an issue to which we will return.

In 1927 Mussolini declared the creation of a "corporate state." Corporatism—his coordinating principle—comes from the Latin *corpus,* which means one body. It is beautifully symbolized by the *fasces,* a bundle of rods. Like National Socialism, Italian Fascism involved a hierarchy from leader to party to state. The Fascist Party also controlled the people through front organizations, though less effectively than the Nazis. Mussolini was most successful in coordinating the economy, specifically in harmonizing the interests of capital and labor. He defined Fascism in economic terms as "the dictatorship of the state over many classes competing." State corporations representing occupational categories were his coordinating mechanism. "The corporations were the links in the chain which bound the citizens tightly to the state."[62] An adequate treatment of them takes us from politics to economics.

Before turning there, we briefly reconsider the questions: How does nationalism go wrong? Why did the Germans and the Italians elect fascist governments? To the appeal of symbolic politics and to specific historical conditions, we can add another important argument. According to Theodor Adorno, fascism has the greatest psychological appeal in a "mass society." Its basic features include reified politics, manifest in a distant state run by "the experts"; the breakdown of intermediate groups like church, family, guild, and town; and the atomization of individuals into "self-sufficient units" or "mere cogs" in a vast machine. Adorno concludes that "mass society" leads "modern men [to] revert to patterns of behavior which flagrantly contradict their own rational level and the present stage of enlightened technological civilization."[63] To overcome their loneliness and powerlessness, the democratic masses identify with a charismatic leader and embrace a totalitarian state.

Against arguments that fascism reflects a specifically Italian or German problem, Adorno portrays it as a reaction against liberalism itself. Joan Tronto has recently noted Hannah Arendt's similar argument in *The Origins of Totalitarianism.* As Tronto construes it, Arendt claims that "the problems of tribalism, of racism, and of conceiving of the other with hatred, is an understandable response to the tremendous moral burden placed upon people by the claims that all share in the 'rights of man.'"[64] A liberal society may be intolerable to many people because of the responsibility that real freedom requires. According to David Calleo, without a sense of mutual responsibility, a liberal society may be ungovernable. He claims that the liberal model did fit late Weimar Germany: "the Reichstag was ineffective not because its deputies were always pursuing the general good to the neglect of particular needs, but because the parties could seldom rise above the vigorous advocacy of selfish interests."[65] In the next section, we consider fascists' solution to the problem of competing interests.

Corporatism: Reconciling Class and Nation

Corporatism predates and postdates fascism, beginning with medieval guilds and continuing through neoliberalism. According to Philippe Schmitter, all of the following ideologies advocate corporatist economics: "romantic, organic theorists of the state; pre-Marxist, protosocialists; Social Christian[s]; fascist authoritarianism; secular modernizing nationalism; radical bourgeois solidarism; mystical universalism; internationalist functionalism; pseudo-Catholic integralism; technocratic, procapitalist reformism; anticapitalist syndicalism; guild socialism; and communitarianism."[66] Schmitter concludes that corporatism might be more usefully conceptualized as "a system of interest representation," rather than an "ideological label." He provides the classic definition of the term:

> corporatism can be defined as a system of interest representation in which the constituent units are organized into a limited number of singular, compulsory, noncompetitive, hierarchically ordered and functionally differentiated categories, recognized or licensed (if not created) by the state and granted a deliberate representational monopoly within their respective categories in exchange for observing certain controls on their selection of leaders and articulation of demands and supports.[67]

Within this definition, he distinguishes two subtypes of corporatism —societal and state—based on the extent and type of state control over interest groups. Societal corporatism evolves alongside a liberal democratic welfare state, as the requirements of maintaining economic prosperity and political loyalty begin to exceed the coordinating capacities of free markets. State corporatism is more often imposed from above as part of a revolutionary program to facilitate industrial development. It can accompany authoritarian or totalitarian politics. Italian and, to a lesser extent, German Fascism fit Schmitter's definition of state corporatism.

Mussolini contrasts his corporate state with liberal's economic man whose individual rights, especially to property, are protected by a limited government. His Fascism "leaves the individual adequate elbow room," and he notes that "even Adam Smith left the door ajar—however cautiously—for government intervention in business."[68] But Fascist "man is integral, he is political, he is economic, he is religious, he is saint, he is warrior."[69] Corporatism solves the "crisis of capitalism" by (re)directing human energies toward the nation-state. Mussolini claims economic needs are best served when classes are "coordinated and harmonised in the unity of the State."[70]

Mussolini's Fascist state created twenty-two corporations to represent different economic areas (e.g., chemical trades, credit and insurance, building trades, cereal, fruit, and vegetables, lumber and woods, air and sea). Each corporation included all relevant economic actors —workers, employers, managers, and owners. "Public" members also served on the corporations that were led by a state-appointed minister. The corporations elected an 800-member General Corporate Assembly, which later became the Italian Chamber of Fasces and Corporations.[71] According to Mussolini, "the corporation ... is formed to expand the wealth, the political power, and the well-being of the Italian people."[72] It coordinates activities and resolves conflicts among economic groups, regulates jobs and training, sets prices and wages, and monitors working conditions—all subject to state approval. Mussolini declared that "the worker, the tiller of the soil, must be able to say ... if I am really better off to-day, it is due to the institutions which the Fascist Revolution has created."[73] In practice, however, the corporations placated business, industry, and the state while they controlled labor. Italian Fascism brought classes together as a nation *without* abolishing capitalism and its attendant inequalities. Italian corporatism was far from socialism, at least as Marx envisioned it.

National Socialism also subordinated class interests to the nation and, in the German case, race. According to Hitler, the Aryan "no longer works directly for himself, but with his activity articulates himself with the community, not only for his own advantage, but for the advantage of all."[74] Hitler asks workers and employers to moderate their demands for the sake of national unity:

> Just as surely as a worker sins against the spirit of a real national community when, without regard for the common welfare and the survival of a national economy, he uses his power to raise extortionate demands, an employer breaks this community to the same extent when he conducts his business in an inhuman, exploiting way, misuses the national labor force and makes millions out of its sweat.[75]

Although the National Socialists organized state "superagencies" (e.g., the Estate of Industry and Trade, the German Food Estate, and a trade union association, the Labour Front), German corporatism was less extensive than in Italy. Hitler implemented his labor and social policies with the cooperation of relatively autonomous agricultural, business, and industrial elites. His successes are striking. In 1933–34, 6.04 million people were "on the dole." This figure dropped steadily to 3.7 million (1935), 2.5 million (1936), 1.8 million (1937), 1.05 million (1938), 300,000 (1939). By the summer of 1939, a developing labor shortage could serve as a rationale for Germany's war effort.[76] By providing jobs, Hitler did not abolish class inequality or private property. Newly employed German workers faced longer hours and harder jobs—without collective bargaining rights. As Hitler saw it, the state "only had to make certain that capital remain the handmaiden of the state and not fancy itself the mistress of the nation." This established two limits: "preservation of a solvent, national, and independent economy on the one hand, assurance of the social rights of the workers on the other."[77] In Germany, like Italy, the first concern took priority over the second.

In 1939, Max Horkheimer wrote, "he who does not wish to speak of capitalism should also be silent about Fascism."[78] Marxists continue to argue that Fascism is "the offspring of a crisis of advanced capitalism."[79] In a controversial study of Weimar Germany, David Abraham argues that in order to reproduce capitalism, a liberal democracy must (1) organize dominant class(es) behind a coherent economic policy; and (2) disorganize the dominated class(es) through social programs that limit discontent.[80] From 1924 to 1928, the Weimar Republic succeeded in both tasks, realizing what has been called a "corporatist equilibrium." But it did so only by displacing political decisions from a fragmented Reichstag to "ministerial bureaucracies" and "interest-group representatives." Abraham sees nothing "neutral" or "classless" about this equilibrium; it was thoroughly "late" capitalist.[81] But it did provide economic stability, until the 1929 depression exacerbated class antagonisms and polarized political parties. Only then did the Weimar Republic fall because "the functions of facilitating private accumulation and guaranteeing mass legitimacy could not be reconciled," at least not by a fragmented Reichstag, incapable of marshaling a capitalist response to socialist demands.[82] In Abraham's words, "as guarantors of capitalism, as proponents of a strong, imperialist Germany, the Nazis appeared to be the best available possibility."[83]

From a Marxist perspective, fascists' call for class compromise or conciliation is bourgeois ideology. Under fascism, the capitalists continue to claim that their class interests really serve the whole society. To support those interests, however, the once invisible hand must become a highly visible state. Marxists' interpretation of fascism as the child of capitalism remains controversial. But it does suggest caution when comparing fascist and socialist regimes or, more specifically, Hitler's and Stalin's leadership. Although fascists and socialists criticize liberal capitalism, significant differences exist between their alternatives to it. Both support a strong party state and a "cult of personality." Yet fascist state corporatist arrangements retained the capitalist economy that socialists would destroy. Fascism triumphed with the support of business, industrial, and military elites, as well as the middle classes, rather than socialists' proletarian and peasant-based revolutions. Trotsky captures the difference (though too starkly, since fascism mixed new and old elites): "Stalinism was the Bolshevik Bonapartism of a young class, Fascism that of an old and dying class."[84] Fascists' power base served to limit their control over socioeconomic forces and their capacity to build a new state. Differences in the use of propaganda are perhaps most important. As Charles Lindblom characterizes them:

> Communist persuasion differs from fascist. It does not unambiguously exalt unilateral authority. Instead it promises a democratic future. Nor does it exalt elitism. Instead it actively practices a reduction of inequalities on some fronts and promises it on some others. And it appeals ... far more than does fascist persuasion, to the rational in man.[85]

For socialists, symbolic politics remains a means to a future society, and not an end in itself.

The Politics of Hate in America Today

We have now considered four related causes of fascism: (1) the specific historical circumstances in Italy and Germany; (2) the psychological appeal of aesthetic(ized) politics; (3) the atomistic individualism of mass democracies; (4) the inability of "free" markets to guarantee economic prosperity. Under fascist rule, we argued, nationalism goes terribly wrong. The nation-state becomes a self-defining, self-justifying power, and superpatriotism replaces real patriotism. On 19 April 1995, right-wing extremists bombed the Federal Building in Oklahoma City. To conclude this chapter, we might ask: Is nationalism going wrong in America today? Do any of the explanations above fit our circumstances?

Hate crimes are steadily rising in America, and most are committed by right-wing extremists. Although state and federal laws vary, hate crimes are generally defined as those "prompted by the victims' race, ethnicity, religion or sexual orientation."[86] They are crimes motivated by hatred not of the victim but of the group to which the victim belongs. According to *Klanwatch,* bias-motivated murders declined from thirty (1993) to eighteen (1994), but other assaults increased by 26 percent. Over 25 percent of the assault victims were gay or lesbian, and almost two-thirds of the verified murders were motivated by antigay bias. The Anti-Defamation League also reports that anti-Semitic acts increased 10.6 percent from 1993 to 1994. Cross-burnings declined from 117 (1992) to 87 (1993) to 52 (1994). Acts of vandalism also dropped, from 405 (1993) to 341 (1994). Since national data on hate crimes are not yet systematically collected, *Klanwatch* cautions "our figures understate the true level of violent hate crime."[87]

The overall number of active hate groups fell slightly, from 299 (1993) to 270 (1994), though their membership probably increased simultaneously. Neo-Nazi organizations grew from fifty-nine (1993) to seventy-six (1994). The Aryan Nation, the neo-Nazis' primary organization, extended its chapters from three states (1993) to eighteen states (1994) and formed an alliance with the National Socialist German Workers Party–Overseas Organization, the major distributor of neo-Nazi literature worldwide. The number of active Ku Klux Klan groups held relatively steady: 100 (1993) and 98 (1994). Skinhead groups declined by 50 percent from eighty-seven (1993) to thirty-four (1994). Identity groups are difficult to assess because they primarily operate underground, but they seem to be increasingly influential in the white supremacist movement. *Klanwatch* observers claim that white supremacists are shifting loyalties from the more traditional Ku Klux Klan to "Aryan Nations, militias, states' rights groups and a growing Identity movement." These groups are now "exploiting the broader issues of immigration, gun control, states rights, abortion and homosexuality" to reach the mass public.[88]

Elinor Langer categorizes the vast array of hate groups into five basic types:[89]

1. The neo-Nazis descend from the American Nazi Party, though they include other Nazi-identified groups. They advocate a "third position," Aryan national socialism, as an alternative to liberal capitalism and traditional Marxism. They claim to defend the white working class against the federal government ruled by race traitors (the ZOG, or Zionist Occupational Government) and a Jewish media conspiracy.
2. The skinheads are youth gangs, originally concentrated in urban areas on the East and West coasts. Many belonged to White Aryan Race (WAR), the organization of Tom Metzgar,

who was convicted of murder in 1990. They are "front-line warriors" for the white race.

3. The Ku Klux Klan is increasingly split into two subgroups. A militant branch affiliated with the neo-Nazis has proclaimed the "Fifth Era," a period of underground activity, government resistance, and racial genocide. A more domesticated branch engages in electoral politics (e.g., the senatorial campaign of David Duke) and espouses a "kinder, gentler white supremacy."

4. The Posse Comitatus is a largely rural, very decentralized, paramilitary and survivalist movement. Its members are tax resisters and local vigilantes, who recognize only county-level government.

5. The Christian Identity movement is a religious "denomination" that sees white Anglo-Saxons as God's "chosen people," the Jews as a Satanic race, and nonwhites as a lesser species of "mud people."

Like the neo-Nazis and the Klan, Identity groups vehemently oppose interracial marriage and homosexual relationships. Klan members pledge to uphold the principles of white supremacy and the purity of white womanhood.[90] They regard feminism as a "Jew-dyke" conspiracy against the white race.[91] In *The Turner Diaries,* a neo-Nazi portrait of the coming revolution, "White women who [are] married to or living with Blacks, with Jews, or with other non-white males are hanged with placards reading 'I betrayed my race' around their necks."[92] With this imagery, the neo-Nazis follow Hitler's edict that "marriage cannot be an end in itself, but must serve the one higher goal, the increase and preservation of the species and the race."[93] Despite such statements, women are active members of many hate groups, enjoying the white privilege and male protection they seemingly provide. We explore the complex links between racial and sexual politics further in the next chapter.

Many scholars treat political extremism as primarily a matter of style or tactics. They argue that extremism spans the spectrum from far left to far right politics—with lack of respect for individual rights and democratic processes as its common theme. Seymour Martin Lipset says, "extremism describes the violation, through action or advocacy, of the democratic political process." Roger Scruton defines extremism as "adoption of means to political ends which show disregard for the life, liberty and human rights of others."[94] Such definitions focus attention on the behavioral or psychological characteristics of individuals. As Daniel Bell puts it, "The way you hold beliefs is more important than what you hold. If somebody's been a rigid Communist, he becomes a rigid anti-Communist—the rigidity being constant."[95] Extremists are authoritarian, dogmatic, intolerant, and unreasonable individuals, the "true believers" of any ideology. Laird Wilcox argues that extreme positions can enrich debate, but extremists' style and tactics only impede it.[96] It is difficult, if not impossible, to argue effectively with condensation symbols! That is the point.

But by defining extremism as an illiberal style or tactic, scholars miss some important aspects of the phenomenon. First, as we discussed in chapter 2, liberals generally refuse to tolerate intolerance. But on what grounds? Isn't intolerance of intolerance also intolerant, at least in liberal terms? What allows liberals to claim political neutrality? Do they really occupy the "ever elusive" political center? Second, we now know that under certain conditions liberals' negative freedom may allow, even prompt, extremist responses. Not only have liberal democratic states constructed political enemies to maintain popular loyalty, but Italian Fascism and German National Socialism were, in part, reactions against liberal capitalists' self-interested individualism. Third, by emphasizing extremists' style, critics ironically may concede too much. In advocating a "politics of style," fascists reduce political issues to aesthetic concerns. Their opponents are obligated to argue against them on more substantive grounds. Yet liberals find it difficult to argue on principle, precisely because they are "tolerant."

It seems appropriate to ask whether American nationalism is going wrong because of a crisis in liberal democracy. David Calleo has argued that liberal democracies offer politicoeconomic stability only under certain circumstances: international peace and domestic prosperity. Writing in 1978, he feared that the United States—citizens and politicians —would refuse to adjust expectations to a new global reality in which more states compete for fewer resources. He feared that our present paralleled the Germans' past. As he put it, "for it is not to Germany that we would go today to find the most egregious examples of ambitions outrunning resources, nor, it might be argued, is it the Germans whose arrogant failure to adjust to a new world strains the international system beyond endurance."[97]

Neoliberalism is an ongoing attempt to adjust American capitalism to a new international order—and to prevail. Neoliberals emphasize the necessity of economic growth, renewed faith in national government, and continued technological progress.[98] They propose coordinated efforts by business, labor, and government on behalf of economic renewal and social justice. A central feature of their proposals is a coordinated industrial policy that identifies priority industries, pursues trade agreements, and rebuilds America's decaying infrastructure. Accompanying this is a renewed commitment to a quality education that includes communitarian themes. American neoliberals join the tradition of "societal corporatism" that began, according to Schmitter, in 1926 with John Maynard Keynes. Schmitter notes that Keynes "first debunks the orthodox claims of liberalism" when he writes, "it is *not* a correct deduction from the Principles of Economics that enlightened self-interest always operates in the public interest."[99] According to Keynes, government participation in economic planning was entirely consistent with capitalist and democratic principles, as long as representative institutions (in his case, the British Parliament) ultimately remained sovereign.

As we saw in chapter 2, Theodore Lowi argues that "interest group liberalism" (or "societal corporatism") has gradually eroded democratic institutions. Since neoliberals stress technical expertise, their rise to power is especially insidious. Bertram Gross dubbs technocratic politics "friendly fascism" to suggest the fuzzy line between societal and state corporatism.[100] But neoliberals have not gained widespread support from either the business community or the mass public. This distinguishes them, in important ways, from German and Italian Fascists. It is the "new right" that espouses an ideology of religious messianism, national supremacy, and natural aristocracy. If the neoconservatives can master the "American vernacular," as Charles Kesler suggests, and build a mass base in middle America among grassroots conservatives, then Calleo's fears might be realized. Could such an alliance be formed?

This question returns us to the psychological appeal of fascism. At the deepest level, symbolic politics addresses the psychological need for a stable identity. To a great extent, our identity has depended on the existence of an Other class, gender, nation, or race. That is, Americans have defined themselves by exclusion and domination —"we" are different from and better than "them." To dismiss hate crimes and hate groups as the style or tactics of psychologically disturbed individuals is to deny this deep-seated identity within many "normal" Americans. In her award-winning study *Women of the Klan,* Kathleen Blee acknowledges her discomfort when she could not easily regard her interviewee as an "Other."[101] Klanswomen were not fearful or hateful, but surprisingly "like" her, except for their racism. They obscured this with their "facile ability to fold bitter racial and religious bigotry into progressive politics."[102] I quote her conclusion at length:

The mainstay of the 1920s Klan was not the pathological individual; rather, Klan promoters effectively tapped a pathological vein of racism, intolerance, and bigotry deep within white Protestant communities. In this sense, the history of the 1920's Klan, though distant in time, is frighteningly close in spirit to the pervasive strands of racism and unacknowledged privilege that exist among dominant groups in the United States today.[103]

Milton Mayer's reaction to his Nazi "friends" was strikingly similar. Although Nazi anti-Semitism gradually took more violent forms after Hitler's election, they "knew" nothing about it, at least not with enough certainty to compel resistance.[104] Their lives continued as before, in many cases better than before. All they had to do was not interfere with the regime. They dismissed stories of the death camps as "enemy propaganda," perhaps because the horror was beyond belief. Though they felt sorry for their Jewish neighbors, they were primarily relieved that they were not Jews. As Mayer describes their quandary: "Responsible men never shirk responsibility, and so, when they must reject it, they deny it. They draw the curtain. They detach themselves altogether from the consideration of the evil they ought to, but cannot, contend with."[105] Partly in self-defense, they asked Mayer, "what would you have done?" In his preface, he answers, "I came back home a little afraid for my country, afraid of what it might want, and get, and like, under pressure of combined reality and illusion. I felt—and feel—that it was not German Man that I had met, but Man. He happened to be in Germany under certain conditions. He might be here, under certain conditions. He might, under certain conditions, be I."[106]

In the *Federalist Papers,* James Madison recognizes that constitutions, including our own, are only as good as their citizens. If liberals' center is to hold, Americans must reject the symbolic politics of superpatriotism. Though psychologically appealing, history shows that aesthetic politics ultimately offers neither safety nor beauty. To "know" this, Americans need to see the violence around them and find ways to build bridges across their differences. Writing about America today, the editors of *Klanwatch* echo Blee's and Mayer's insights:

We have dodged the most terrifying of all truths: that the problem of militant bigotry in America is *our* problem. It is not only the rural South that is the scene of brutal racial killings; it is Brooklyn, Portland, Raleigh—*our* towns. The hate that inspires these acts is not simply the product of a depraved environment or mental illness; it is the outcome of *our own* naiveté and neglect.[107]

In the next two chapters, we examine feminists' and environmentalists' attempts to develop other alternatives to personal and national identities based on the exclusion and oppression of an Other.

An Addendum: Ethnic Nationalism and the European Community

In December 1995 the Serbs and Croats signed the Dayton peace accord, agreeing to partition war-torn Bosnia into separate territories whose boundaries would be patrolled by a NATO peacekeeping force. The fate of the former Yugoslavia is an especially striking illustration of how the politics of nation-states is increasingly being supplanted by, on the one hand, regional and/or global organizations and, on the other hand, more localized ethnic-national movements. The 1990 declaration of the European Community ("Union" after 1992) that coincided with a resurgence of ethnic violence in former communist nations and the violent reaction of many European nationals to the presence of foreign guest-workers in their countries are other examples. What explains these simultaneous trends toward international coordination and ethnic fragmentation? What do both trends portend for the future of nation-states?

Although events continue to unfold, it is not too early to offer speculative answers to these questions. We began this chapter by distinguishing the nation, as a "felt sense" of communal identity, from the state, a governing body with a monopoly over the use of legitimate force within its territory. We saw that the term *nation-state* is a recent and a curious amalgam. Only since the late-eighteenth-century development of liberal democracies have nations been closely associated with states. Walker Connor argues that by "interutilizing," nation and state scholars obscure their very different meanings.[108] The Latin root of nation is *nasci*, which means "to be born of" and suggests "common blood ties." Few nations so defined—roughly 12 percent —have their own states. Instead, most nation-states are "imagined communities" or assemblages of many national groups.[109] They are created by a variety of political techniques, including educational, immigration, and linguistic policies along with more diffuse forms of socialization, including the symbolic politics of myth and ritual discussed above. What scholars frequently refer to as nation-building is, then, really state-building, and nationalism more accurately describes citizens' sense of identity with and loyalty toward their polyethnic state. In contrast, the Latin origins of the term *nation* suggest that it should be reserved for a "self-aware ethnic group"—with *or* without a state.[110] As Connor recognizes, however, ethnic self-awareness is a long-term developmental project that often initially proceeds through definition by opposition: "a group of people must know ethnically what they *are not* before they know what they *are*."[111] The territorial boundaries of a nation-state system have served to separate, and thereby define, the world's various people.

From this perspective, the ethnic unrest that accompanies the decreasing importance of European nation-states may reflect a human need for communal identity that cannot (yet?) be met by international organizations. Descriptions of ethnic-national politics as "neo-tribalism" recall Hannah Arendt's fear: when the moral responsibility of universal rights becomes too great, citizens may retreat to xenophobic, even genocidal, forms of self-definition. Fascist ideology may be seen as such a shortcut on the path to ethnic-national identity. It employs "fanatical devotion" to the state, or what we have called "superpatriotism," to compensate for the absence of a deeply rooted German or Italian national identity.[112] Not surprisingly, ethnic hatred is most virulent in Europe today where former communist regimes similarly supplanted processes of ethnic-national self-definition. In Yugoslavia, Tito's communist policies papered over multiple ethnic divisions to create a fragile Yugoslav nation-state. The current conflict is, in part, a return to the past, a resurgence of old hatreds left unresolved during years of communist rule. According to one author, "The mentality of Balkan warriors in 1995 is little different than it was in 1945. . . . Ask Bosnian Serb fighter Cvetko Kikic, for example, who started Bosnia's war . . . and [he] replies, 'The Vatican and the Nazis.'"[113] In Eastern Europe, territorial debates have emerged where state boundaries divided national groups, e.g., Hungary and Romania, and where national groups were subsumed under a single state, e.g., Czecho-Slovakia. The presence of significant Muslim minorities in former Soviet territories has also raised questions about their membership in the new European order, in short, about their "Europeanness."[114]

Problems defining the new European order only represent another side of the coin. According to Philip Schlesinger, the European Union offers the various peoples of Europe few "points of identification." This is especially true now that "Europeanism" can no longer be defined against an opposing "communist" superideology. The benchmarks of European civilization—market economies, civil societies, and liberal democracies—seem far removed from the politics of identity. Schlesinger expects crises of national identity from below to accompany the integration of the European Union from above. Although tensions between *demos* (universal rights) and *ethnos* (particular identities) can no longer be supplanted by nation-state substitutes, "the production of an overarching collective identity can only seriously be conceived as the outcome of a long-standing social and political practice."[115] For this reason, Schlesinger sounds a potentially pessimistic note: "collective belief in the virtue of a civic order ... does not seem to be the most compelling mobilising cry for Europe in the 1990s." Instead, "culture is ... going to be one of the key political battlefields in the 1990s."[116]

Other scholars offer more optimistic interpretations of recent developments. They suggest various ways ethnic-national groups might sustain a sense of identity in a new world order without nation-states. New communications technologies, like the Internet, may decrease the importance of geographical proximity for sustaining communal ties. They offer ethnic groups the (perhaps troubling) opportunity to live in two worlds, one foreign, one familiar, at the same time.[117] They also bring to the fore the tendency of nationalist movements to conflate cultural and political claims. According to Yael Tamir, the former is the essence of nationalism, not the latter. She argues that "at the core of nationalism lies a cultural rather than a political claim, that national movements are motivated by a desire to assure the existence and flourishing of a particular community, to preserve its culture, tradition, and language, rather than merely to seize state power."[118]

Tamir defends a liberal nationalism that recognizes the right of all ethnic groups to self-determination, including cultural representation in the public sphere. She distinguishes self-determination from the right to self-rule. Ethnic minorities do not have a right to determine policy within a nation-state. Nor do oppressed people have a right to their own nation-states. Liberal nationalism assumes that ethnic groups need not affect *all* levels of the political process to sustain their cultural identities. So understood, self-rule can only lead "either to a postnational, integrated, and peaceful world or to a Balkanised world of small states involved in relentless war."[119] Ironically, neither alternative adequately supports the right of ethnic groups to self-determination. In contrast, "ensuring the ability of all nations to implement their right to national self-determination would ... lead to a world in which traditional nation-states wither away, surrendering their power to make economic, strategic, and ecological decisions to regional organizations and their power to structure cultural policies to local national communities."[120]

According to Tamir, the tension between universal rights (*demos*) and particular identities (*ethnos*) begins and ends with the nation-state system. The decoupling of nations from states reveals global and local alternatives to a "virulent ethnocentrism." Tamir offers the European Community as a case in point. Unlike standard interpretations that stress its potential for international economic and strategic cooperation, Tamir argues that the European Community also provides a framework for cultural identity. Its institutional arrangements and current policies allow "different national groups a broad range of national autonomy."[121] This "alternative national view" is, she argues, the real legacy of liberals' respect for equal rights.

Notes

1. Hans Kohn, *Nationalism: Its Meaning and History* (Princeton, N.J.: Van Nostrand, 1965), 9. Kohn provides an excellent, though brief, history of nationalism.

2. Max Weber, "Politics as a Vocation," in *From Max Weber: Essays in Sociology,* ed. Hans Gerth and C. Wright Mills (New York: Oxford University Press, 1958), 78.

3. Kohn, *Nationalism,* 10.

4. Quoted in Michael Parenti, *Land of Idols: Political Mythology in America* (New York: St. Martin's Press, 1994), 38.

5. Ibid., 26.

6. Ibid., 38.

7. F.L. Carsten, *The Rise of Fascism* (Berkeley: University of California Press, 1982), 47.

8. Quoted in ibid., 80.

9. Ibid.

10. Benito Mussolini, *The Doctrine of Fascism,* in Kohn, *Nationalism,* 174.

11. Murray Edelman, *The Symbolic Uses of Politics* (Urbana: University of Illinois Press, 1972), 2.

12. Ibid., 6.

13. Ibid.

14. Ibid., 7–8.

15. Murray Edelman, *Constructing the Political Spectacle* (Chicago: University of Chicago Press, 1988), chap. 4.

16. Edelman, *Symbolic Uses,* 16.

17. Ibid., 18.

18. Ibid.

19. Ibid., 19.

20. Walter Benjamin, "The Work of Art in the Age of Mechanical Reproduction," in *Illuminations,* trans. Harry Zohn (New York: Schocken Books, 1969), 217–52.

21. Edelman, *Symbolic Uses,* 2.

22. Simonetta Falasca-Zamponi, "The Aesthetics of Politics: Symbol, Power, and Narrative in Mussolini's Fascist Italy," *Theory, Culture, and Society* 9 (1992): 80.

23. Ibid., 90.

24. Parenti, *Land of Idols,* 33.

25. Carsten, *Rise of Fascism,* 10. Carsten's account of the origins of Italian and German Fascism informs much of my analysis below.

26. Quoted in Leon P. Baradat, *Political Ideologies: Their Origins and Impact,* 3d ed. (Englewood Cliffs, N.J.: Prentice Hall, 1988), 253.

27. Adolf Hitler, *Mein Kampf,* trans. Ralph Manheim (Boston: Houghton Mifflin, 1971), 171.

28. Ibid., 180–81.

29. Ibid., 118.

30. Quoted in Carsten, *Rise of Fascism,* 30–31.

31. Quoted in ibid., 23.

32. Quoted in ibid., 34.

33. Quoted in ibid., 36.

34. Hitler, *Mein Kampf,* 308–27.

35. Milton Mayer, *They Thought They Were Free: The Germans 1933–1945,* 2d ed. (Chicago: University of Chicago Press, 1966), 51.

36. Quoted in Carsten, *Rise of Fascism,* 62.

37. The king capitulated before the famed march actually occurred. The Fascists then took the city without struggle.

38. Quoted in Carsten, *Rise of Fascism,* 75.

39. Benito Mussolini, "Fascism: Doctrine and Institutions," in *Dogmas and Dreams: A Reader in Modern Political Ideologies,* 2d ed., ed. Nancy S. Love (Chatham, N.J.: Chatham House, 1998), 441.

40. Benjamin, *Illuminations,* 241.

41. Quoted by Baradat in *Political Ideologies,* 240.

42. Quoted in Carsten, *Rise of Fascism,* 21.

43. Quoted by Falasca-Zamponi, "Aesthetics of Politics," 83.

44. Ibid.

45. Seymour Martin Lipset, *Political Man: The Social Bases of Politics* (Garden City, N.Y.: Doubleday, 1963), 148.

46. Hindenburg had appointed Hitler chancellor expecting him to govern in a coalition with the nationalists. Instead, Hitler called for another election. One week prior to it, the Reichstag building caught fire. The socialists were widely believed, probably incorrectly, to be responsible. Hitler used this incident, as well as general instability, as the basis for his request.

47. Hitler, *Mein Kampf,* 77–79.

48. Ibid., 88.

49. Ibid., 81.

50. Ibid., 91.

51. Ernst Hubber, a Nazi philosopher, as quoted by Baradat in *Political Ideologies,* 251.

52. Hitler, *Mein Kampf,* 394. I am indebted for this quote to Lyman Tower Sargent, *Contemporary Political Ideologies: A Comparative Analysis,* 10th ed. (Belmont, Calif.: Wadsworth, 1996), 202.

53. Hitler, *Mein Kampf,* 298.

54. Benito Mussolini, *The Doctrine of Fascism,* quoted in Kohn, *Nationalism,* 171.

55. Quoted in Roy C. Macridis, *Contemporary Political Ideologies: Movements and Regimes* (Boston: Scott, Foresman/Little, Brown, 1989), 215.

56. Mussolini, *Doctrine of Fascism,* 174.

57. Quoted in Falasca-Zamponi, "Aesthetics of Politics," 81–82.

58. Ibid., 82.

59. Quoted in Theodor Adorno, "Freudian Theory and the Pattern of Fascist Propaganda," in *The Essential Frankfurt School Reader,* ed. Andrew Arato and Eike Gebhardt (New York: Continuum, 1982), 128.

60. Mayer, *They Thought They Were Free,* 45.

61. Ibid., 50.

62. Quoted in Macridis, *Contemporary Political Ideologies,* 218.

63. Adorno, "Freudian Theory," 121.

64. Joan Tronto, *Moral Boundaries: A Political Argument for an Ethic of Care* (New York: Routledge, 1993), 58.

65. David Calleo, "The German Problem Reconsidered," in *The German Problem Reconsidered* (Cambridge, England: Cambridge University Press, 1978), 153.

66. Philippe C. Schmitter, "Still the Century of Corporatism?" *Review of Politics* 36, no. 1 (January 1974): 87. The list of ideologies is Schmitter's; I have omitted the individuals he cites as examples of each type, since many are quite obscure.

67. Ibid., 93. Schmitter distinguishes corporatism from pluralist, monist, and syndicalist forms of interest representation. For him, the most important comparison is between corporatism and pluralism. He defines the latter as "a system of interest representation in which the constituent units are organized into an unspecified number of multiple, voluntary, competitive, nonhierarchically ordered and self-determined (as to type or scope of interest) categories which are not specially licensed, recognized, subsidized, created or otherwise controlled in leadership selection or interest articulation by the state and which do not exercise a monopoly of representational activity within their respective categories" (p. 96). In contrast to pluralists' belief that "private vices lead to public virtues," corporatists rely on the guidance of an "authoritarian leader" or "technocratic planners" to unify society.

68. Mussolini, *Fascism: Doctrine and Institutions,* 440.

69. Ibid., 442.

70. Ibid., 436.

71. I am indebted to Roy Macridis, *Modern Political Regimes: Patterns and Institutions* (Boston: Little, Brown, 1986), for some of these details.

72. Mussolini, *Fascism: Doctrine and Institutions,* 441.

73. Ibid., 442.

74. Hitler, *Mein Kampf,* 297–98.

75. Ibid., 340.

76. V.R. Berghahn, *Modern Germany: Society, Economy, and Politics in the Twentieth Century,* 2d ed. (Cambridge, England: Cambridge University Press, 1987), 138.

77. Hitler, *Mein Kampf,* 209.

78. Quoted in David McLellan, *Marxism after Marx* (Boston: Houghton

Mifflin, 1979), 265.

79. Alex Callinicos, *The Revenge of History: Marxism and the East European Revolutions* (University Park: Pennsylvania State University Press, 1991), 86.

80. David Abraham, *The Collapse of the Weimar Republic: Political Economy and Crisis,* rev. ed. (New York: Holmes and Meier, 1986). Abraham identified five economic functions a liberal democracy must perform to reproduce capitalism: "(1) Guarantee of the organizational and legal principles of the capitalist system.... (2) Establishment and construction of some material preconditions for production.... (3) Occasional and regular participation and intervention in the course of economic activity and growth.... (4) Regulation of conflicts between capital and labor.... (5) Maintenance of the legitimacy of, and mass loyalty to, the social system as a whole" (pp. 5–6). Representatives of capital wholeheartedly support the first two, but some, if not all, may oppose the last three.

81. Ibid., 28.

82. Ibid., 37.

83. Ibid., 41.

84. Quoted in McLellan, *Marxism after Marx,* 139.

85. Charles E. Lindblom, *Politics and Markets: The World's Political-Economic Systems* (New York: Basic Books, 1977), 54.

86. *Klanwatch: Intelligence Report* 77, no. 1 (March 1995): 4.

87. Ibid. The figures cited are also from the *Klanwatch* project of the Southern Poverty Law Center. Their figures are compiled from direct reports, newspaper articles, and court cases. The 1991 Hate Crimes Statistics Act requires the FBI to compile figures on hate crimes; the first comprehensive report appeared in 1995.

88. Ibid., 9, 11.

89. Elinor Langer, "The American Neo-Nazi Movement Today," *The Nation* 251, no. 3 (16 July 1990): 82–83.

90. *Constitution and Laws of the Knights of the Ku Klux Klan* (Atlanta: Knights of the Ku Klux Klan, 1921), 5.

91. Helen Zia, "Women in Hate Groups," *Ms.* 1, no. 5 (March/April 1991): 23.

92. Andrew Macdonald, *The Turner Diaries,* 2d ed. (Washington, D.C.: National Alliance, 1980), 161.

93. Hitler, *Mein Kampf,* 252.

94. Both Lipset and Scruton are quoted in John George and Laird Wilcox, *Nazis, Communists, Klansmen, and Others on the Fringe* (Buffalo, N.Y.: Prometheus Books, 1992), 54.

95. Quoted in ibid., 55.

96. Ibid., 54–56.

97. Calleo, "German Problem Reconsidered," 209.

98. I am indebted to Kenneth Dolbeare and Linda Medcalf, *American Ideologies Today: Shaping the New Politics of the 1990's,* 2d ed. (New York: McGraw-Hill, 1993), 72–82, for this characterization of neoliberalism.

99. Quoted by Schmitter, "Century of Corporatism?" 108–9.

100. Bertram Gross, *Friendly Fascism: The New Face of Power in America* (New York: M. Evans, 1980).

101. Kathleen M. Blee, *Women of the Klan: Racism and Gender in the 1920s* (Berkeley: University of California Press, 1991), 6.

102. Ibid.

103. Ibid., 7.

104. For a discussion, again see Berghahn, *Modern Germany*, chap. 4.

105. Mayer, *They Thought They Were Free*, 76.

106. Ibid., xix.

107. *Hate Violence and White Supremacy: A Decade Review 1980–1990* (a project of the Southern Poverty Law Center, December 1989), 1.

108. Walker Connor, "A Nation Is a Nation, Is a State, Is an Ethnic Group, Is a . . . ," in *Nationalism,* ed. John Hutchinson and Anthony D. Smith (New York: Oxford University Press, 1994), 36–46.

109. The term comes from Benedict Anderson's *Imagined Communities* (London: Verso, 1991).

110. Connor, "A Nation Is a Nation . . . ," 45.

111. Ibid.

112. Ibid., 41.

113. John Pomfret, "Between War and Peace: Facing Up to the History of Hatred in Bosnia and Its Neighbors," *Washington Post Weekly* 13, no. 8 (25–31 December 1995): 7.

114. Philip Schlesinger makes these points in "Europeanness: A New Cultural Battlefield?" in Hutchinson and Smith, *Nationalism,* 316–25.

115. Ibid., 321.

116. Ibid., 325.

117. William H. McNeill, "Reasserting the Polyethnic Norm," in Hutchinson and Smith, *Nationalism,* 300–305.

118. Yael Tamir, *Liberal Nationalism* (Princeton: Princeton University Press, 1993), xiii.

119. Ibid., 151.

120. Ibid.

121. Ibid., 165.

7

Feminism

Advocating the mere tolerance of difference between women is the grossest reformism. It is a total denial of the creative function of difference in our lives. Difference must be not merely tolerated, but seen as a fund of necessary polarities between which our creativity can spark like a dialectic. Only then does the necessity for interdependence become unthreatening.

— Audre Lorde

Feminism in America: Past, Present, and Post?

In a recent symposium, "Let's Get Real about Feminism," sponsored by *Ms.* magazine, Naomi Wolf said, "something's not translating, and what is not translating has to do with the way in which feminism has been defined too narrowly."[1] Wolf's words capture what opinion polls have shown for some time. Three-quarters of American women support efforts to "strengthen and change women's status in society," but only 40 percent say feminism reflects their concerns, and fewer still, a mere one-third, identify themselves as feminists.[2] No wonder feminism has become "the new 'F' word." Yet a full two-thirds of American women say that the United States needs a strong women's movement to improve their status.[3] Gay Bryant, editor of *Mirabella,* responds to these figures by saying, "We assume our readers are feminists with a small 'f.' We think of them as strong, independent, smart women; we think of them as pro-woman, although not all of them would define themselves as feminists politically."[4] Susan McHenry, senior editor at *Working Woman,* addresses the discomfort with feminism by replacing the term "women's movement" with "women moving." She defines the latter as women "who are getting things done, regardless of what they call themselves."[5]

So, why doesn't "feminism" translate well? What is the problem? According to Wendy Kaminer, feminism suffers not only from a bad image but from an identity crisis. The feminist movement has yet to resolve the tensions—the phrases vary—between equality and difference, or rights and responsibility, or justice and care. Is it possible, many women ask, to be feminine and a feminist? Feminists' tendency to prioritize issues central to white heterosexual career women makes matters worse. As Gloria Steinem puts it, "The real opposition comes when you say, 'I'm a feminist, I'm for equal power for all women,' which is a revolution, instead of 'I'm for equal rights for me,' which is a reform."[6] To succeed, perhaps simply to survive, the feminist movement must learn to address the needs of more women. A reexamination of its history, especially its more exclusionary moments, provides a starting point.

The roots of feminists' current identity crisis run through the history of the American women's movement. In *Moral Boundaries,* Joan Tronto identifies a paradox the powerless often face when they try to convince the powerful that they too should have power.[7] Their arguments can take two forms: (1) include me because I am really just like you, or (2) include me because I am different in ways of value to you. Both strategies result in limited success, at best, for feminists. To see why, we need only ask: Which women are most like the men in power? Which women would powerful men value most? The answers: men in power value women who are similar to them or whose differences complement, without challenging, them. In either case, women are defined in relation to men and divided from each other.

The history of American feminism supports Tronto's insights. Standard sources organize that history into three major periods: (1) the early women's movement (1848–75); (2) the suffrage movement (1890–1925); (3) the women's rights movement (1966–present).[8] Within each period, while some women were struggling for equality with men, others were stressing women's differences from men. In various ways, this disagreement overlapped with other differences between women (i.e., by class, race, and sexuality).

Our first period begins in 1848 at the Seneca Falls Women's Rights Convention where American feminism became an organized movement. Seventy-four years had elapsed since 1776, when Abigail Adams exhorted her husband John to "Remember the Ladies" and declared we "will not hold ourselves bound by any Laws in which we have no voice or Representation."[9] Lucretia Mott and Elizabeth Cady Stanton organized Seneca Falls after they were prevented from speaking at the 1840 World Anti-Slavery Convention. Without a voice, they concluded that women could not work effectively to liberate themselves or others. In Seneca Falls, women wrote their own "Declaration of Rights and Sentiments," which amended Thomas Jefferson's words. They declared that "we hold these truths to be self-evident that all men *and women* are created equal." They then discussed the "history of repeated injuries and usurpations on the part of man toward woman, having in direct object the establishment of an absolute tyranny over her." A call for a woman's right to vote, to own property, to divorce, to attend college, to join the professions of law, medicine, and religion, and, more generally, to determine her own "sphere of action" according "to her conscience and to her God" followed.[10]

Throughout the mid-nineteenth century, American women organized to fight for the many rights they claimed at Seneca Falls. The women's movement only narrowed its focus to the suffrage after the Civil War. In 1866 Congress ratified the Fourteenth Amendment, giving black *men* the vote. For the first time, the Constitution specified that political representation was "for men only." During the congressional debates, Wendell Phillips, president of the American Anti-Slavery Society, opposed woman suffrage, arguing that "this hour belongs to the Negro." Elizabeth Cady Stanton replied, "do you believe the African race is composed entirely of males?"[11] At Seneca Falls, Stanton had described voting rights as "not even half a loaf . . . only a crust, a crumb." Now it became a higher priority. From 1869 to 1916, women waged suffrage campaigns in forty-one states with only nine victories. They gradually concluded that woman suffrage required another constitutional amendment.

A second period begins in 1890 with the formation of the National American Woman Suffrage Association (NAWSA). The NAWSA merged the National Woman Suffrage Association (NWSA) and the American Woman Suffrage Association (AWSA), suffrage organizations already involved in state campaigns. From 1893 to 1917, the NAWSA grew in membership from 13,150 to 2 million members. It received support from the Women's Christian Temperance Union (WCTU), which backed Prohibition and other moral reforms. The General Federation of Women's Clubs, which represented the multiracial women's club movement, also joined its ranks. So did other business, professional, and working women's organizations. Together these groups formed an alliance powerful enough to prompt passage of the Nineteenth Amendment.

Carrie Chapman Catt led the NAWSA to victory. But her winning strategies were very costly for American feminism. Antisuffragists often argued that women were not informed about politics and hence did not deserve the vote. One "anti" pamphlet read: "if the great mass of ignorant women's votes are added to the great mass of ignorant men's votes, there will be constant demands for work, money, bread, leisure, in short, 'all kinds of laws to favor all kinds of persons.'"[12] As we saw, Stanton's response was to stress how all women deserved equal rights. If women lacked information about politics, then they needed opportunities to learn. Given a chance, women, like men, would overcome their ignorance. According to Stanton, woman suffrage was simply an extension of liberal principles to all American citizens.

Catt's approach was more strategic and less ethical. She claimed not to know whether suffrage was "a right, a duty, or a privilege, but ... whatever it is the women want it."[13] To get it, Catt invoked a deeply prejudiced 1893 NAWSA resolution. It read: "in every State there are more ... white women who can read and write than all negro voters; more American women who can read and write than all foreign voters; so that the enfranchisement of such women would settle the vexed question of rule by illiteracy whether of home-grown or foreign-born production."[14] She combined this with other appeals to (some) women's differences (i.e., their moral virtue). Women in the social reform and settlement movements knew that without a voting constituency they had limited power over their elected representatives. Florence Kelly related Mayor Van Wyck's response to their appeals for more factory inspectors: "Ladies, why do you waste your time year after year in coming before us and asking for this appropriation? You have not a voter in your constituency and you know it, and we know it, and you know we know it."[15] Catt claimed that woman suffrage would force congressmen [sic] to support the Progressives' legislative agenda.

In 1920, Tennessee became the thirty-sixth state to ratify the Nineteenth Amendment. Harry Burns, who cast the swing vote, was later accused of accepting a suffragist bribe. He replied that he had voted as his mother said he should, adding, "I know that a mother's advice is always safest for her boy to follow."[16] Unfortunately, newly enfranchised women tended to vote like their husbands or fathers—if they voted at all. Following the suffrage struggle, American women were less unified and less visible in national politics. Although the National Women's Party continued to fight for constitutional equality, it only became the focus of a revitalized women's movement in the 1960s.

Three very different events begin this period. First, in 1961 President Kennedy created the Commission on the Status of Women, with fifty state branches, to report on the status of women's rights in Amer-

ica. Second, Congress included sex in Title VII of the 1964 Civil Rights
Act, prohibiting discrimination in employment, and the Equal Opportunity Employment Commission (EEOC) was created to enforce the
act. It failed adequately to do so. (Its first director, Herman Edelsberg,
claimed that "men were entitled to female secretaries.") Third, Betty
Friedan published *The Feminine Mystique,* naming the vague sense of
dissatisfaction shared by white middle-class women who were full-time
wives and mothers.

In 1966 these factors converged at the Third National Conference
of Commissions on the Status of Women. When its delegates refused to
consider a resolution to urge the EEOC to enforce sex discrimination
legislation, Friedan walked out. She decided to form the National Organization for Women (NOW). As its origins suggest, NOW has focused on gaining women equal rights. It led the unsuccessful campaign
for the Equal Rights Amendment, which reads: "Equality of rights under the law shall not be denied or abridged by the United States or by
any state on account of sex." An extended ratification period elapsed in
1973 with the amendment still three states short of the required three-
quarters majority. NOW has fought to protect abortion rights and, under Molly Yard, to form a third Women's Party.

NOW's orientation is liberal feminist, and it has been less than inclusive of lesbian and bisexual women, working-class women, and
women of color. As in earlier periods, another women's movement,
composed of many small groups, sustained more radical visions of
women's liberation.[17] These groups' members often found themselves
taking a back seat in the civil rights, ecology, gay and lesbian rights,
and peace movements. Refusing to be housewives to the revolution,
they formed their own organizations. Their feminism is associated with
grassroots politics, community issues, and holistic change. According
to Eileen Paul, NOW follows a white male model when it makes legal
change the first priority. In contrast, the base work she does involves
women from different classes and races in a shared process of social
change. As she puts it, "we came to it [organizing] as women, although
this doesn't mean it is the exclusive property of women."[18]

In *Women, Politics, and American Society,* Nancy McGlen and
Karen O'Connor argue that the gap between NOW's rights-based strategy and more radical groups parallels the nineteenth-century split between the NAWSA and social reformers. They see parallels as well between the decline of organized feminism in national politics from the
1920s through the 1950s and from the late 1970s to the mid-1990s. In
both cases, a period of successful reforms was followed by dispersed
energies. They also compare current antifeminist backlash, documented

by Susan Faludi, to the 1950s feminine mystique. Recent ties between feminism and the "recovery" movement, which portrays women as victims, a disempowering difference, unite backlash and decline in an especially disturbing way. According to Wendy Kaminer, "put very simply, women need a feminist movement that makes them feel strong."[19]

Although the 1973 defeat of the ERA and recent conservative trends have discouraged some feminists, McGlen and O'Connor do not think that we live in a "post-" or "anti-" feminist age. Many goals of 1848 and 1966—not to mention 1776—are still unmet. Americans also continue to express support for a women's movement to improve women's status. Feminists can reach their potential supporters with a new agenda that is less biased toward white women leaders' priorities. A recent study, the Women's Voices Project, identified combining work and family (30 percent), discrimination in hiring (20 percent), and low pay (19 percent) as the "biggest problems said to be facing *most women*." Working-class women and women of color in particular ranked these issues as very important. National health care was also a high priority. Abortion rights, child support, and crime ranked lower.[20]

McGlen and O'Connor see a clear message in these results. In order for recent events, like the *Webster* decision, the Thomas hearings, and the Clinton presidency, to remobilize American women, "I'm not a feminist, but . . ." must become the rallying cry of a new movement. A new feminist politics also would require new theoretical frameworks. To what extent can feminist theory meet the challenges necessary to revitalize feminist politics? What do those challenges reveal about how feminist theory too often replicates old oppression in subtler forms? These questions guide the rest of the chapter.

The Sex-Gender System

To understand feminist theorists' explanations of women's oppression in male-dominated societies, some basic definitions are required. Despite their differences, feminist theories have a common focus: the sex-gender system. This distinguishes them from the other ideologies we have discussed whose emphases are primarily economic, political, or both. As feminists' famous phrase "the personal is political" suggests, their theories question the distinction between public and private life that other ideologies, except anarchism, presuppose.

Feminist theorists tend to define sex in biological terms (i.e., male or female) and to distinguish it from gender (i.e., masculine or feminine, a closely related social construct). They do not argue that sex causes gender. Instead, gender is how women's (and men's) bodies are constructed and interpreted by society, that is, we expect males to be more masculine and females to be more feminine. Virginia Sapiro's definition of the sex-gender system conveys the complex interaction between these concepts: "the system or structure of roles, power, and activities predominant within a society that are based on the biological distinctions between males and females and further elaborated and interpreted through culturally defined gender norms."[21]

Recently, feminists have begun to explore more complex relationships between sex, gender, and other aspects of identity. They have begun to consider not only how gender is an extension of sex but also how sex is an interpretation of gender. According to Elizabeth Minnich, references to the sex-gender system tend to blur sex, sexuality, reproduction, and gender. To make male or female the basic characteristic of human beings is also to privilege heterosexuality as natural and to restrict women's sexuality to reproductive functions. As a result, "woman was seen only insofar as she was part of the condition of men's lives, locked on the biological or 'natural' level, denied the central defining quality of humanness." More bluntly put, woman is defined as "for-man" and "not-man," and denied any autonomous reality.[22]

Feminists' concern is how the sex-gender system expresses and reinforces male power. To understand this concern, we need to define another term: patriarchy. Heidi Hartmann defines it as follows: "patriarchy [is] . . . a set of social relations between men, which have a material base, and which, though hierarchical, establish or create interdependence and solidarity among men that enable them to dominate women."[23] According to Hartmann, the material base of patriarchy is men's control over women's labor—productive and reproductive. *All* men have this power over some women, in part because they define women by (hetero)sex or define heterosexuality as "normal." This allows *all* men to restrict women's sexuality (e.g., to monogamous heterosexual marriage) and to sexualize women's work (e.g., to caretaking professions, a mommy track, and/or childrearer and homemaker). Of course, all men are not created equal under patriarchy. Class, ethnic, and racial distinctions give some men power over other men, as well as "their" women. The sex-gender system is always inflected by other hierarchies, which affect men and women from different groups in different ways. Under patriarchy, however, men cooperate with one another in order to dominate women, despite other conflicts between them. Minnich sums up patriarchy in all its complexity:

> The peculiar construction of the meanings of woman-as-natural-creature whose essence is somehow expressed as it is locked into sex, sexuality,

and reproduction within a hierarchical gender/class/race system has perpetuated the root error of taking the few to be the norm, the inclusive term, and the ideal.[24]

Feminist theorists examine the interactions between class, race, and sexuality, which patriarchy often obscures.

We might briefly return to the suffrage struggle to illustrate the sex-gender system in operation. According to Aileen Kraditor, there were three related types of arguments against woman suffrage: (1) theological, (2) biological, and (3) sociological. (All three should remind you of conservative themes, especially Phyllis Schlafly's arguments.) The first type claimed that to grant women the vote would violate the divine order of nature. "Anti's" based this argument on biblical texts, specifically Genesis and St. Paul, which distinguish a male public sphere from a female private one. Woman's place was the home, where her role was to serve her husband; he was to protect their common interests in the outside world. In 1906, Grover Cleveland argued that by denying women the vote the United States followed this divinely ordained division of labor (except for Wyoming, Colorado, Utah, and Idaho, which were suffrage states).

Second, "anti's" argued that women's loyalty to family, a result of their biological functions, made them more emotional, intuitive, illogical, and hence unsuitable for political activity. These feminine qualities did have their place. According to one "anti,"

A woman's brain evolves emotion rather than intellect; and whilst this feature fits her admirably as a creature burdened with the preservation and happiness of the human species, it painfully disqualifies her for the sterner duties to be performed by the intellectual faculties. The best wife and mother and sister would make the worse legislator, judge and police.[25]

But precisely because of her feminine virtues, woman was a threat to political order. Her patriotic duties were best fulfilled by raising future citizen-soldiers (i.e., through republican motherhood). Some "anti's" also feared that women's "weakness, nervousness, and proneness to fainting" would be disruptive at "polling booths and party conventions."[26]

Third, "anti's" argued that political activity detracted from women's family responsibilities and was unnecessary for women to perform these tasks well. Kraditor quotes from a leaflet entitled "Household Hints":

Housewives. You do not need a ballot to clean out your sink spout. A handful of potash and some boiling water is quicker and cheaper.... Control of the temper makes a happier home than control of elections.... Good cooking lessens alcoholic craving quicker than a vote on local option.[27]

Good wives and mothers, this suggests, were the best social reformers, not members of the Progressive Party.

Today, it is relatively easy to see these arguments as expressions of patriarchal power, that is, men's attempts to control women's labor. Unfortunately, current analogues are less obvious, in part, because the sex-gender system operates to a great extent unconsciously. As Minnich puts it, they are both "out there" and "within us." This means that feminist theorists must simultaneously work inside and outside of the system they study. In different ways, their theories attempt to expose the seemingly "natural, neutral, and necessary"—sex-gender—as a construct of patriarchy.

Traditional Theories: Liberal and Marxist Feminism

"Traditional" may seem inappropriate as a characterization of any feminist theory. Yet liberal and Marxist feminism are traditional in two senses: they share the basic framework of their "parent" ideologies, and they would include women in it. In the introduction, we outlined a basic framework of political ideologies. It included four components: (1) a set of moral values; (2) a vision of the good society; (3) a critique of the existing society; (4) a strategy for getting from here to there. Traditional feminist theorists criticize the exclusion of women from liberalism and Marxism, but not the basic framework. They are examples of what Kathy Ferguson calls "me too" feminism.[28]

Liberalism and the Rights of Man

As we saw in chapter 2, early liberals were far from democratic. John Locke excluded women (along with children and laborers) from politics; they were among "those who cannot know and must believe." In his remarks on women's roles, Jean-Jacques Rousseau reveals how patriarchy benefits men. Women, he says, are "to please us, to be useful to us, to make us love and esteem them, to educate us when young, to take care of us when grown up; to advise, to console us, to render our lives easy and agreeable."[29] But we have also seen the democratic potential contained in liberals' principle of equal rights. According to Mary Wollstonecraft, the first liberal feminist and the author of *A Vin-*

dication of the Rights of Woman (1792), "the divine right of husbands, like the divine right of kings, may, it is to be hoped, in this enlightened age be contested without danger...."[30] When women demanded equal rights, liberals could not refuse them without violating their basic principles.

Liberal feminists' challenges to the "rights of man" begin with redefinitions of women's nature. According to Wollstonecraft, the nature that ill suits women for politics is an artificial one created by and for men. The ideal woman—by patriarchal standards—has only "negative virtues" (i.e., "patience, docility, good-humor, and flexibility; virtues incompatible with any vigorous exertion of intellect").[31] Wollstonecraft urges women to compete like men in the "race of life." By achieving economic independence, women can develop their potential for full rationality and, with it, political responsibility.

Although Wollstonecraft's argument is primarily rights-based, her focus on social conditions that inhibit women's development suggests utilitarian arguments for women's rights as well. A half century later, John Stuart Mill and Harriet Taylor developed those arguments further. In their *Essay on the Subjection of Women,* they claim that society cannot afford to waste the talents of half its members. They ask:

> Is there so great a superfluity of men fit for high duties, that society can afford to reject the service of any competent person? Are we so certain of always finding a man made to our hands for any duty or function of social importance which falls vacant, that we lose nothing by putting a ban upon one-half of mankind, and refusing before hand to make their faculties available ... ?[32]

Like Wollstonecraft, Mill and Taylor argue that the supposed "mental inferiorities" of women are the result of their limited opportunities: "they [women] have always hitherto been kept ... in so unnatural a state, that their nature cannot but have been greatly distorted and disguised."[33] Only after women have experienced equal rights can real differences between the sexes begin to emerge.

Betty Friedan, founder of the National Organization for Women, echoes these early liberal feminist arguments a century later. In *The Feminine Mystique* she portrays the "problem that has no name" as, in part, the juxtaposition of the talented individual and the successful woman.[34] The "feminine mystique" suggests that for women to gain education, independence, and equality with men is to become unfeminine. Real women, patriarchy says, are wives and mothers. According to Friedan, liberal feminists seek the "*right* of every woman in America to become all she is capable of becoming." As she puts it, "the real sexual revolution is the emergence of women from passivity, from thingness, to full self-determination, to full dignity."[35] This revolution need not pit women against men, but it does require changes in sex roles, namely that men assume equal family responsibilities and that women gain equal employment opportunities. NOW's legislative agenda, which includes support for affirmative action, day care, no-fault divorce, and comparable worth, as well as more controversial reproductive freedoms (i.e., public funding for abortion on demand), is directed toward this goal.

As the most prominent strain of American feminism, liberal feminism is also the most frequent target of attack. Many of the criticisms echo those against liberal ideology we discussed earlier. The central tensions of liberalism, between individual and community, between liberty and equality, and between groups and nations, also involve feminists in complex balancing acts. But some criticisms also reveal the limits of liberalism as a framework for liberating women. A major problem is liberals' somatophobia, or fear of the body, especially women's bodies. Liberal definitions of the individual as a rational citizen with equal rights ignore biological differences between men and women. Liberal feminism, critics claim, implies that real women are just like men. This feminist ideal excludes and implicitly denigrates those women who choose to bear and raise children. It also makes it difficult to take biological differences between the sexes into account when formulating public policy. Health insurance plans provide a striking example of how formal equality is far from neutral. Many health plans include maternity benefits, but they do so by defining pregnancy as an illness.[36] Once again, the healthy adult is presumed male.

Liberals' rights of man, even in their more inclusive feminist form, have quite limited applications. Liberal feminists' vision of liberation best fits the experience of the subset of women (i.e., white, middle-class, and heterosexual) on which it is based.

Marxist Feminism and Proletarian Revolution

Although Marx mentions reproduction (as well as production) among human beings' first historical acts, he never wrote a systematic study of relations between the sexes. That task he left to Engels in *The Origin of the Family, Private Property, and the State*.[37] There Engels undertakes an extensive survey of precapitalist forms of the family and society. He argues that the oppression of women is not a natural phenomenon but a historical one. It does not reflect biological differences between the sexes, but results from major changes in property relations. According to Engels, matrilineal right characterized primitive societies. A division of labor existed between the sexes that roughly corresponded to their reproductive functions. Women managed the household, while men hunted for food and protected the *gens*. These separate spheres had equal power. Since women held the family name, they may have been superior, at least in the household. Wealth increased in the male sphere with the beginnings of domestic agriculture, especially livestock. Now men wanted to control who inherited their property. To do so, they overthrew "mother right" and instituted a system of monogamous marriage. For Engels, monogamy refers to an economic relation in which men control women's sexuality to ensure the undisputed paternity of their heirs. In this system, a wife differs from a prostitute only because "she does not hire out her body, like a wage-worker, on piecework, but sells it into slavery once and for all."[38]

From a Marxist perspective, liberal feminists' proposals for equal rights are extremely naive. They ignore the many functions the patriarchal family performs in capitalist societies. These range beyond the accumulation and inheritance of private property. Women, as wives and mothers, also provide a great deal of socially necessary work without pay. They are a source of cheap labor, as short-term, part-time workers. In addition, a society organized in nuclear families has artificially high consumption, since each small unit needs a car, a home, a lawnmower, a washing machine. As the emotional center of many families, women also offer men a haven from the heartless world of economic competition.

A Marxist analysis suggests that capitalist economies simply cannot afford the legal reforms liberal feminists advocate. Comparable worth threatens the labor pool of less expensive women workers. Abortion rights undermine men's control of women's sexuality and, with it, their family responsibilities. Liberal feminism, Marxist feminists conclude, is a form of bourgeois ideology. It conceals the power relations that undergird equal rights and undermines the socialist revolution by dividing proletarian women from men. For Marxist feminists, sex-specific exploitation of women is a function of capitalism, not patriarchy. Lenin's (in)famous attack on Clara Zetkin is best understood in this context. To her insistence that the German Social Democrats consider "sexual issues," he responded,

> The record of your sins, Clara, is even worse. I have been told that at the evenings arranged for reading and discussion with working women, sex and marriage problems come first.... I could not believe my ears when I heard that. The first state of proletarian dictatorship is battling with the

counter-revolutionaries of the whole world. The situation in Germany itself calls for the greatest unity of all proletarian revolutionary forces. . . .
But active Communist women are busy discussing sex problems and the
forms of marriage—"past, present, and future." They consider it their
most important task to enlighten working women on these questions.[39]

Following Engels, Lenin argues that monogamy, as an economic relation, will be abolished only when women can freely join men in public
industry. Proletarian revolution, not legal reform, will accomplish this
goal. Socialism is the solution to women's sex-specific exploitation under capitalism. Yet "actually existing socialism" provided ample evidence that sexism postdates the proletarian revolution.

Like liberals, Marxists argue that women can, and should, be like
men, that is, proletarian revolutionaries. As a "me too" feminism,
Marxism also replicates the oppression it would overcome. Recognizing its limits, some feminists have examined the relationship between
sex and class—without subsuming one under the other. They call themselves socialist feminists to distinguish themselves from more orthodox
Marxists. Heidi Hartmann's definition of patriarchy discussed above
fits this approach. As a socialist feminist, she argues that patriarchy
and capitalism have a symbiotic or interactive relationship. They are
joined on many issues, but often with internal tensions. For example,
the wage differentials that accompany a sex-segregated workforce give
men, as primary breadwinners, some power over women's labor at
home and at work. But men's interests as capitalists and patriarchs are
at odds. A husband may want "his" wife to earn more money *and* to
be home with the kids more. Hartmann argues that these internal tensions are also flash points, potential sites of social change. She urges
women and (male?) workers to organize separately and collectively to
abolish patriarchy and capitalism:

> While men and women share a need to overthrow capitalism they retain
> interests particular to their gender group. It is not clear . . . that the social-
> ism being struggled for is the same for both men and women. For a hu-
> man socialism would require not only consensus on what the new society
> should look like and what a healthy person should look like, but more
> concretely, it would require that men relinquish their privilege.[40]

Marxism may identify what men and women should struggle
against, but it is feminism that suggests what they should struggle
for—a human socialism.

Although their analyses are more complex, socialist feminists also face the limits of "me too" feminism. My phrase "women and (male?) workers" above illustrates their problem. What, we might ask, of women who work? How are they oppressed? By sex? By class? With whom do they unite? Women? Workers? In order to be inclusive, "me too" feminism can only add up their oppressions. Nevertheless, as Elizabeth Spelman puts it,

> Selves are not made up of separable units of identity strung together to constitute a whole person. It is not as if there is a goddess somewhere who made lots of little identical "woman" units and then, in order to spruce up the world a bit for herself, decided to put some of those units in black bodies, some in white bodies, some in the bodies of kitchen maids. . . .[41]

To include women on these terms (i.e., as a sum of parts) is hardly liberating. According to Minnich, such feminisms internalize a model of the self that is liberal, modern—and masculine. The "thin self" becomes a "modular self," that is, a self of many units. Many oppressions are still omitted from the calculations (e.g., ageism, ethnocentrism, racism, heterosexism). With her brilliant title, *All the Women Are White, All the Blacks Are Men, but Some of Us Are Brave*, Gloria Hull reveals that existing categories *cannot* include black women's complex identities.[42] They, and many other women, do not fit into any single box.

Radical feminists, to whom we turn next, retain some aspects of the basic framework shared by Marxism and liberalism. They continue to regard one form of oppression as primary: sex supersedes class, gender, and race in their analyses. But radical feminism tries to invert the social order, rather than merely include women in it. Inversion turns out to be inseparable from transformation. Since their transformations often emphasize language, radical feminists also set the stage for postmoderns' analyses of feminist discourse. They reveal how all theories, including feminist ones, involve relations of power.

From Radical to Postmodern Feminism

According to radical feminists, the oppression of women is fundamental throughout human history. By *fundamental,* they mean that women's oppression came first, runs deepest, hurts most, extends farthest, and will probably last longest, since it is hardest to eradicate.[43] Radical feminists claim that every culture is really two cultures, a dominant male one and a subordinate female one. Men dominate women primarily by controlling their sexuality. They devise the sex-gender system, which limits women's sexuality to heterosexual and reproductive functions. Heterosexism makes relations with men crucial for women's fulfillment and divides women from one another, since they must compete for men. As Adrienne Rich puts it, "heterosexuality for women [is] a means of assuring male right of physical, economical, and emotional access."[44] Women's desires and pleasures have no place in this sexual imaginary, according to Luce Irigaray. As "the sex which is not one"—a hole/lack/slit—"woman lives her desire only as an attempt to possess at long last the equivalent of the male sex organ." She becomes "a more or less complacent facilitator for the working out of man's fantasies."[45]

She exists to satisfy his emotional, as well as sexual, fantasies. Patriarchy associates the following qualities with women: "weak, 'night,' passive, emotional, intuitive, mysterious, unresponsible, quarrelsome, childish, dependent, evil, submissive, etc."[46] Radical feminists do not argue that women should overcome these "negative" qualities, that is, become "just like men." Instead, they reconceive feminine virtues in ways that empower women. Lesbianism is their reconception not only of sex but also of gender, especially of the connection between women and care.

Caring activities are crucial for human life, but patriarchy gives care second-rate status. Care is women's work; it is self-sacrificing; it is confined to the private sphere or low-status jobs. Radical feminists argue that women should care for themselves and other women—instead of men. Lesbianism, then, means far more than sex between women. As Charlotte Bunch puts it, "to be a Lesbian is to love oneself, woman, in a culture that denigrates and despises women."[47] She identifies a lesbian continuum of women-identified-women whose explicit commitments range from personal relations to political action. The entire continuum is implicitly political, however. As the self-affirmation of women, lesbianism attacks patriarchal power and heterosexual privilege.

As we saw, radical feminists often draw on anarchist ideas in their political activities. They have formed mutual aid organizations run by consensus (e.g., women's health collectives, shelters for battered women). Radical feminists also have created worker-managed, worker-owned businesses (e.g., Holly Near's Redwood Cultural Work). Their opposition to sexual violence has ranged from direct action to legal reform. Radical feminists have staged "take back the night" marches and fought pornography as a civil rights violation. In most cases, their politics involves simultaneous efforts to separate from and to engage with the patriarchal system. The former strategy creates space where women are empowered, and the latter one increases pressure for social change.

Radical feminists' argument that "sisterhood is global" causes some critics to accuse them of overgeneralizing across cultures, of positing an "Essential Woman." Most recently, postmoderns have asked: are there women? They answer with a resounding no, except as culturally specific sex-gender systems construct them. Postmoderns suggest that "woman" is an assumed or imposed identity. "Women" who adopt it are in "drag."[48] By questioning the existence of "women," except as language constructs "them," postmoderns open themselves to attack as anti- or postfeminist. Their critics argue that feminists need the category "women," at least for practical politics. Without it, it becomes difficult to identify sources of women's (whose?) oppression and to organize a feminist (which?) movement against it. Nancie Caraway suggests that postmodernism be viewed not as a feminist theory but as an attitude or tendency within it.[49] From this perspective, postmoderns' concerns can inform feminists without putting feminism at risk.

But what is postmodernism? Its sources range from art to literature to philosophy, making any single definition seem woefully inadequate. Matei Calinescu identifies "weak thought" as postmoderns' common feature.[50] Postmoderns give up the pretense of "having a relation to values that is not governed by memory, nostalgia, supplication. . ." and they make an "effort not to impose [their] own 'rationality'" on society. They offer "a new framework for asking questions about modernity." Their questions include: What is a world? What kinds of worlds are there? How are they constituted? How do they differ? For postmoderns, worlds are constructed in/with language, that is, through concepts, frames, texts, and words. To question dominant constructs, postmoderns employ literary techniques more than philosophical ones. According to Calinescu, postmodernism is predominantly a style, which includes ironic engagement, narrative perspectivism, contextual interventions, and so on. Regarding feminism, postmoderns question the categories, "Man," "Woman," and "Sex-Gender." As Joan Tronto puts it, they show us why those categories often do not work well.[51]

First, as we have seen, traditional feminism presumes a "preexisting person unit"—the "thin self"—that is then classed, gendered, raced, and sexed. Postmoderns point out that this "preexisting person unit" is already defined in specific terms, that is, as an autonomous, rational individual. "It" is a modern—and male—subject. When feminists merely add the "woman unit" to "its" ("his?") attributes, they implicitly accept not only a male-defined self but also women's inferiority. Kathy Ferguson describes the standpoint of the modern male subject as "We are One and the One is Me." From this perspective, "woman" is an "Other" to "man." She can be other as opposite of him or in addition to him or both. But her self-definition as "otherness" simply mirrors "Him."[52] No wonder "me too" feminism cannot include many women's experience of selfhood.

Second, some feminists' tendency to overgeneralize about women, to essentialize "Woman," is closely related. As "Other" to "Man," women are defined by their sameness-in-difference from him. All too often, the sameness to which feminists point is women's identity as men's victims. More important, feminists who speak for women risk replicating the tendency of patriarchy to dominate an "Other." Only now the "Other" is those "Other Women" who do not or will not fit our category "Woman." As Kathy Ferguson puts it, postmoderns ask feminists, "Why not thematize the possibilities of participation in life with others who are neither identical with the self nor inferior to it?"[53] In other words, why not let "women" include the rich variety of women's experience and women's resistance—even under patriarchy?

By revealing the limits of "Man" and "Woman," postmoderns suggest that feminists must question the very categories of sex and gender. As we have seen, patriarchy invests these categories with great importance. To invert patriarchy, as some radical feminists do, is also to replicate it. Instead, postmoderns would explode the sex-gender system and, with it, traditional feminist frameworks. Only then can feminists challenge their identity as "not-men" and "for-men," and become women. Monique Wittig insists that "one is not born a woman," that male/female are social constructs, and that "a lesbian *has* to be something else, not woman, not man." "Lesbian," she claims, is the only concept "beyond the categories of sex (woman and man)." It destroys "heterosexuality—the political system based on women's oppression, which produces the body of thought on the difference between the sexes to explain women's oppression." It also creates "for the first time in history . . . the necessity of existing as a person."[54]

Postmoderns intend their criticisms of "Man," "Woman," and "sex-gender" to create space for a plurality of differences. They envision a society without top-bottom, center-margin, deep-shallow, inner-outer, nature-culture: without dualism as dominance. A postmodern feminism would disavow firm foundations for its vision of women's liberation, and it would oppose a problem-solving political orientation. It would tolerate "ambiguity, ambivalence, and contradiction" between, among, and within feminist theories. According to Kirstie McClure,

> . . . what is at stake . . . is a matter neither of explanatory adequacy nor of political efficacy as conventionally understood, but a matter of breathing room for the articulation of new knowledges, new agencies, and new

practices—a matter, in short, of working toward a new configuration of "the political."[55]

Yet many feminists disagree and argue that postmodernism undermines both the explanatory adequacy and the political efficacy of feminism. Without the collective "women," critics ask, what remains of feminism? Postmoderns themselves recognize the problem when they continue to deploy the category "women" for political purposes, referring to it as an operational or a strategic essentialism. According to Kathy Ferguson, feminists' real concern runs deeper: postmodernism cannot identify the differences that matter among women, and between men and women. Postmodernism, she concludes, lacks ethical and political direction.[56]

This raises more questions: Why did postmoderns begin to question the subject just when (some) women began to join men as political subjects? What of women who still live the "paradox of nonbeing"? Who have no identity to question? Who do not fit any of the boxes? Whose oppression is literally unspeakable?[57] Might postmodernism have a deeply classist, racist, and sexist subtext? Might it replicate its modern context? As Christine Di Stefano puts it, "it is as if postmodernism has returned us to the falsely innocent indifference of the very humanism to which it stands opposed; a rerun, in updated garb, of the modernist case of the incredible shrinking woman."[58] The postmodern rerun downplays the real costs of imposed identities and feminists' real need for theories to guide and justify political struggles against them. But postmodernism has influenced the kind of theory feminists seek. Many now are looking for nonessentialist concepts of women and posthumanist concepts of humanity. Only such concepts, they argue, allow genuine connections among different women. Not surprisingly, multicultural feminism provides a site for these new feminisms.

Multicultural Feminism and Coalition Work

"It [survival] is learning how to take our differences and make them strengths. *For the master's tools will never dismantle the master's house.*"[59] Audre Lorde's words have profound implications for feminist theory. What if the modern male subject *and* postmodern deconstructions of it/him are the master's tools? How can feminists avoid appeals to an essential woman *and* the "paradox of nonbeing"? Even to ask these questions is to begin to turn women's differences into strengths, as Lorde says feminists must. It is also to begin to explore what Donna Haraway calls "the spiritual and political meaning of postmodernism."

It is to recognize that "nobody is self-made, least of all man."[60] The question then becomes how "we" (any and all of us) can create a feminist movement with others who are neither identical to nor inferior to ourselves?

Nancie Caraway has suggested that feminists treat postmodernism as a tendency because it "lacks that quality of *soulfulness* which full-fledged political theories of recovery require...."[61] We might see multicultural feminism as bringing the soul back into feminism after postmodernism. Gloria Anzaldúa speaks in these terms in "*La conciencia de la mestiza*: Towards a New Consciousness."[62] She distinguishes *mestiza* consciousness from the counterstances more typical of the feminist theories we have discussed. The latter "lock-in" dualisms, joining oppressor and oppressed in mortal combat. Although such feminisms can be liberating, Anzaldúa argues that they cannot be a "way of life." The *mestiza* sees this because for her self—Anglo, Hispanic, Indian, lesbian, woman—"rigidity is death." She must learn to live on the borderlands, to cross over, to link people, to be a "total self," but without being a (w)hole.

According to Anzaldúa, "The work takes place underground—subconsciously. It is work that the soul performs." Her description of the learning process speaks directly to the problems of "me too" feminists' "person unit" with its/his separate parts:

> That focal point or fulcrum, that juncture where the *mestiza* stands, is where phenomena tend to collide. It is where the possibility of uniting all that is separate occurs. This assembly is not one where severed or separated pieces merely come together. Nor is it a balancing of opposing powers. In attempting to work out a synthesis, the self has added a third element which is greater than the sum of its severed parts. That third element is a new consciousness—a *mestiza* consciousness—and though it is a source of intense pain, its energy comes from a continual creative motion that keeps breaking down the unitary aspect of each new paradigm.[63]

Anzaldúa describes a consciousness that is not stable, simple, or safe. The new *mestiza* refuses the roles of subject or object "woman." Neither can express her body or her being: "In our flesh, (r)evolution works out the clash of cultures."[64] Yet Anzaldúa's consciousness is feminist. She claims that "as long as woman is put down, the Indian and the Black in all of us is put down. The struggle of the *mestiza* is above all a feminist one."[65] It is also a human one. The *mestiza's* flesh reveals that "all blood is intricately woven together, and that we are spawned out of similar souls."[66]

With her words, which I consciously quote at length, Anzaldúa challenges white feminists to the core. White women have not fought racism or homophobia with the same vigor as they fight sexism. Many nonetheless expect women of color to join with them as sisters in solidarity. The list of white feminists' betrayals and blunders goes on and on. White feminists invoked racism in order to win the vote. Margaret Sanger sought contraceptives partly for eugenics. Angela Davis names the "myth of the black male rapist" and challenges feminists to address not only rape but also fraudulent rape charges. Many women of color see involuntary sterilization as a more serious issue than abortion rights.

Elizabeth Hood states the problem starkly: "white women as a group continue to value their whiteness above their sex."[67] The writer bell hooks describes white women's racism in terms reminiscent of Anzaldúa's blood and soul. White women suffer from an "angel complex":

> You thought that you was more a white woman, you had this kind of angel feeling that you were untouchable. You know that? There's nothing under the sun that made you believe that you was just like me, that under this white pigment of skin is red blood, just like under this black skin of mine. So we was used as black women over and over and over.
>
> In the past, I don't care how poor this white woman was in the South, she felt like she was more than us. In the North, I don't care how poor or how rich this white woman has been, she still felt like she was more than us. But coming to the realization of the thing, her freedom is shackled in chains to mine, and she realizes for the first time that she is not free until I am free.[68]

Many women of color would still allow white women to learn to be their allies. Nancie Caraway calls this learning process "cross-over politics." By decentering the subject, postmoderns anticipate it, but it involves a different orientation. Following Bettina Aptheker and Elsa Barkley Brown, Caraway asks feminists to "pivot the center." Brown describes the process:

> I do not mean that white or male students can learn to feel what it is like to be a Black woman. Rather, I believe that all people can learn to center in another experience, validate it, and judge it by its own standards without need of comparison or need to adopt that framework as their own. Thus, one has no need to "decenter" anyone in order to center someone else, one has only to constantly, appropriately, "pivot the center."[69]

Caraway recognizes the limits of empathy, imagination, and perception. I cannot know "just how you feel" and to claim otherwise is to enshrine my (mis)understanding. Yet "cross-over politics" involves greater understanding than a liberal view of multiculturalism suggests. In chapter 2, we discussed Diane Ravitch's phrase "pluralism with unity," which characterizes liberal toleration as a balance of cultural pluralism and the public good. According to multicultural feminists, mere toleration of cultural differences will not suffice. It continues to conceal the ongoing oppression in our deeply classist, racist, and (hetero)sexist society. To "pivot the center" is to agree to see and to fight that oppression. It is also to begin to recognize difference as an opportunity for creative collective action.

Multicultural feminists suggest coalition politics as an organizing strategy for feminists. The identity politics, which liberals fear, not only involves an oppositional consciousness but also risks new exclusionary practices and cultural insensitivities—now from the margins. Nancie Caraway discusses the danger of "other privilege."[70] It manifests itself in the attitude that the oppressed can do no wrong. It can make white women, who would be allies, feel like they can do no right. This too silences women, though different ones. Caraway asks all women to be generous *and* accountable. This is the deeper meaning of Bernice Johnson Reagon's message that "we've pretty much come to the end of a time when you can have a space that is 'yours only'—just for the people you want to be there."[71] Spaces for those "just like us"—"homes"—probably were necessary, but we can no longer survive in them; they will be conquered and destroyed. Since culture crisscrosses sex-gender, the latter alone cannot create solidarity among women. "We are not from our base acculturated to be women people, capable of crossing our first people boundaries—Black, White, Indian, etc." "Women," she says, was only a "code word."[72] What will follow?

We began this chapter questioning claims that ours is a "post-feminist" age. A new feminist movement, we saw, requires a more inclusive agenda. Now we can see that it is possible only with a new consciousness beyond the self/other dichotomies of modern male theory and society. According to Reagon, the social movements of the 1960s, civil rights, feminist, gay/lesbian rights, antiwar and peace, have not failed, but they are stumbling: "The reason we are stumbling is that we are at the point where in order to take the next step we've got to do it with some folk we don't care too much about."[73] Will feminists take the next step? Of *real* coalition work, Reagon says, "I feel as if I'm gonna keel over any minute and die. Most of the time you feel threatened to the core and if you don't, you're not really doing no coalescing."[74] Yet it is also the only way to be—and stay—alive. To reinvoke Lorde, divide and conquer are the master's tools. It is in interdependency that feminists' courage, strength, and vision reside.

Notes

1. *Ms.* 4, no. 2 (September/October 1993): 43.

2. Quoted by Wendy Kaminer in "Feminism's Identity Crisis," *Atlantic Monthly* 272 (October 1993): 52.

3. Nancy E. McGlen and Karen O'Connor, *Women, Politics, and American Society* (Englewood Cliffs, N.J.: Prentice Hall, 1995), 304; Kalia Doner, "Women's Magazines: Slouching toward Feminism," *Social Policy* 23, no. 4 (Summer 1993): 41.

4. Quoted by Kaminer, "Feminism's Identity Crisis," 53.

5. Quoted in ibid., 56.

6. "Let's Get Real about Feminism," *Ms.,* 35.

7. Joan Tronto, *Moral Boundaries: A Political Argument for an Ethic of Care* (New York: Routledge, 1993), 14–15.

8. McGlen and O'Connor, *Women, Politics, and American Society,* chap. 1.

9. Abigail Adams, "Letter to John, March 31, 1776," quoted by McGlen and O'Connor, *Women, Politics, and American Society,* 2.

10. "Declaration of Sentiments," quoted by McGlen and O'Connor, *Women, Politics, and American Society,* 295–96.

11. Quoted by William L. O'Neill, "The Fight for Suffrage," *Wilson Quarterly* 10, no. 4 (Autumn 1986): 100.

12. Quoted by Aileen Kraditor, *Ideas of the Woman Suffrage Movement, 1890–1920* (New York: Columbia University Press, 1965), 31.

13. Ibid., 45.

14. Ibid., 131.

15. William O'Neill, *Feminism in America: A History,* 2d rev. ed. (New Brunswick, N.J.: Transaction, 1989), 54.

16. Quoted by O'Neill, "Fight for Suffrage," 99.

17. Jo Freeman, *The Politics of Women's Liberation: A Case Study of an Emerging Social Movement and Its Relation to the Policy Process* (New York: Longman, 1975).

18. Eileen Paul, "The Women's Movement and the Movement of Women," *Social Policy* 44 (Summer 1993): 48.

19. Kaminer, "Feminism's Identity Crisis," 66.

20. McGlen and O'Connor, *Women, Politics, and American Society,* 305–8.

21. Virginia Sapiro, *Women in American Society,* 3d ed. (Mayfield, Calif.: Mayfield, 1994), 65.

22. Elizabeth Minnich, *Transforming Knowledge* (Philadelphia: Temple University Press, 1990), 126.

23. Heidi Hartmann, "The Unhappy Marriage of Marxism and Feminism: Towards a More Progressive Union," in *Dogmas and Dreams: A Reader in Modern Political Ideologies,* 2d ed., ed. Nancy S. Love (Chatham, N.J.: Chatham House, 1998), 507–8.

24. Minnich, *Transforming Knowledge,* 125–26.

25. Kraditor, *Ideas,* 20.

26. Ibid.

27. Ibid., 24.

28. Kathy Ferguson, *The Man Question: Visions of Subjectivity in Feminist Theory* (Berkeley: University of California Press, 1993), 60.

29. Jean-Jacques Rousseau, *Emile,* quoted by Sheila Rowbotham in *Women, Resistance, and Revolution* (New York: Random House, 1974), 36.

30. Quoted by Alison Jaggar, *Feminist Politics and Human Nature* (Totowa, N.J.: Rowman and Allenheld, 1983), 28.

31. Mary Wollstonecraft, "A Vindication of the Rights of Woman," in *Philosophy of Woman: An Anthology of Classic and Current Concepts,* ed. Mary Briody Mahowald (Indianapolis: Hackett, 1983), 219.

32. J.S. Mill, "On the Subjection of Women," quoted by Jaggar, *Feminist Politics,* 178.

33. Ibid., 36.

34. Betty Friedan, *The Feminine Mystique* (New York: Norton, 1963).

35. Betty Friedan, "Our Revolution Is Unique," in Mahowald, *Philosophy of Woman,* 14, 18.

36. Alison Jaggar provides another example of the occasional absurdity of formal equality. In 1976, the U.S. Supreme Court ruled in *Gilbert* v. *General Electric* that the exclusion of pregnancy-related disabilities from GE's disability plan did not constitute sex discrimination. The Court reasoned that the exclusion was not in itself "gender-based," but only removed one "physical condition" from coverage. It seems the fact that only women experienced the condition was irrelevant (p. 47).

37. Friedrich Engels, *The Origin of the Family, Private Property, and the State* (New York: International Publishers, 1972).

38. Ibid., 134–35.

39. Quoted in Jaggar, *Feminist Politics,* 243.

40. Hartmann, "Unhappy Marriage," 517.

41. Elizabeth Spelman, *Inessential Woman: Problems of Exclusion in Feminist Thought* (Boston: Beacon Press, 1988), 158.

42. Gloria T. Hull, Patricia Bell Scott, and Barbara Smith, eds., *All the Women Are White, All the Blacks Are Men, but Some of Us Are Brave* (Old Westbury, N.Y.: Feminist Press, 1982).

43. Jaggar offers this interpretation of *fundamental* in *Feminist Politics,* chap. 9.

44. Adrienne Rich, "Compulsory Heterosexuality and Lesbian Existence," in *Feminist Frameworks: Alternative Theoretical Accounts of the Relations between Women and Men,* 2d ed., ed. Alison M. Jaggar and Paula S. Rothenberg (New York: McGraw-Hill, 1984), 416.

45. Luce Irigaray, "This Sex Which Is Not One," in *New French Femi-*

nism: An Anthology, ed. Elaine Marks and Isabelle de Courtivron (New York: Schocken Books, 1980), 100.

46. Anne Koedt, Ellen Levine, and Anita Rapone, eds., *Radical Feminism* (New York: Quadrangle Books, 1973), 342. Quoted by Jaggar, *Feminist Politics,* 250.

47. Charlotte Bunch, "Lesbians in Revolt," in Jaggar and Rothenberg, *Feminist Frameworks,* 144.

48. Christine Di Stefano, "Am I That Performance? Vicissitudes of Gender" (paper presented at the 1991 American Political Science Association Convention).

49. Nancie Caraway, *Segregated Sisterhood: Racism and the Politics of American Feminism* (Knoxville: University of Tennese Press, 1991), 60.

50. Matei Calinescu, *Five Faces of Modernity: Modernism, Avant-Garde, Decadence, Kitsch, Postmodernism* (Durham, N.C.: Duke University Press, 1987), 272.

51. Tronto, *Moral Boundaries,* 19.

52. Ferguson, *Man Question,* 54.

53. Ibid., 47.

54. Monique Wittig, "One Is Not Born a Woman," in Love, *Dogmas and Dreams,* 527.

55. Kirstie McClure, "The Issue of Foundations: Scientized Politics, Politicized Science, and Feminist Critical Practice," in *Feminists Theorize the Political,* ed. Judith Butler and Joan Scott (New York: Routledge, 1992), 365.

56. Ferguson, *Man Question,* 29.

57. Caraway, *Segregated Sisterhood,* 63.

58. Di Stefano, "Dilemmas of Difference: Feminism, Modernity, and Postmodernism," in *Feminism/Postmodernism,* ed. Linda J. Nicholson (New York: Routledge, 1990), 77.

59. Audre Lorde, "The Master's Tools Will Never Dismantle the Master's House," in *Sister Outsider: Essays and Speeches* (Freedom, Calif.: Crossing Press, 1984), 112.

60. Donna Haraway, "Ecce Homo, Ain't (Ar'n't) I a Woman, and Inappropriate/d Others: The Human in a Post-Humanist Landscape," in Butler and Scott, *Feminists Theorize the Political,* 88.

61. Caraway, *Segregated Sisterhood,* 60.

62. Gloria Anzaldúa, "*La conciencia de la mestiza:* Towards a New Consciousness," in *Making Face, Making Soul: Haciendo Caras, Creative and Critical Perspectives by Women of Color,* ed. Gloria Anzaldúa (San Francisco: Aunt Lute Press, 1990), 377–89.

63. Ibid., 379.

64. Ibid., 380.

65. Ibid., 383.

66. Ibid.

67. Fanny Lou Hamer, quoted by Elizabeth Hood, "Black Women, White Women: Separate Paths to Liberation," in Jaggar and Rothenberg, *Feminist Frameworks,* 201.

68. Ibid., 199.

69. Quoted by Caraway, *Segregated Sisterhood,* 192.

70. Ibid., 180–82.

71. Bernice Johnson Reagon, "Coalition Politics: Turning the Century," in *Home Girls: A Black Feminist Anthology,* ed. Barbara Smith (Latham, N.Y.: Kitchen Table/Women of Color Press, 1983), 357.

72. Ibid., 360.

73. Ibid., 368.

74. Ibid., 356.

8

Ecology and Ideology

We know that the white man does not understand our ways. He is a stranger who comes in the night, and takes from the land whatever he needs. The earth is not his friend, but his enemy, and when he's conquered it he moves on. He kidnaps the earth from his children. His appetite will devour the earth and leave behind a desert. If all the beasts were gone, we would die from a great loneliness of the spirit, for whatever happens to the beasts also happens to us. All things are connected. Whatever befalls the Earth, befalls the children of the Earth.

— Chief Seattle, 1855

Environmentalism and Ecologism

According to Andrew Dobson, "the first and most important point to be made about ecologism is that it is not the same as environmentalism."[1] Environmentalism refers to the wise management of the natural world for human purposes. Although environmentalists propose new policies, they do not require fundamentally new values. Most of the ideologies we have studied can incorporate environmental concerns without changing their existing frameworks. Unlike environmentalism, ecologism is an ideology of its own, one that challenges the dominant values of the modern Western world. Its etymological origin is the Greek word, *Oekologie,* referring to the "web of life," or the relatedness of things.[2] It is also associated with ethology (animal behavior) and *oekonomie* (household management). The ecology movement began in late-nineteenth-century Europe as a challenge to mechanism, the dominant scientific paradigm associated with Enlightenment reason. We have already seen how mechanistic science constructs a world of hierarchical dualisms—mind/body, matter/spirit, man/nature—in which interactions occur between discrete subjects that cause effects on discrete objects, and vice versa. In contrast, ecologism is organic or holistic and focuses on "energy flows within a closed system."[3] Among its central principles are "everything is connected to everything else" and "the whole is greater than the sum of the parts."[4] Ecologism portrays humanity as a partner with/in nature, not as its ruler or steward. It also sounds a warning call. As Chief Seattle put it, "continue to contaminate your bed, and you will one night suffocate in your own waste."[5]

Carolyn Merchant has identified three different ethics—egocentrism, homocentrism, and ecocentrism—that characterize human relationships with the natural world.[6] By applying her typology to other ideologies we have studied, we can further clarify how ecologism differs from environmentalism, and why ecologism is a distinct ideology. Classical liberalism is an example of egocentrism, the first ethic. In his famous chapter on property, John Locke declares "the Earth, and all that is therein, is given to Men for the Support and Comfort of their being." He continues, "God and his Reason commanded him to subdue the Earth, i.e., improve it for the benefit of life."[7] A century later, Adam Smith reaffirmed the "industry of mankind," which creates "a general plenty [that] diffuses itself through all the different ranks of the society."[8] Milton Friedman, Smith's heir, includes pollution among the "neighborhood effects" that the state should regulate. But he justifies government intervention on market principles, not out of a concern for environmental protection. As he puts it, "The man who pollutes a stream is in effect forcing others to exchange good water for bad. These others might be willing to make the exchange at a price. But it is not feasible for them, acting individually, to avoid the exchange or to enforce appropriate compensation."[9] From an egocentric perspective, the natural world exists for human use and profit.

The second ethic, homocentrism, still puts humanity on the top of the biological pyramid, but it also recognizes human connections with and obligations to "lower" life forms. Merchant portrays utilitarianism as a homocentric ethic. By employing sensory experience (a pleasure/pain calculus) in making decisions, Jeremy Bentham places human beings among the animal species. Still, John Stuart Mill insists that moral sentiments people cultivate in society are "higher pleasures" that anyone who has experienced both would prefer. Where utilitarians agree is on their basic principle: "the greatest good for the greatest number." It suggests that public policies should balance multiple interests, values, and, by extension, species.

Al Gore's *Earth in the Balance* applies utilitarian principles to environmental issues.[10] Gore discusses the disastrous effects of capitalist development on the natural world. Global warming, soil depletion, water pollution, species extinction, toxic chemicals, nuclear radiation, and so on, pose serious threats to the survival of life on earth. Gore argues that market principles and environmental protection are potentially compatible. If hidden costs are included in prices of products and standards of productivity, then industries that waste and pollute natural resources will have an incentive to reform. Citizens could also better determine the costs of "progress" and assess tradeoffs between their "standard of living" and "quality of life." As a collective response to environmental problems, Gore proposes a Global Marshall Plan in which wealthier nations support sustainable development in the Second and Third Worlds. Through regular summit meetings, political leaders would coordinate environmental policies to meet mutually agreed upon strategic goals. Gore identifies population control, appropriate technology development, new accounting methods, international regulatory agreements, and comprehensive educational programs among the most pressing current needs. Gore's homocentrism appears in his emphasis on shared management of the global environment to balance the needs of different regions.

Socialism and, to a lesser extent, anarchism also espouse homocentric ethics. By declaring that man is a "species-being," a "*corporeal*, living, real, sensuous, objective being," Marx places humanity in nature.[11] "Nature is man's *inorganic body*," but "man [also] *lives* on nature."[12] According to Robert Goodin, Marx applies his "producer-based" theory of value to nature.[13] For Marx, labor is man's "species-activity" and nature gains value as the object of human labor. "Nature fixed in isolation from man—is *nothing* for man."[14] Although Marx occasionally criticizes its effects on the environment, he associates industrial development with human progress, even under capitalism. He says, "subjection of Nature's forces to man, machinery, application of chemistry to industry and agriculture, steam-navigation, [etc.]—what earlier century had even a presentiment that such productive forces slumbered in the lap of social labour?"[15] Dobson argues that capitalism and socialism share the same "superideology" of "industrialism."[16] In this sense, both are homocentric, at best.

So are many anarchists, including some who claim to be ecocentric. According to Merchant, social anarchists continue to assume "a dialectic between society (especially economics) and ecology."[17] Murray

Bookchin's *Post-Scarcity Anarchism* illustrates her point.[18] Bookchin sees the hierarchical divisions of past societies as necessary results of scarce resources. In order to rule over nature, some men ruled over other men, women, and children. Modern technology now offers humanity the possibility of a society that not only overcomes scarcity (a relative condition, in any case) but also "transcends all the splits of the past."[19] According to Bookchin, "postscarcity society ... is the fulfillment of the social and cultural potentialities latent in a technology of abundance."[20] Neither capitalism nor socialism can fulfill this potential. The former is increasingly irrational in its attempts "to uphold scarcity, toil, poverty, and subjugation against the growing potential for postscarcity, leisure, abundance, and freedom."[21] The latter continues "to loiter ... around the issues of a 'planned economy' and a 'socialist state'—issues created by an earlier stage of capitalism and by a lower stage of technological development.... "[22] Bookchin is an anarchist in his commitment to a "wholistic" revolution to be followed by a "stateless, classless, decentralized society."[23] As a step toward revolution, he counsels "dropping out" as a "mode of dropping in—into the tentative, experimental, and as yet highly ambiguous social relations of utopia."[24] Bookchin's ecological utopia is not a "return to [man's] ancestral immediacy with nature," however. Return is neither possible nor desirable: "Whether now or in the future, human relationships with nature are always mediated by science, technology, and knowledge."[25] By assuming that humanity is separate from nature, and seeking a balance between human and natural needs, Bookchin remains homocentric.

"We do not seek a 'back to nature' movement; instead we emphasize the realization that we can never leave nature."[26] With these words, Jan Hartke conveys the essence of ecocentrism. Humanity and the societies we create are inextricable parts of the natural world. Of the ideologies we have studied, conservatism and fascism might initially seem ecocentric. Conservatives emphasize the limits of reason, the complexity of life, the need for balance, and the ties between generations. Nevertheless, economic conservatism parallels the egocentrism of classical liberalism. Social conservatives' commitment to "natural aristocracy" also violates the egalitarian orientation of an ecological perspective.[27] With fascism, the case is less clear. Anna Bramwell identifies a "green streak in Nazism."[28] She traces the origins of ecologism to late-nineteenth-century German vitalism (or *lebensphilosophie),* which influenced Nazi ideology with its emphasis on "being versus thinking." In idealizing rural life, criticizing modern culture, and appealing to natural laws, fascism resembles ecocentrism, and vice versa. But ecologists' monism—"the oneness of life"—is the most disturbing parallel, according to Bramwell. By blurring boundaries between nature, self, and society, ecocentrism may legitimate authoritarian politics. As we later see, the democratic politics of the Green movement calls Bramwell's argument into question. Holism (the recognition of interdependence) also differs from monism (the obliteration of difference.) Ecologists' emphasis on species survival counters the tendencies some have toward romantic idealism.

Among the ideologies we have studied, some feminisms are closest to ecocentrism. Not all, however. Liberal, socialist, and radical feminisms often replicate, as well as reverse, the dualities and hierarchies of male-ordered ideologies. In contrast, ecofeminism stresses "the interrelationship and unity of all life on earth."[29] Ynestra King describes its ethos: "it's a way of being which understands there are connections between all living things and indeed we women are the fact and flesh of connectedness ... feminism and ecology are where politics come face to face with biology, and where the spiritual and the political come together."[30] According to ecofeminists, the domination of nature and the domination of women are closely connected. "Women and nature are the original 'others' in patriarchy—those who are feared, the reminders of mortality, those who must be objectified and dominated."[31] Some feminists fear that ecologists' celebration of women and nature only replicates patriarchal constructions of women as mothers. For others, ecologists' emphasis on overcoming all forms of oppression, including the control of "Man" over "Nature," is a positive step. Not surprisingly, anarchafeminism and multicultural feminism, which emphasize difference(s), have the strongest ties to ecocentrism.

With the exception of feminism, ecologism evades the categories of other ideologies, as well as standard right/left political formulas. Of efforts to classify ecologists, Bramwell says, "they sit stubbornly in their pro-nature box while political categories swirl around them."[32] Unlike environmentalism, ecologism is not easily incorporated by other ideologies. As a critique of mechanistic science, industrial development, and hierarchical politics, it is an ideology in its own right. In the next section, we explore the role of ecocentric values in Green politics.

Shades of Green: A Brief History

It is difficult to give the emergence of Green politics an exact date. Many "Big Ten" environmental organizations, such as the Sierra Club and the National Audubon Society, originated in the late nineteenth century and influenced the early-twentieth-century Progressive Movement.[33] Then, as now, they appealed to middle-class supporters, engaged in interest-group politics, and cooperated with major corporations. Emphasizing the preservation of natural resources for human use, they employ(ed) a homocentric ethic.

In 1962, Rachel Carson's *Silent Spring* focused public attention on the potentially disastrous effects of chemical insecticides on the planetary ecosystem.[34] Carson attacked the arrogance of human efforts to alter natural balances that have evolved over the ages, and she stressed the duty of humanity to live in harmony with other species. During the 1960s, Aldo Leopold's earlier argument for a "land ethic" was also rediscovered.[35] Like Carson, Leopold portrays humanity as "member and citizen" of the earth, not its "conqueror." By accepting our obligation to the land and the life it sustains, humanity can take the next step in its ethical evolution. We can transcend a strictly economic relationship to land-as-property and recognize that we belong to a larger land-community. Echoing Kropotkin, Leopold describes a land ethic as "a kind of community instinct in-the-making."[36] He proposes the following approach to environmental issues: "Examine each question in terms of what is ethically and esthetically right, as well as what is economically expedient. A thing is right when it tends to preserve the integrity, stability, and beauty of the biotic community. It is wrong when it tends otherwise."[37]

Carson's and Leopold's ecocentrism influenced a variety of single-issue, grassroots groups that emerged with other social movements of the 1960s. Many have anarchist roots and employ direct-action techniques. In 1976 the Clamshell Alliance formed to oppose construction of the Seabrook nuclear power plant in New Hampshire. "The Clams" brought the antinuke movement national attention when they occupied the Seabrook site using nonviolent tactics and anarchist politics.[38] In the early 1980s, Earth First began to engage in peaceful forms of civil disobedience and more controversial tactics, like "monkeywrenching." Earth First claims that monkeywrenching, including tree-spiking, is nonviolent, since "it is aimed at inanimate machines and tools." David Foreman, its founder, states his ecocentrism in radical terms: "I am a product of the Pleistocene epoch, the age of large mammals. . . . I do not want to live in a world without jaguars and great blue whales and redwoods and rain forests. . . . I only have meaning *in situ,* in the age I live in, the late Pleistocene."[39]

Ecocentrism gained international prominence with the 1983 electoral success of the German Greens. Today, many Western democracies have Green parties or movements. *Die Grünen* began in 1968 as a social movement engaged in direct action on local issues. In 1979, they founded a political party and in 1983 gained 5.6 percent of the vote, earning them twenty-seven seats in the West German National Assembly. They won on a party platform with "four main pillars: (1) Ecology; (2) Social Justice; (3) Grassroots Democracy; (4) Nonviolence." To these four pillars, they add "six additional principles: (5) Decentralization; (6) Community-based Economics; (7) Postpatriarchal Principles; (8) Respect for Diversity; (9) Global Responsibility; (10) Future Focus."[40] As this comprehensive program suggests, "Green politics is not only different in *what* it has to say: it is equally different in the *way* it says it."[41] According to Robert Goodin, "what" differs is the Greens' "natural resource-based theory of value." The assumption that nature has some intrinsic value, independent of human use, undergirds the Green platform. They are neither a "single-issue" nor a "catchall" party.[42] Ecocentrism unifies their many policy positions, which together pose a fundamental challenge to current values. For example, the Greens link their positions on ecology, feminism, and democracy, since all concern human survival. A relevant plank reads: "The aim of the Greens is a humane society built on complete equality of the sexes in the context of an overall ecological policy. Carrying through this survival policy will require the utmost participation of women in safeguarding the life of the next generation together with men in the political arena."[43]

Jonathan Porritt's description of the contrast between traditional Bundestag members "soberly dressed in black" and the Greens, who "decided not only to wear their ordinary, everyday clothes, but to bring with them some symbolic token of the Earth itself, a small tree or plant" illustrates the "way" they differ from other parties. More seriously put, the Greens' "theory of value" implies a "theory of agency."[44] They regard ecocentric politics as inseparable from participatory democracy. As Porritt puts it, "the exploitation of the biosphere is inextricably linked to the exploitation of people; to fight for the rights of those people, one must fight for the rights of the planet."[45] In other platform planks, Greens defend the rights of old people, children, immigrants, sexual outsiders, and the disabled. They also mandate rotation of offices, open party meetings, citizen initiatives, and decentralized administration. Their Preamble reads: "we need a political movement in which the interrelated values of human solidarity and democracy are fundamental, and which thoroughly repudiates a way of thinking oriented to output and hierarchy and governed by lethal competition."[46]

Scholars disagree about the future implications of the connections Greens make between ecological values and political processes. Although their platform proposals are not easily co-opted by other parties, the Greens' unified vision does limit their political options. The Greens have also had numerous problems coordinating party activities. These suggest to some that their grassroots approach is impractical, at least, in national and international politics. Following their 1983 electoral success, the Greens split into two camps over political strategy. "Realos" worked within the existing system, forming red/green coalitions. "Fundis" continue to insist that Green values also require radical changes in political processes. On the assumption that outcomes supersede processes, Goodin urges the Greens to work in coalition with other parties.[47]

The debate between "fundis" and "realos" in the German Greens reflects a choice facing the larger movement today. Pale greens support "a cleaner service economy, sustained by cleaner technology and producing cleaner affluence" to "fix" the environment.[48] A darker "green politics explicitly seeks to decentre the human being, to question mechanistic science and its technological consequences, to refuse to believe that the world was made for human beings—and it does this because it has been led to wonder whether dominant post-industrialism's project of material affluence is either desirable or sustainable."[49] The choice is clear: either human reason controls the natural world or human beings apply "nature's lessons" to modern life. According to Merchant, "the environment movement in the 1990s has arrived at a crossroads."[50] Environmentalists travel one road, to the right. Ecologists travel another, to the left. The second road has many sideroads, for example, deep ecology, ecofeminism, "fundi" Green, and social ecology. Merchant also identifies a third way: "at the center of the crossroads, a new road is still in the planning stage."[51] This road leads to the future, and its builders say, "we are neither left nor right, we are in front."[52] It is here—at the crossroads—where the greatest challenge to modern politics is found.

Ecology and Ideology

Nature poses that challenge to humanity. According to Dobson, the natural world teaches ecologists four lessons applicable to modern politics.[53] First, stability is a function of diversity. He says, "the 'healthy society' (organic metaphor intended) is one in which a range of opinions is not only tolerated but celebrated, in that this provides for a repository of ideas and forms of behaviour from which to draw when confronted with political or social problems."[54] By extension, active, broad participation makes adequate debate, wise policy, and genuine consent possible in politics. Second, the interdependence of life forms suggests the equality of all beings. Only an abstract or "thin" self could feign autonomy from and superiority over its bodily existence. Ecocentrism serves to remind humanity that life is a universal value. Nature places the burden of proof on those who oppose the basic equality of being(s). Third, nature teaches respect for what endures or survives over time. Compared to natural history, human history is all too brief and much too bold. Ecologists caution mankind to "live with, rather than against, the natural world."[55] This means living with other communities, instead of imposing our relatively recent ways on them. Fourth, nature is "female" or, more precisely, the giving and nurturing of life is associated with the "feminine." As we saw, some feminists challenge this teaching as a cultural stereotype. Others embrace it out of respect for the fertility of Mother Earth.

To explore fully the meaning of these natural lessons for modern politics would require another book. But we might conclude by considering some of their implications for the study of ideology. The first lesson—diversity yields stability—directly relates to definitions of ideology, especially pejorative ones. Used pejoratively, ideology refers to deceptive or dogmatic belief systems. The negative connotations of the term have arisen, in part, from the role ideology plays in politics. As Daniel Bell says, "ideology is the conversion of ideas into social levers."[56] As ideology, ideas are converted into bases for action, the essence of politics. This conversion process requires that ideas assume relatively fixed, even simplified, meanings. Michael Freeden refers to ideologies as "configurations of *decontested* meanings" and says their purpose is to "cement the word-concept relationship."[57] To extend the metaphor, nature provides many kinds of glue. The NASA scientist charged with inventing a spaceworthy superglue "failed" completely —and developed the adhesive now used on "post-it" notes. Perhaps the "cement" of ideologies only "posts" our current values. By temporarily fixing meanings, ideologies enable collective action. Those meanings also remain open to other ideas from other contexts.

A likely objection to this argument runs, "that's not ideology any more, is it?" or "that's the end of ideology again, isn't it?" But nature's second and third lessons remind us that living things are interdependent and ephemeral. According to Habermas, human beings possess the unique capacity to reflect on their values, when necessary, to modify or replace them. The capacity to reflect is primarily mental, but people separate it from physical existence at their peril. Freeden chooses a biological term—morphology—to characterize the structure of an ideology.[58] With this, he implies that human ideas, like human beings, live and die. As "decontested meanings," ideologies are of temporary, sometimes momentary, significance. To admit this does not mean the "end of ideology," but it does situate ideology in history. In response to postmodern attacks on "essentialism," Elizabeth Minnich defends what we have called "decontested meanings," even "ideological" claims to universality. She says, "it may not be universals that are the problem but, simply and profoundly, *faulty* universals and the particularities they frame."[59] She urges humanity to "risk" universalizing:

> A universal idea of humankind ... is useful, perhaps particularly on a moral level, as long as we remember that no content it has yet had is adequately inclusive, on the one hand, and that even much more inclusive thinking cannot "fill" an idea that is inspirational, regulative, evocative—that raises rather than answers questions.[60]

In studying ideologies, we have considered their uses (and abuses) through history. That knowledge should enable you to "begin to rethink what universals are *for,* and when and how we wish to use rather than submit to them."[61]

This brings us to the fourth lesson from nature: the "feminine" quality of giving and nurturing life. All the ideologies we discussed had their moments of openness—and closure. The latter emerged most clearly in their negative remarks on ideology per se. Each ideology we studied accused others of being "ideological" and denied its own status as ideology. Liberals sought an "elusive center" to avoid the "curse of either/or" and simultaneously espoused a market model of political freedom. Conservatives defended the "familiar present" against "metaphysical abstractions," but their "nonideational ideology" conveniently affirmed their privileges. Socialists attacked "bourgeois ideology" as false consciousness and distinguished it from their materialist science of proletarian revolution. Anarchists refused to prescribe the new social order, but they maintained a perfectionist idea of human freedom. Fascists consciously created a mythical politics and claimed that war between nations or races was the essence of life. Feminists attacked dualisms and hierarchies, but often continued to construct all men and some women as "Others."

Nonetheless, feminist impulses came closest to remaining open to life—nature's fourth lesson. According to Kathy Ferguson, "one of the goals of feminist discourse ... is, in Foucault's words, to 'call into question our will to truth, [and] restore to discourse its character as an event.'"[62] To achieve this goal, feminists try to resist their own will to truth, to refuse to privilege women's experience. In Ursula King's words, "seen in its widest dimension, feminism is ultimately a challenge to reflect on what it means to be human today in quite new ways and under new conditions."[63] For Susan Griffin, this is how a theory differs from an ideology:

> . . . when a theory is transformed into an ideology, it begins to destroy the self and self-knowledge. Originally born of feeling, it pretends to float above and around feeling. Above sensation. It organizes experience according to itself, without touching experience. By virtue of being itself, it is supposed to know. To invoke the name of this ideology is to confer truthfulness. No one can tell it anything new. Experience ceases to surprise it, inform it, transform it. It is annoyed by any detail which does not fit into its worldview. Begun as a way to restore one's sense of reality, now it attempts to discipline real people, to remake natural beings after its own image. All that it fails to explain it records as dangerous. Begun as a theory of liberation, it is threatened by new theories of liberation; slowly, it builds a prison for the mind.[64]

So defined, ideology deserves the negative connotations attributed to it.

Nevertheless, its original meaning combined the "will to truth" of mechanistic science with the participatory ethos of democratic politics. The new science of ecology that stresses "webs of life" better characterizes the relationship between democracy and ideology. It replaces Destutt de Tracy's self-evident truths with "webs of meaning" created through democratic discourse.[65] As shared meanings, ideologies simultaneously order democratic politics and touch citizens' lives. In doing so, they can counter the despair modern citizens feel over the unreality of "democratic" politics. As we saw, Vaclav Havel warned Western democracies: those who "live within a lie" do not live in harmony—with themselves or others. For Havel, ideology "offers human beings the illusion of an identity, of dignity, and of morality while making it easier for them to *part* with them."[66] But the alternative—"to live within *the* truth"—is no longer available to us. At best, we can continually question our "will to truth" and continually create new "webs of meaning." When they are understood this way, political ideologies can continue to infuse our politics with hope for life.

Notes

1. Quoted in Andrew Dobson, *Green Political Thought: An Introduction* (Boston: Unwin Hyman, 1990), 13.

2. Anna Bramwell, *Ecology in the 20th Century: A History* (New Haven: Yale University Press, 1989), chap. 1, p. 14.

3. Ibid., 4.

4. Carolyn Merchant, *Radical Ecology: The Search for a Livable World* (New York: Routledge, 1992), 64–65.

5. Quoted in Ed McGaa, *Mother Earth Spirituality: Native American Paths to Healing Ourselves and Our World* (San Francisco: HarperCollins, 1990), xii.

6. Merchant, *Radical Ecology*, chap. 2.

7. John Locke, *The Second Treatise of Government*, in *Two Treatises of Government*, ed. Peter Laslett (New York: Cambridge University Press, 1963), 26, 32.

8. Adam Smith, *The Wealth of Nations*, ed. Edwin Cannan (New York: Modern Library, 1937), 11.

9. Milton Friedman, *Capitalism and Freedom* (Chicago: University of Chicago Press, 1962), 30.

10. Al Gore, *Earth in the Balance: Ecology and the Human Spirit* (New York: Penguin, 1993).

11. Karl Marx, *Economic and Philosophical Manuscripts of 1844*, in *The Marx-Engels Reader*, 2d ed., ed. Robert C. Tucker (New York: Norton, 1978), 115.

12. Ibid., 75.

13. Robert E. Goodin, *Green Political Theory* (Cambridge, England: Polity Press, 1992), chap. 2. Goodin distinguishes "three distinct bases on which we might ground a theory of value—consumer satisfaction, labour inputs, or natural resource inputs. These options correspond to a 'capitalist' theory of value, a 'Marxist' theory of value, and a 'green' theory of value, respectively" (p. 22).

14. Marx, *Economic and Philosophical Manuscripts*, 124.

15. Karl Marx, *Manifesto of the Communist Party*, in Tucker, *Marx-Engels Reader*, 477.

16. Dobson, *Green Political Thought*, 29–30.

17. Merchant, *Radical Ecology*, 146.

18. Murray Bookchin, *Post-Scarcity Anarchism* (Berkeley, Calif.: Ramparts Press, 1971).

19. Ibid., 18.

20. Ibid., 11.

21. Ibid., 15.

22. Ibid., 13.

23. Ibid., 18.

24. Ibid., 16.

25. Ibid., 21.

26. Quoted in McGaa, *Mother Earth Spirituality*, xv.

27. Dobson, *Green Political Thought*, 30.

28. Bramwell, *Ecology*, 161.

29. Ursula King, *Women and Spirituality: Voices of Protest and Promise* (University Park: Pennsylvania State University Press, 1993), 208.

30. Quoted in ibid., 209.

31. Ibid.

32. Bramwell, *Ecology*, 124.

33. Merchant refers to "Big Ten" environmental organizations (*Radical Ecology*, 159).

34. Rachel Carson, *Silent Spring* (Boston: Houghton Mifflin, 1962).

35. Aldo Leopold, "The Land Ethic," in *A Sand County Almanac* (New York: Ballantine Books, 1966), 237–61.

36. Ibid., 240.

37. Ibid., 262.

38. Murray Rosenblith, "Surrounded by Acres of Clams," in *Reinventing Anarchy: What Are Anarchists Thinking These Days?* ed. Howard J. Ehrlich, Carol Ehrlich, David De Leon, and Glenda Morris (Boston: Routledge and Kegan Paul, 1979), 347–60.

39. Quoted in Merchant, *Radical Ecology*, 175. Monkeywrenching, or "throwing a wrench in the works," is an anarchist strategy for sabotaging industrial operations. By driving spikes into trees marked for "harvesting," members of Earth First destroy logging equipment. Unfortunately, the process also endangers loggers.

40. Merchant provides this concise summary of the Greens' fifty-plus-page 1983 party platform (*Radical Ecology*, 167–68).

41. Jonathan Porritt, preface to *Die Grünen: Programme of the German Green Party* (London: Heretic Books, 1983), 3.

42. Goodin, *Green Political Theory*, 84–93.

43. Porritt, *Programme*, 40.

44. Goodin, *Green Political Theory*, 113–15.

45. Porritt, preface to *Programme*, 4.

46. Porritt, *Programme*, 7.

47. Goodin, *Green Political Theory*, chap. 5.

48. The green/Green distinction is Dobson's in *Green Political Thought*, 5.

49. Ibid., 9.

50. Merchant, *Radical Ecology*, 157.

51. Ibid., 158.

52. Ibid.

53. Dobson, *Green Political Thought*, 24.

54. Ibid., 25.

55. Ibid., 27–28.

56. Daniel Bell, "The End of Ideology in the West," in *The End of Ideology Debate*, ed. Chaim J. Waxman (New York: Funk and Wagnalls, 1968), 96.

57. Michael Freeden, "Political Concepts and Ideological Morphology," *Journal of Political Philosophy* 2, no. 1 (1994): 156.

58. Ibid.

59. Elizabeth Kamarck Minnich, *Transforming Knowledge* (Philadelphia: Temple University Press, 1990), 56.

60. Ibid., 57.

61. Ibid.

62. Kathy Ferguson, "Male-Ordered Politics: Feminism and Political Science," in *Idioms of Inquiry: Critique and Renewal in Political Science,* ed. Terence Ball (Albany, N.Y.: SUNY Press, 1987), 223.

63. King, *Women and Spirituality,* 215.

64. Quoted in Ferguson, "Male-Ordered Politics," 216.

65. My language here parallels Ferguson's description of democratic discourse, though I suspect she would object to the term *ideology.*

66. Vaclav Havel, *The Power of the Powerless: Citizens against the State in Central-Eastern Europe* (Armonk, N.Y.: M.E. Sharpe, 1985), 28.

Bibliography

Abraham, David. *The Collapse of the Weimar Republic: Political Economy and Crisis.* Rev. ed. New York: Holmes and Meier, 1986.

Adams, William. "Aesthetics: Liberating the Senses." In *The Cambridge Companion to Marx,* ed. Terrell Carver, 246–74. Cambridge, England: Cambridge University Press, 1991.

Adorno, Theodor. "Freudian Theory and the Pattern of Fascist Propaganda." In *The Essential Frankfurt School Reader,* ed. Andrew Arato and Eike Gebhardt, 118–37. New York: Continuum, 1982.

Ames, Fisher. "The Dangers of American Liberty." In *The Portable Conservative Reader,* ed. Russell Kirk, 84–112. New York: Viking Penguin, 1982.

Anderson, Benedict. *Imagined Communities.* London: Verso, 1991.

Anzaldúa, Gloria. "*La conciencia de la mestiza:* Towards a New Consciousness." In *Making Face, Making Soul: Haciendo Caras, Creative and Critical Perspectives by Women of Color,* ed. Gloria Anzaldúa, 377–89. San Francisco: Aunt Lute Press, 1990.

Arato, Andrew, and Eike Gebhardt, eds. *The Essential Frankfurt School Reader.* New York: Continuum, 1982.

Arblaster, Anthony. *Democracy.* Minneapolis: University of Minnesota Press, 1987.

Aristotle. *Politics.* Trans. and ed. Ernest Barker. New York: Oxford University Press, 1973.

Ashcraft, Richard. "Political Theory and the Problem of Ideology." *Journal of Politics* 42 (August 1980): 687–705.

Bakunin, Mikhail. *The Political Philosophy of Bakunin, Scientific Anarchism.* Ed. G.P. Maximoff. Glencoe, Ill.: Free Press, 1953.

Ball, Terence. *Transforming Political Discourse: Political Theory and Critical Conceptual History.* Oxford: Basil Blackwell, 1988.

Baradat, Leon P. *Political Ideologies: Their Origins and Impact.* 3d ed. Englewood Cliffs, N.J.: Prentice Hall, 1988.

Barber, Benjamin. *Strong Democracy: Participatory Politics for a New Age.* Berkeley: University of California Press, 1984.

———. *The Conquest of Politics: Liberal Philosophy in Democratic Times.* Princeton: Princeton University Press, 1988.

Barber, James David, and Barbara Kellerman, eds. *Women Leaders in American Politics.* Englewood Cliffs, N.J.: Prentice Hall, 1986.

Beecher, Jonathan, and Richard Bienvenu. *The Utopian Vision of Charles Fourier.* Boston: Beacon Press, 1971.

Belenky, Mary Field, Blythe McVicker Clinchy, Nancy Rule Goldberger, and Jill Mattuck Tarule. *Women's Ways of Knowing: The Development of Self, Love, and Mind.* New York: Basic Books, 1986.

Bell, Daniel. "The End of Ideology in the West." In *The End of Ideology Debate,* ed. Chaim J. Waxman. New York: Funk and Wagnalls, 1968.

Bellah, Robert N. "The Quest for the Self." In *Rights and the Common Good: A Communitarian Perspective,* ed. Amitai Etzioni, 45–58. New York: St. Martin's Press, 1995.

Bellah, Robert N., Richard Madsen, William M. Sullivan, Ann Swidler, and Steven M. Tipton. *Habits of the Heart: Individualism and Commitment in American Life.* Berkeley: University of California Press, 1985.

Bem, Sandra L., and Daryl J. Bem. "Homogenizing the American Woman: The Power of an Unconscious Ideology." In *Feminist Frameworks: Alternative Theoretical Accounts of the Relations between Women and Men,* 2d ed., ed. Alison M. Jaggar and Paula S. Rothenberg, 10–24. New York: McGraw-Hill, 1984.

Benhabib, Seyla. "Feminism and Postmodernism." In *Feminist Contentions: A Philosophical Exchange,* ed. Linda Nicholson, 15–36. New York: Routledge, 1995.

Benjamin, Walter. "The Work of Art in the Age of Mechanical Reproduction." In *Illuminations,* trans. Harry Zohn, 217–52. New York: Schocken Books, 1969.

Berghahn, V.R. *Modern Germany: Society, Economy, and Politics in the Twentieth Century.* 2d ed. Cambridge, England: Cambridge University Press, 1987.

Berlin, Isaiah. "Two Concepts of Liberty." In *Four Essays on Liberty,* ed. Isaiah Berlin, 118–72. London: Oxford University Press, 1969.

Bernstein, Eduard. *Evolutionary Socialism: A Criticism and Affirmation.* Trans. Edith C. Harvey. New York: Stockholm Books, 1961.

Blackburn, Robin, ed. *After the Fall: The Failure of Communism and the Future of Socialism.* London: New Left Books, 1991.

Blee, Kathleen M. *Women of the Klan: Racism and Gender in the 1920s.* Berkeley: University of California Press, 1991.

Bloom, Allan. "The Democratization of the University." In *How Democratic Is America?* ed. Robert A. Goldwin, 109–36. Chicago: Rand McNally, 1971.

———. *The Closing of the American Mind.* New York: Simon and Schuster, 1987.

Bookchin, Murray. *Post-Scarcity Anarchism*. Berkeley, Calif.: Ramparts Press, 1971.

Bramwell, Anna. *Ecology in the 20th Century: A History*. New Haven: Yale University Press, 1989.

Bronner, Stephen Eric. *Socialism Unbound*. New York: Routledge, 1990.

Buckley, William F. Jr. "Did You Ever See a Dream Walking?" In *Keeping the Tablets: Modern American Conservative Thought*, ed. William F. Buckley Jr. and Charles R. Kesler, 19–36. New York: Harper & Row, 1988.

Buckley, William F. Jr., and Charles R. Kesler, eds. *Keeping the Tablets: Modern American Conservative Thought*. New York: Harper & Row, 1988.

Bunch, Charlotte. "Lesbians in Revolt." In *Feminist Frameworks: Alternative Theoretical Accounts of the Relations between Women and Men*, 2d ed., ed. Alison M. Jaggar and Paula S. Rothenberg, 377–89. New York: McGraw-Hill, 1984.

Burke, Edmund. *Reflections on the Revolution in France*. Ed. Conor Cruise O'Brien. New York: Penguin, 1982.

Burnham, James. "Communism: The Struggle for the World." In *Keeping the Tablets: Modern American Conservative Thought*, ed. William F. Buckley Jr. and Charles R. Kesler, 353–78. New York: Harper & Row, 1988.

Calhoun, John C. "On the Veto Power." In *The Portable Conservative Reader*, ed. Russell Kirk, 155–80. New York: Viking Penguin, 1982.

Calinescu, Matei. *Five Faces of Modernity: Modernism, Avant-Garde, Decadence, Kitsch, Postmodernism*. Durham, N.C.: Duke University Press, 1987.

Calleo, David. *The German Problem Reconsidered: Germany and the World Order, 1870 to the Present*. Cambridge, England: Cambridge University Press, 1978.

Callinicos, Alex. *The Revenge of History: Marxism and the East European Revolutions*. University Park: Pennsylvania State University Press, 1991.

Caraway, Nancie. *Segregated Sisterhood: Racism and the Politics of American Feminism*. Knoxville: University of Tennessee Press, 1991.

Carson, Rachel. *Silent Spring*. Boston: Houghton Mifflin, 1962.

Carsten, F.L. *The Rise of Fascism*. Berkeley: University of California Press, 1982.

Carver, Terrell, ed. *The Cambridge Companion to Marx*. Cambridge, England: Cambridge University Press, 1991.

Chambers, Whittaker. "The Direct Glance." In *Keeping the Tablets: Modern American Conservative Thought*, ed. William F. Buckley Jr. and Charles R. Kesler, 417–31. New York: Harper & Row, 1988.

Chytry, Joseph. *The Aesthetic State*. Berkeley: University of California Press, 1992.

Clark, John P. "What Is Anarchism?" In *Anarchism,* ed. J. Roland Pennock and John W. Chapman. New York: New York University Press, 1978.

Cohen, G.A. *Karl Marx's Theory of History: A Defense.* Princeton: Princeton University Press, 1978.

Connolly, William. *Political Science and Ideology.* New York: Atherton Press, 1967.

Connor, Walker. "A Nation Is a Nation, Is a State, Is an Ethnic Group, Is a . . . ." In *Nationalism,* ed. John Hutchinson and Anthony D. Smith, 36–46. New York: Oxford University Press, 1994.

Constitution and Laws of the Knights of the Ku Klux Klan. Atlanta: Knights of the Ku Klux Klan, 1921.

Crowder, George. *Classical Anarchist Theory.* New York: Oxford University Press, 1994.

Dahl, Robert. *Who Governs? Democracy and Power in an American City.* New Haven: Yale University Press, 1961.

———. "The Concept of Power." *Behavioral Science* 2, no. 3 (July 1966): 202–3.

Di Stefano, Christine. "Dilemmas of Difference: Feminism, Modernity, and Postmodernism." In *Feminism/Postmodernism,* ed. Linda J. Nicholson. New York: Routledge, 1990.

———. "Am I That Performance? Vicissitudes of Gender." Paper presented at the 1991 American Political Science Association Convention.

Dobson, Andrew. *Green Political Thought: An Introduction.* Boston: Unwin Hyman, 1990.

Dolbeare, Kenneth M., ed. *American Political Thought.* 3d ed. Chatham, N.J.: Chatham House, 1996.

Dolbeare, Kenneth M., and Linda J. Medcalf. *American Ideologies Today: Shaping the New Politics of the 1990s.* 2d ed. New York: McGraw-Hill, 1993.

Doner, Kalia. "Women's Magazines: Slouching toward Feminism." *Social Policy* 23, no. 4 (Summer 1993): 37–43.

Edelman, Murray. *The Symbolic Uses of Politics.* Urbana: University of Illinois Press, 1972.

———. *Constructing the Political Spectacle.* Chicago: University of Chicago Press, 1988.

Ehrlich, Carol. "Socialism, Anarchism, Feminism." In *Reinventing Anarchy: What Are Anarchists Thinking These Days?* ed. Howard J. Ehrlich, Carol Ehrlich, David De Leon, and Glenda Morris, 259–77. Boston: Routledge and Kegan Paul, 1979.

Eley, Geoff. "Reviewing the Socialist Tradition." In *The Crisis of Socialism in Europe,* ed. Christine Lemke and Gary Marks, 21–60. Durham, N.C.: Duke University Press, 1992.

Elster, Jon. *Making Sense of Marx.* New York: Cambridge University Press, 1985.

Engels, Friedrich. *Ludwig Feuerbach and the Age of Classical German Phi-*

losophy. In *Karl Marx and Friedrich Engels: Selected Works,* 594–632. New York: International Publishers, 1968.

———. *The Origin of the Family, Private Property, and the State.* New York: International Publishers, 1972.

———. "Socialism: Utopian and Scientific." In *The Marx-Engels Reader,* ed. Robert C. Tucker, 638–717. New York: Norton, 1972.

———. "The Tactics of Social Democracy." In *Marx-Engels Reader,* 556–73.

———. "Versus the Anarchists." In *Marx-Engels Reader,* 728–30.

Etzioni, Amitai, ed. *Rights and the Common Good: A Communitarian Perspective.* New York: St. Martin's Press, 1995.

Falasca-Zamponi, Simonetta. "The Aesthetics of Politics: Symbol, Power, and Narrative in Mussolini's Fascist Italy," *Theory, Culture, and Society* 9 (1992): 74–91.

Falk, Richard A. "Anarchism and World Order." In *Anarchism,* ed. J. Roland Pennock and John W. Chapman, 63–87. New York: New York University Press, 1978.

Farr, James, and Raymond Seidelman. *Discipline and History.* Ann Arbor: University of Michigan Press, 1993.

Ferguson, Kathy E. *The Feminist Case against Bureaucracy.* Philadelphia: Temple University Press, 1984.

———. "Male-Ordered Politics." In *Idioms of Inquiry: Critique and Renewal in Political Science,* ed. Terence Ball, 209–29. Albany: SUNY Press, 1987.

———. *The Man Question: Visions of Subjectivity in Feminist Theory.* Berkeley: University of California Press, 1993.

Fischman, Dennis. *Political Discourse in Exile: Karl Marx and the Jewish Question.* Amherst: University of Massachusetts Press, 1991.

Fourier, Charles. *The Utopian Vision of Charles Fourier.* Trans. and ed. Jonathan Beecher and Richard Bienvenu. Boston: Beacon Press, 1971.

Freeden, Michael. "Political Concepts and Ideological Morphology." *Journal of Political Philosophy* 2, no. 1 (1994).

Freeman, Jo. *The Politics of Women's Liberation: A Case Study of an Emerging Social Movement and Its Relation to the Policy Process.* New York: Longman, 1975.

Freud, Sigmund. *The Future of an Illusion.* Trans. W.D. Robson-Scott. New York: Liveright, 1955.

Fried, Albert. "The Course of American Socialism: A Synoptic View." In *Socialism in America: From the Shakers to the Third International—A Documentary History,* ed. Albert Fried, 1–15. New York: Columbia University Press, 1992.

Friedan, Betty. *The Feminine Mystique.* New York: Norton, 1963.

———. "Our Revolution Is Unique." In *Voices of the New Feminism,* ed. Mary Lou Thompson, 31–43. Boston: Beacon Press, 1970.

Friedman, Milton. *Capitalism and Freedom.* Chicago: University of Chicago Press, 1962.

Friedman, Milton, and Rose Friedman. *Free to Choose: A Personal Statement.* New York: Avon Books, 1981.

Fromm, Erich. *Escape From Freedom.* New York: Avon Books, 1965.

Fukuyama, Francis. *The End of History and the Last Man.* New York: Free Press, 1992.

Gale, Mary Ellen. "Free Speech, Equal Rights, and Water Buffaloes: University Regulation of Discriminatory Verbal Harassment." In *Rights and the Common Good: A Communitarian Perspective,* ed. Amitai Etzioni, 93–106. New York: St. Martin's Press, 1995.

George, John, and Laird Wilcox. *Nazis, Communists, Klansmen, and Others on the Fringe.* Buffalo, N.Y.: Prometheus Books, 1992.

Ginsberg, Benjamin. *The Consequences of Consent: Elections, Citizen Control, and Popular Acquiescence.* Reading, Mass.: Addison-Wesley, 1982.

Godwin, William. "The Rights of Man and the Principles of Society." In *The Anarchists,* ed. Irving Horowitz, 106–19. New York: Dell, 1964.

Goldman, Emma. *Anarchism and Other Essays.* New York: Dover, 1969.

Goodin, Robert E. *Green Political Theory.* Cambridge, England: Polity Press, 1992.

Gore, Al. *Earth in the Balance: Ecology and the Human Spirit.* New York: Penguin, 1993.

Gouldner, Alvin W. "Marx's Last Battle: Bakunin and the First International." *Theory and Society* 11 (1982): 853–84.

Gray, John. *Liberalism.* Minneapolis: University of Minnesota Press, 1986.

Gross, Bertram. *Friendly Fascism: The New Face of Power in America.* New York: M. Evans, 1980.

Guerin, Daniel. *Anarchism.* New York: Monthly Review Press, 1970.

Guinier, Lani. *The Tyranny of the Majority: Fundamental Fairness in Representative Democracy.* New York: Free Press, 1994.

Gunn-Allen, Paula. *The Sacred Hoop: Recovering the Feminine in American Indian Traditions.* Boston: Beacon Press, 1986.

Haber, Robert. "The End of Ideology as Ideology." In *The End of Ideology Debate,* ed. Chaim Waxman. New York: Funk and Wagnalls, 1968.

Habermas, Jürgen. "Towards a Theory of Communicative Competence." *Inquiry* 13 (1970): 360–75.

———. *Theory of Communicative Action.* Vol. 2, *Lifeworld and System.* Trans. Thomas McCarthy. Boston: Beacon Press, 1987.

———. "What Does Socialism Mean Today? The Revolutions of Recuperation and the Need for New Thinking." In *After the Fall: The Failure of Communism and the Future of Socialism,* ed. Robin Blackburn, 25–46. London: New Left Books, 1991.

Hamilton, Alexander. "Report on Manufactures." In *American Political Thought.* 3d ed., ed. Kenneth M. Dolbeare, 166–70. Chatham, N.J.: Chatham House, 1996.

Haraway, Donna. "Ecce Homo, Ain't (Ar'n't) I a Woman, and Inappropriate/d Others: The Human in a Post-Humanist Landscape." In *Feminists Theorize the Political,* ed. Judith Butler and Joan Scott, 86–100. New York: Routledge, 1992.

Hartmann, Heidi. "The Unhappy Marriage of Marxism and Feminism: Towards a More Progressive Union." In *Dogmas and Dreams: Political Ideologies in the Modern World,* 2d ed., ed. Nancy S. Love, 503–22. Chatham, N.J.: Chatham House, 1998.

Hate Violence and White Supremacy: A Decade Review 1980–1990. Montgomery, Ala.: Southern Poverty Law Center, December 1989.

Havel, Vaclav. *The Power of the Powerless: Citizens against the State in Central-Eastern Europe.* Armonk, N.Y.: M.E. Sharpe, 1985.

Heider, Ulrike. *Anarchism: Left, Right, and Green.* Trans. Danny Lewis and Ulrike Bode. San Francisco: City Lights Books, 1994.

Hitler, Adolf. *Mein Kampf.* Trans. Ralph Manheim. Boston: Houghton Mifflin, 1971.

———. *The Speeches of Adolf Hitler.* Ed. Norman H. Baynes. Oxford: Oxford University Press, 1942.

Hobbes, Thomas. *Leviathan: Or the Matter, Forme and Power of a Commonwealth, Ecclesiastical and Civil.* Ed. Michael Oakeshott. New York: Collier Books, 1962.

Hobsbawm, Eric. "Lost Horizons." *New Statesman & Society* 3 (14 September 1990): 16–18.

———. "Goodbye to All That." In *After the Fall: The Failure of Communism and the Future of Socialism,* ed. Robin Blackburn, 115–25. London: New Left Books, 1991.

———. "Out of the Ashes." In *After the Fall,* 315–25.

Hochschild, Jennifer. "Disjunction and Ambivalence in Citizens' Political Outlooks." In *Reconsidering the Democratic Public,* ed. George Marcus and Russell Hanson, 187–210. University Park: Pennsylvania State University Press, 1994.

Hodges, Donald Clark. "The End of 'The End of Ideology.'" In *The End of Ideology Debate,* ed. Chaim J. Waxman. New York: Funk and Wagnalls, 1968.

Hofstadter, Richard. *The American Political Tradition.* New York: Knopf, 1948.

Hood, Elizabeth. "Black Women, White Women: Separate Paths to Liberation." In *Feminist Frameworks: Alternative Theoretical Accounts of the Relations between Women and Men,* 2d ed., ed. Alison M. Jaggar and Paula S. Rothenberg, 189–202. New York: McGraw-Hill, 1984.

Horowitz, Irving, ed. *The Anarchists.* New York: Dell, 1964.

Hull, Gloria T., Patricia Bell Scott, and Barbara Smith, eds. *All the Women Are White, All the Blacks Are Men, but Some of Us Are Brave.* Old Westbury, N.Y.: Feminist Press, 1982.

Huntington, Samuel. "Conservatism as an Ideology." *American Political Science Review* 51 (June 1957): 454–73.

Iannello, Kathleen P. *Decisions without Hierarchy: Feminist Interventions in Organization Theory and Practice.* New York: Routledge, 1992.

Ingersoll, David, and Donald Matthews. *The Philosophic Roots of Modern Ideology: Liberalism, Communism, Fascism.* Englewood Cliffs, N.J.: Prentice Hall, 1986.

Irigaray, Luce. "The Sex Which Is Not One." In *New French Feminisms: An Anthology,* ed. Elaine Marks and Isabelle de Courtivron, 99–106. New York: Schocken Books, 1980.

Jaggar, Alison M. *Feminist Politics and Human Nature.* Totowa, N.J.: Rowman and Allenheld, 1983.

Jaggar, Alison M., and Paula S. Rothenberg. *Feminist Frameworks: Alternative Theoretical Accounts of the Relations between Women and Men,* 2d ed. New York: McGraw-Hill, 1984.

Jefferson, Thomas. "The First Inaugural." In *The Portable Thomas Jefferson,* ed. Merrill Peterson, 290–95. New York: Viking Press, 1977.

Johansen, Bruce E. *Forgotten Founders: How the American Indian Helped Shape Democracy.* Cambridge: Harvard University Press, 1982.

Jones, Kathleen. *Compassionate Authority: Democracy and the Representation of Women.* New York: Routledge, 1993.

Kaminer, Wendy. "Feminism's Identity Crisis." *Atlantic Monthly* 272 (October 1993): 51–68.

Kennedy, Emmet. "'Ideology' from Destutt de Tracy to Marx." *Journal of the History of Ideas* 40, no. 3 (July–September 1979): 353–68.

Kesler, Charles R. Introduction to *Keeping the Tablets: Modern American Conservative Thought,* ed. William F. Buckley Jr. and Charles R. Kesler, 3–18. New York: Harper & Row, 1988.

King, Ursula. *Women and Spirituality: Voices of Protest and Promise.* University Park: Pennsylvania State University Press, 1993.

Kirk, Russell. *The Conservative Mind: From Burke to Santayana.* Chicago: Henry Regnery, 1953.

———, ed. *The Portable Conservative Reader.* New York: Viking Penguin, 1982.

Kirkpatrick, Jeane. "Dictatorships and Double Standards." In *Keeping the Tablets: Modern American Conservative Thought,* ed. William F. Buckley Jr. and Charles R. Kesler, 392–414. New York: Harper & Row, 1988.

Klanwatch: Intelligence Report 77, no. 1 (March 1995). Montgomery, Ala.: Klanwatch Project.

Kohn, Hans. *Nationalism: Its Meaning and History.* Princeton, N.J.: Van Nostrand, 1965.

Kraditor, Aileen. *Ideas of the Woman Suffrage Movement, 1890–1920.* New York: Columbia University Press, 1965.

Kramnick, Isaac. "Equal Opportunity and the 'Race of Life.'" *Dissent* 28, no. 2 (Spring 1981): 178–87.

Kramnick, Isaac, and Frederick Watkins. *The Age of Ideology: Political*

Thought, 1750 to the Present. 2d ed. Englewood Cliffs, N.J.: Prentice Hall, 1979.

Krauthammer, Charles. "Is Reagan Conservative?" *New Republic* 197, no. 4 (27 July 1987).

Kristol, Irving. "What Is a Neo-Conservative?" *Newsweek* 87 (19 January 1976): 17.

———. "Capitalism, Socialism, Nihilism." In *The Portable Conservative Reader,* ed. Russell Kirk, 627–43. New York: Viking Penguin, 1982.

Kropotkin, Petyr. *Mutual Aid: A Factor in Evolution.* Boston: Porter Sargent, 1914.

Lakoff, Sanford. *Equality in Political Philosophy.* Cambridge: Harvard University Press, 1964.

Langer, Elinor. "The American Neo-Nazi Movement Today." *The Nation* 251, no. 3 (16 July 1990): 82–107.

Lapham, Lewis. "Democracy in America." *Harper's Magazine,* November 1990, 47–56.

Lasch, Christopher. *The Agony of the American Left.* New York: Knopf, 1967.

———. "Communitarianism or Populism?" In *Rights and the Common Good: A Communitarian Perspective,* ed. Amitai Etzioni, 59–66. New York: St. Martin's Press, 1995.

Lemke, Christine, and Gary Marks, eds. *The Crisis of Socialism in Europe.* Durham, N.C.: Duke University Press, 1992.

Lenin, Vladimir Il'ich. "Better Fewer, but Better." In *The Lenin Anthology,* ed. Robert C. Tucker, 736–46. New York: Norton, 1975.

———. *State and Revolution: The Marxist Theory of the State and the Tasks of the Proletariat in the Revolution.* In *Lenin Anthology,* 311–98.

———. *What Is to Be Done? Burning Questions of Our Movement.* In *Lenin Anthology,* 12–114.

Leopold, Aldo. *A Sand County Almanac.* New York: Ballantine Books, 1966.

Lindblom, Charles E. *Politics and Markets: The World's Political-Economic Systems.* New York: Basic Books, 1977.

Lipset, Seymour Martin. *Political Man: The Social Bases of Politics.* Garden City, N.Y.: Doubleday, 1963.

Locke, John. *A Letter Concerning Toleration.* Ed. Patrick Romanell. Indianapolis: Bobbs-Merrill, 1955.

———. *The Reasonableness of Christianity.* Ed. I.T. Ramsey. Stanford, Calif.: Stanford University Press, 1958.

———. *The Second Treatise of Government.* In *Two Treatises of Government,* ed. Peter Laslett. New York: Cambridge University Press, 1960.

Lorde, Audre. *Sister Outsider: Essays and Speeches.* Freedom, Calif.: Crossing Press, 1984.

Love, Nancy S., ed. *Dogmas and Dreams: A Reader in Modern Political Ideologies.* 2d ed. Chatham, N.J.: Chatham House, 1998.

Lowi, Theodore. *The End of Liberalism: The Second Republic of the United States.* 2d ed. New York: Norton, 1979.

———. "The State of Political Science: How We Become What We Study." In *Discipline and History,* ed. James Farr and Raymond Seidelman, 383–95. Ann Arbor: University of Michigan Press, 1993.

Macdonald, Andrew. *The Turner Diaries.* 2d ed. Washington, D.C.: National Alliance, 1980.

MacIntyre, Alasdair. *Three Rival Versions of Moral Enquiry: Encyclopaedia, Genealogy, and Tradition.* Notre Dame, Ind.: University of Notre Dame Press, 1990.

Mackie, Thomas T., and Richard Rose. *International Almanac of Electoral History.* 3d ed. Washington, D.C.: CQ Press, 1992.

MacPherson, C.B. *The Political Theory of Possessive Individualism: Hobbes to Locke.* New York: Oxford University Press, 1962.

———. *The Real World of Democracy.* New York: Oxford University Press, 1972.

Macridis, Roy. *Modern Political Regimes: Patterns and Institutions.* Boston: Little, Brown, 1986.

———. *Contemporary Political Ideologies: Movements and Regimes.* 4th ed. Boston: Scott, Foresman/Little, Brown, 1989.

Madison, James. *Federalist* nos. 10, 51. In *The Federalist Papers,* ed. Clinton Rossiter. New York: Mentor Books, 1961.

Mahowald, Mary Briody, ed. *Philosophy of Woman: An Anthology of Classic and Current Concepts.* Indianapolis: Hackett, 1983.

Mannheim, Karl. *Ideology and Utopia.* Trans. Louis Wirth and Edward Shils. London: Routledge and Kegan Paul, 1948.

Marcus, George, and George Hansen. *Reconsidering the Democratic Public.* University Park: Pennsylvania State University Press, 1994.

Marks, Elaine, and Isabelle de Courtivron, eds. *New French Feminisms: An Anthology.* New York: Schocken Books, 1980.

Marx, Karl. "Address to the Communist League." In *The Marx-Engels Reader,* 2d ed., ed. Robert C. Tucker, 501–11. New York: Norton, 1978.

———. "After the Revolution: Marx Debates Bakunin." In *Marx-Engels Reader,* 542–49.

———. *Capital.* Vol. 1. In *Marx-Engels Reader,* 294–438.

———. *Capital.* Trans. Ben Fowkes. Vol. 1. New York: Random House, 1977.

———. "The Civil War in France." In *Marx-Engels Reader,* 618–52.

———. "Critique of the Gotha Program." In *Marx-Engels Reader,* 525–41.

———. *The Eighteenth Brumaire of Louis Bonaparte.* In *Marx-Engels Reader,* 594–617.

———. *Economic and Philosophical Manuscripts of 1844.* In *Marx-Engels Reader,* 66–125.

———. *Grundrisse.* In *Marx-Engels Reader,* 221–93.

————. "Inaugural Address of the Working Men's International Association." In *Marx-Engels Reader,* 512–19.

————. "Letter to Bebel, Liebknecht, Bracke." In *Marx-Engels Reader,* 549–55.

————. "Letter to Ruge (March 13, 1843)." In *Selected Correspondence.* Moscow: Foreign Language Publishers, 1956.

————. *Manifesto of the Communist Party.* In *Marx-Engels Reader,* 469–500.

————. Preface to *A Contribution to the Critique of Political Economy.* In *Marx-Engels Reader,* 3–6.

Marx, Karl, and Friedrich Engels. *The German Ideology.* Ed. C.J. Arthur. New York: International Publishers, 1977.

————. *The German Ideology.* In *Marx-Engels Reader,* 146–200.

Maximoff, G.P., ed. *The Political Philosophy of Bakunin: Scientific Anarchism.* Glencoe, Ill.: Free Press, 1953.

May, Todd. *The Political Philosophy of Poststructuralist Anarchism.* University Park: Pennsylvania State University Press, 1994.

Mayer, Milton. *They Thought They Were Free: The Germans 1933–1945.* 2d ed. Chicago: University of Chicago Press, 1966.

McClure, Kirstie. "The Issue of Foundations: Scientized Politics, Politicized Science, and Feminists' Critical Practice." In *Feminists Theorize the Political,* ed. Judith Butler and Joan Scott, 341–68. New York: Routledge, 1992.

McGaa, Ed. *Mother Earth Spirituality: Native American Paths to Healing Ourselves and Our World.* San Francisco: HarperCollins, 1990.

McGlen, Nancy E., and Karen O'Connor. *Women, Politics, and American Society.* Englewood Cliffs, N.J.: Prentice Hall, 1995.

McLellan, David. *Karl Marx: His Life and Thought.* New York: Harper & Row, 1973.

————. *Marxism after Marx.* Boston: Houghton Mifflin, 1979.

————, ed. *Marxism: Essential Writings.* New York: Oxford University Press, 1988.

McNeill, William. "Reasserting the Polyethnic Norm." In *Nationalism,* ed. John Hutchinson and Anthony D. Smith, 300–305. New York: Oxford University Press, 1994.

Medcalf, Linda J., and Kenneth M. Dolbeare. *Neopolitics: American Political Ideas in the 1980s.* Philadelphia: Temple University Press, 1985.

Mehring, Franz. *Karl Marx: The Story of His Life.* Trans. Edward Fitzgerald. Atlantic Highlands, N.J.: Humanities Press, 1966.

Merchant, Carolyn. *Radical Ecology: The Search for a Livable World.* New York: Routledge, 1992.

Mill, J.S. *On Liberty.* In *Utilitarianism, On Liberty, and Considerations on Representative Government,* ed. H.B. Acton. London: J.M. Dent, 1972.

Minnich, Elizabeth Kamarck. *Transforming Knowledge.* Philadelphia:

Temple University Press, 1990.

Murray, Charles. "The Constraints on Helping." In *Keeping the Tablets: Modern American Conservative Thought,* ed. William F. Buckley Jr. and Charles R. Kesler, 240–66. New York: Harper & Row, 1988.

Mussolini, Benito. *The Doctrine of Fascism.* In Hans Kohn, *Nationalism: Its Meaning and History,* 170–75. Princeton, N.J.: Van Nostrand, 1965.

Nicholson, Linda J., ed. *Feminism/Postmodernism.* New York: Routledge, 1990.

Niemeyer, Gerhart. "The Communist Mind." In *Keeping the Tablets: Modern American Conservative Thought,* ed. William F. Buckley Jr. and Charles R. Kesler, 343–52. New York: Harper & Row, 1988.

Nietzsche, Friedrich. *On the Advantage and Disadvantage of History for Life.* Trans. Peter Preuss. Indianapolis: Hackett, 1980.

Oakeshott, Michael. "On Being Conservative." In *The Portable Conservative Reader,* ed. Russell Kirk, 567–99. New York: Viking Penguin, 1982.

O'Brien, Sharon. *American Indian Tribal Governments.* Norman: University of Oklahoma Press, 1989.

O'Neill, William. *Feminism in America: A History.* 2d rev. ed. New Brunswick, N.J.: Transaction, 1989.

O'Neill, William L. "The Fight for Suffrage." *Wilson Quarterly* 10, no. 4 (Autumn 1986): 99–109.

Orwell, George. *Homage to Catalonia.* New York: Harcourt Brace Jovanovich, 1952.

Parenti, Michael. *Land of Idols: Political Mythology in America.* New York: St. Martin's Press, 1994.

Paul, Eileen. "The Women's Movement and the Movement of Women." *Social Policy* 44 (Summer 1993): 44–50.

Pennock, J. Roland, and John W. Chapman, eds. *Anarchism.* New York: New York University Press, 1978.

Peterson, Merrill, ed. *The Portable Thomas Jefferson.* New York: Viking Press, 1977.

Phillips, Derek. *Looking Backwards: A Critical Appraisal of Communitarian Thought.* Princeton: Princeton University Press, 1993.

Piven, Frances Fox, and Richard Cloward. *The New Class War.* New York: Pantheon, 1982.

———. *Why Americans Don't Vote.* New York: Pantheon, 1989.

Plamenatz, John. *Ideology.* New York: Praeger, 1970.

Poguntke, Thomas. *Alternative Politics: The German Green Party.* Edinburgh: Edinburgh University Press, 1994.

Pomfret, John. "Between War and Peace: Facing Up to the History of Hatred in Bosnia and Its Neighbors," *Washington Post Weekly* 13, no. 8 (25–31 December 1995): 7.

Porritt, Jonathan. *Die Grünen: Programme of the German Green Party.*

London: Heretic Books, 1983.

Proudhon, Pierre-Joseph. *What Is Property? An Inquiry into the Principle of Right and of Government.* Ed. George Woodcock. New York: Dover, 1970.

Ravitch, Diane. "Pluralism within Unity: A Communitarian Version of Multiculturalism." In *Rights and the Common Good: A Communitarian Perspective,* ed. Amitai Etzioni, 179–86. New York: St. Martin's Press, 1995.

Reagon, Bernice Johnson. "Coalition Politics: Turning the Century." In *Home Girls: A Black Feminist Anthology,* ed. Barbara Smith, 356–68. Latham, N.Y.: Kitchen Table/Women of Color Press, 1983.

Reissman, Frank. "A New Political Culture." *Social Policy,* Summer 1987, 2–4.

Rich, Adrienne. "Compulsory Heterosexuality and Lesbian Existence." In *Feminist Frameworks: Alternative Theoretical Accounts of the Relations between Women and Men,* 2d ed., ed. Alison M. Jaggar and Paula S. Rothenberg, 416–19. New York: McGraw-Hill, 1984.

Roberts, Paul Craig. "The Breakdown of the Keynesian Model." In *Keeping the Tablets: Modern American Conservative Thought,* ed. William F. Buckley Jr. and Charles R. Kesler, 220–31. New York: Harper & Row, 1988.

Rosenblith, Murray. "Surrounded by Acres of Clams." In *Reinventing Anarchy: What Are Anarchists Thinking These Days?* ed. Howard J. Ehrlich, Carol Ehrlich, David De Leon, and Glenda Morris, 347–60. Boston: Routledge and Kegan Paul, 1979.

Rossiter, Clinton, ed. *The Federalist Papers.* New York: Mentor Books, 1961.

Rowbotham, Sheila. *Women, Resistance, and Revolution.* New York: Random House, 1974.

Sapiro, Virginia. *Women in American Society.* 3d ed. Mayfield, Calif.: Mayfield, 1994.

Sargent, Lyman Tower. *Contemporary Political Ideologies: A Comparative Analysis.* 10th ed. Belmont, Calif.: Wadsworth, 1996.

Schlafly, Phyllis. "The Power of the Positive Woman." In *Women Leaders in American Politics,* ed. James David Barber and Barbara Kellerman. Englewood Cliffs, N.J.: Prentice Hall, 1986.

Schlesinger, Philip. "Europeanness: A New Cultural Battlefield?" In *Nationalism,* ed. John Hutchinson and Anthony D. Smith, 316–25. New York: Oxford University Press, 1994.

Schmitter, Philippe C. "Still the Century of Corporatism?" *Review of Politics* 36, no. 1 (January 1974): 85–131.

Schumpeter, Joseph. *Capitalism, Socialism, and Democracy.* 3d ed. New York: Harper & Row, 1950.

Smith, Adam. *The Wealth of Nations.* Ed. Edwin Cannan. New York: Modern Library, 1937.

Sobran, Joseph. "The Abortion Culture." In *Keeping the Tablets: Modern American Conservative Thought,* ed. William F. Buckley Jr. and Charles R. Kesler, 327–38. New York: Harper & Row, 1988.

Sowell, Thomas. "The Civil Rights Vision: From Equal Opportunity to 'Affirmative Action.'" In *Keeping the Tablets: Modern American Conservative Thought,* ed. William F. Buckley Jr. and Charles R. Kesler, 308–26. New York: Harper & Row, 1988.

Spelman, Elizabeth. *Inessential Woman: Problems of Exclusion in Feminist Thought.* Boston: Beacon Press, 1988.

Steinfels, Peter. *The Neo-Conservatives: The Men Who Are Changing America's Politics.* New York: Simon and Schuster, 1979.

Stirner, Max. *The Ego and His Own.* In *The Anarchists,* ed. Irving Horowitz, 291–310. New York: Dell, 1964.

Talmon, J.L. *The Origins of Totalitarian Democracy.* London: Secker and Warburg, 1952.

Tamir, Yael. *Liberal Nationalism.* Princeton: Princeton University Press, 1993.

Thomas, Paul. "Critical Reception: Marx Then and Now." In *The Cambridge Companion to Marx,* ed. Terrell Carver, 23–54. Cambridge, England: Cambridge University Press, 1991.

Thompson, John. *Studies in the Theory of Ideology.* Berkeley: University of California Press, 1984.

Thoreau, Henry David. "Essay on Civil Disobedience." In *The Anarchists,* ed. Irving Horowitz, 311–20. New York: Dell, 1964.

Tronto, Joan. *Moral Boundaries: A Political Argument for an Ethic of Care.* New York: Routledge, 1993.

Tucker, Robert C., ed. *The Marx-Engels Reader.* 2d ed. New York: Norton, 1978.

————, ed. *The Lenin Anthology.* New York: Norton, 1975.

Turner, Denys. "Religion: Illusions and Liberation." In *The Cambridge Companion to Marx,* ed. Terrell Carver, 320–38. Cambridge, England: Cambridge University Press, 1991.

Van Dyke, Vernon. *Ideology and Political Choice: The Search for Freedom, Justice, and Virtue.* Chatham, N.J.: Chatham House, 1995.

Waxman, Chaim J., ed. *The End of Ideology Debate.* New York: Funk and Wagnalls, 1968.

Weber, Max. "'Objectivity' in Social Science." In *The Methodology of the Social Sciences,* trans. and ed. Edward Shils and Henry Finch, 50–112. New York: Free Press, 1949.

————. "Politics as a Vocation." In *From Max Weber: Essays in Sociology,* ed. Hans C. Gerth and C. Wright Mills, 77–128. New York: Oxford University Press, 1958.

Wieck, David. "The Habit of Direct Action." In *Reinventing Anarchy: What Are Anarchists Thinking These Days?"* ed. Howard Ehrlich, Carol Ehrlich, David De Leon, and Glenda Morris, 331–32. Boston:

Routledge and Kegan Paul, 1979.

Will, George. "A Conservative Welfare State." In *Keeping the Tablets: Modern American Conservative Thought,* ed. William F. Buckley Jr. and Charles R. Kesler, 232–39. New York: Harper & Row, 1988.

Wittig, Monique. "One Is Not Born a Woman." In *Dogmas and Dreams: Political Ideologies in the Modern World,* 2d ed., ed. Nancy S. Love, 523–27. Chatham, N.J.: Chatham House, 1998.

Wollstonecraft, Mary. "A Vindication of the Rights of Woman." In *Philosophy of Woman: An Anthology of Classic and Current Concepts,* ed. Mary Briody Mahowald, 205–21. Indianapolis: Hackett, 1983.

Wood, Ellen Meiksins. *The Retreat from Class: A New "True" Socialism.* London: New Left Books, 1986.

Wood, Gordon S. *The Creation of the American Republic: 1776–1787.* New York: Norton, 1969.

Woodcock, George. *Anarchism: A History of Libertarian Ideas and Movements.* New York: World, 1972.

Zia, Helen. "Women in Hate Groups." *Ms.* 1, no. 5 (March–April 1991): 20–27.

Index

Abortion, woman's right to, 61
Abraham, David, 139
Adams, Abigail, 155
Adams, John, 155; on balanced government, 53–54; and interpretation of Constitution, 50
Adams, William, 76
Adorno, Theodor, 87; on appeal of fascism, 136
Affirmative action: critique of, 63–64; Johnson on, 35
Agency, theory of, 185
Agony of the American Left, The (Lasch), 88
Alienation, capitalist, 79, 80–81
All the Women Are White, All the Blacks Are Men, but Some of Us Are Brave (Hull), 167
Althusser, Louis, 87
American Anti-Slavery Society, 156
American Nazi Party, 141
American Woman Suffrage Association (AWSA), 156
Ames, Fisher, 58; on democracy, 54–56; on Jefferson election, 52
Anarchafeminism, 114–17; and ecocentrism, 183
Anarchism: definitions of, 95–99; future of, 117–19; as homocentric, 181; as ideal society, 97; individualist, 96, 99–104; socialist, 96, 104–7. *See also* Spanish Anarchists
"Anarchism: What It Really Stands For," (Goldman), 97
"Angel complex," 173
Anti-Defamation League, 141
Antinuke movement, 184
Anti-Semitism, 128, 129, 130
Anzaldúa, Gloria, 173; on *mestiza* consciousness, 172

Aptheker, Bettina, 173
Arendt, Hannah: on reactions to liberalism, 136; on self-definition, 147
Aristotle, 25; on liberality, 18, 36; on role of politics, 17; on role of poor, 17
Aryan Nation, growth of, 141
Ashcraft, Richard, 10
Aura: defined, 127; of Italian Fascism, 131
Authoritarian socialism, 104. *See also* Anarchism; Spanish Anarchists

Bakunin, Mikhail, 98, 99, 104–6
Ball, Terence, 11
Baradat, Leon, 8
Barber, Benjamin, 11; on liberal individualism, 33; on "two democracies," 38
Bell, Daniel, 10, 44, 143; and end-of-ideology thesis, 1–4; on ideology, 187
Bellah, Robert, 20; on challenge to liberals, 33; on citizens' support of market, 37; on "communities of memory and hope," 32–33, 37, 39; on distributive justice, 36
Bem, Daryl J., 7
Bem, Sandra L., 7
Benjamin, Walter, 87; on "aura," 127; quotes Marinetti, 131
Bentham, Jeremy, 180
Berkman, Alexander, 95
Berlin, Isaiah, 100
Bernstein, Eduard, 84
Bill of Rights, FDR's second, 34–35
Blee, Kathleen, 144–45
Bloom, Allan, 62–63
Bonner, Eric, 89
Bookchin, Murray, 181–82
Borkenau, Franz, 112
Bramwell, Anna, 182–83
Brockway, Fenner, 113
Brown, Elsa Barkley, 173

208

About the Author

Nancy S. Love is an associate professor in the Department of Political Science at Pennsylvania State University, where she received the Christian R. and Mary F. Lindback Award for Distinguished Teaching in 1991. She has also taught at Swarthmore College and Cornell University.

Professor Love received her A.B. degree from Kenyon College and her Ph.D. from Cornell University.

She is the author of *Marx, Nietzsche, and Modernity,* published by Columbia University Press in 1986, and editor of *Dogmas and Dreams: A Reader in Modern Political Ideologies,* 2d edition (Chatham House, 1998), to which this volume is a companion text. Her articles have appeared in *The Cambridge Companion to Habermas,* ed. Stephen K. White, *differences: A Journal of Feminist Cultural Studies, New German Critique, Polity,* and *Women and Politics.*

Professor Love is currently at work on a book entitled *The Music of Collective Action.*